Cross-Examination: The Mosaic Art

Cross-Examination Handbook

Other Books By The Author

Fiction:

What's Happening?
Part 35
Sicilian Defense
Courthouse
J. T.

Nonfiction:

Trial : Strategy and Psychology
Disposition by Guilty Plea

Handbook
of
CROSS-EXAMINATION

The Mosaic Art

SECOND EDITION

John Nicholas Iannuzzi

PRENTICE HALL

Library of Congress Cataloging-in-Publication Data
Iannuzzi, John Nicholas,
    Cross-examination handbook / John Nicholas Iannuzzi, — 2nd ed.
      p. cm.
    Rev. ed. of: Cross examination. c1982.
    Includes index.
    ISBN 0-13-779869-5
    1. Cross-examination—United States. I. Iannuzzi, John Nicholas,
  1935–   Cross examination.
  KF8920.I36   1998
  345.73'075—dc21   98-44119
                                                CIP

This publication is designed to provide accurate and authoritative information in regard to the subject matter covered. It is sold with the understanding that the publisher is not engaged in rendering legal, accounting, or other professional service. If legal advice or other expert assistance is required, the services of a competent professional person should be sought.

—From a Declaration of Principles jointly adopted by a Committee of the American Bar Association and a Committee of Publishers and Associations.

Printed in the United States of America

10 9 8 7 6 5 4 3 2 1

ISBN 0-13-779869-5

ATTENTION: CORPORATIONS AND SCHOOLS

Prentice Hall books are available at quantity discounts with bulk purchase for educational, business, or sales promotional use. For information, please write to: Prentice Hall & Special Sales, 240 Frisch Court, Paramus, NJ 07652. Please supply: title of book, ISBN number, quantity, how the book will be used, date needed.

PRENTICE HALL
Paramus, NJ 07652

A Simon & Schuster Company

On the World Wide Web at http://www.phdirect.com

Prentice-Hall International (UK) Limited, *London*
Prentice-Hall of Australia Pty. Limited, *Sydney*
Prentice-Hall Canada, Inc., *Toronto*
Prentice-Hall Hispanoamericana, S.A., *Mexico*
Prentice Hall of India Private Limited, *New Delhi*
Prentice Hall of Japan, Inc., *Tokyo*
Simon & Schuster Asia Pte. Ltd., *Singapore*
Editora Prentice-Hall do Brasil, Ltda., *Rio de Janeiro*

About the Author

John Nicholas Iannuzzi is a partner in Iannuzzi and Iannuzzi. To date, Mr. Iannuzzi has handled more than 200 homicide cases in most of the counties of greater New York, as well as cases in every area of penal law. He has also handled all manner and type of civil cases, including contracts, trademark infringement, tort, and matrimonial. His practice ranges through every jurisdiction—local, federal, and even through the appellate courts up to the United States Supreme Court

Mr. Iannuzzi holds a BS-SS from Fordham College in New York and a JD from New York Law School. In addition to his practice, he has been an adjunct professor of trial advocacy at the Fordham University School of Law since 1988. Mr. Iannuzzi has been recognized by Who's Who in American Law, Editions 1 through 9 (current) and Who's Who in the World (1993 to the present). He is the author of two other law books, *Trial Strategy and Psychology* and *Disposition by Guilty Plea,* as well as five other fiction works.

Contents

Chapter 3   Pre-Trial Discovery   *29*

Chapter 4   Depositions: Cross-Examination of a Different Color   *39*

Chapter 5   On-Trial Discovery   55

PART II

Controlling the Cross-Examined Witness   79

PART III

Prior Inconsistent Statements   175

Chapter 16   Prior Inconsistent Statements   *177*

Chapter 17   Prior Inconsistent Statements Made Under Oath   *183*

PART IV
Special Tools and Tactics   245

Cross-Examination: The Mosaic Art

Cross-Examination Handbook

Opening Statement

The Best Cross-Examination Is One That Never Takes Place

Cross-examination is intended to whittle down your trial Adversary's direct evidence, to hone down the case against your client, and to take testimony and exhibits intended by your Adversary to damage your client and neutralize or dilute them substantially. When your Adversary puts a witness on the stand whose testimony does no harm whatever to your client, there is normally no need to cross-examine that witness as there is nothing you have to overcome and nothing that needs whittling down.

Your aim as trial counsel is to protect your client's interests, not to sharpen the cutting edge of your cross-examiner's blade. Thus, the first tenet of the cross-examiner's creed is that a witness whose evidence is either favorable, neutral, or fits comfortably into your own overview of the ultimate mosaic of your case, should not ordinarily be questioned.

Curtail the Evidence Against You

The next best thing to having no adverse evidence offered against your client is to permit as little harmful evidence as possible to be introduced against your client. The cross-examiner can be instrumental in accomplishing that by curtailing the introductory flow of your Adversary's evidence. Where you have the opportunity to curtail adverse evidence by objecting to its admissibility, you would be very foolish, indeed, to be magnanimous, to be silent, to tacitly permit your Adversary to build a fortress you must ultimately storm.

Knowing the rules of the admissibility of evidence and guarding against improper incursions by your Adversary are superb methods of protecting

1

your client. You do not have to cross-examine a witness on testimony or evidence the judge does not admit.

In the ensuing pages of this book, there will be very little, if any, discussion of the rules for the admissibility of Direct evidence. However, crucial in curtailing your Adversary's Direct case is knowing the rules of admissibility of evidence completely, thus to be in position to limit the case against your client before it ever gets off the ground.

Cross-Examination—A Volatile Weapon

Cross-examination is the basic weapon in the armament of all trial lawyers.

Strangely, despite the basic nature and need of Cross-examination to the trial attorney, it is a weapon rarely used effectively. One need only sit as a spectator at actual trials and hearings to know that most lawyers conduct abysmally ineffective Cross-examinations and, as a result, lose many a case unnecessarily.

This last remark is not intended as an insult to trial lawyers. It is intended, rather, to point out that knowing substantive law and having passed a Bar examination is not preparation enough to match wits with a live witness. In Cross-examination, the trial lawyer is not making a prepared speech as he does—or should do—in an opening statement or a summation; he is not researching a law brief in the quiet of the library, where he can rely upon Blackstone and Cardozzo. You are on your feet, in front of a jury, the center of attention. You must do all the following: remember the Direct examination and attempt to form withering questions for the witness, recall the law of evidence, keep in mind the substantive law, preserve the record for possible appeal, and try to look cool and undisturbed.

Despite the importance and difficulty of Cross-examination, most trial lawyers have had very little, if any, schooling in the art. Professors at law school can usually trace pleasant bromides about trying cases and cross-examining witnesses. However, most professors have not had sufficient trial experience to properly prepare students for the trial, and, even if they have, being told how to cross-examine is a far cry from the real thing. The real school for Cross-examination is the arena, the well of the courtroom; the real teacher is the confrontation, when cap and gown are tossed off, and you grapple cheek to jowl and eyeball to eyeball with the Adverse Witness.

Because neither the inexperienced neophyte nor the busy practicing trial lawyer has the time or opportunity to witness as many talented and able trial lawyers in action as he or she might wish in order to observe, study, and perfect his or her technique, this book reveals some of the methods and disciplines that can be employed to unstring rather than be unstrung.

Cross-Examination—The Mosaic Art

While the legendary big kill, the inquiry which paralyzes the witness, completely destroying his will to resist the cross-examiner's onslaught, and which brings total victory to your cause, is a consummation devoutly to be wished, it is usually just that: a wish. In the course of an ordinary trial, you should not expect, or even try for, a big kill. It just isn't there. Of course, if that rare opportunity to be victorious with one or two poignant questions does present itself, do not hesitate to embrace it.

In the ordinary trial, however, you shall be fighting an Adversary who is probably as aware of the potential good and bad points of the case as you are, and you shall cross-examine a human being who isn't going to easily let you make him look the fool in front of the jury or the court. Both your Adversary and his witness know where you want to go, and they are not going to make it easy for you or be pawns in your march to total victory. Therefore, be aware of your purposes as you rise to cross-examine; it is to whittle down the enemy's evidence, to make it work for you, and to make it fit into your trial strategy. The most important aim of successful Cross-examination is to take the evidence intended by your Adversary to damage your case, and reshape it into a useful piece of information that will fit comfortably, compatibly, into your own case.

Cross-examination is not an end unto itself. Just as an artist, working a mosaic, fits bits and pieces of material together to ultimately create an entire picture, the cross-examiner's aim is the reshaping of an Adversary's evidence into pieces which, by the end of the trial, will, together with your own evidence, either fit into a mosaic of fact supporting your position or that adverse evidence shall be made to appear as innocuous background material.

The Mosaic Need Not Be Worked from Left to Right

It is not necessary for you to assemble the mosaic in a rigid, systematic order.

Disorder or confusion, of course, are not being suggested. You can, however, assemble different sections of the mosaic, with the pieces seeming to be disparate, unconnected, the pattern only beginning to become apparent toward the end of the case. Then, with your own inimitable style, pulled together at the summation. Too ordered a progression of the mosaic before then may telegraph your direction and alert your Adversary to set up road-blocks.

The same principle of not telegraphing trial strategy by too systematic an approach is also true in regard to the individual Cross-examination of a witness. Headlong, didactic, pragmatic, continuous inquiry along a particular line may permit the witness to anticipate your path and prepare his or her mind to deliver harmful answers. It is better, therefore, to have the goal of your Cross-examination clear in your mind. Cover a certain line of inquiry, go on to another aspect of the examination, return to the first line of inquiry, then go to a third, then return to the second. In this way, the witness must be alert to an attack from any quarter, and cannot spend time anticipating the next questions, and cannot prepare to cut your supports out from under you.

The most important thing to understand about Cross-examination is that it is a purposeful method to carefully whittle down your Adversary's evidence and to help form the bits and pieces that will be the mosaic of your client's case on summation.

It is not necessary for either the jury or your Adversary to understand where all the pieces shall ultimately fit. It is only important that you form the pieces and establish the facts carefully and pointedly. Then, in stunning summation, you draw all the pieces together for the jury into an irresistible fabric of logic.

Cross-Examination—A Controlled Discipline

To be an effective cross-examiner, you must know just where you want to go with your Cross-examination, go only there, and not an inch beyond. Simply, you must control every aspect of the examination: its direction, its questions, the witness, and even the answers the witness gives. You must know the answers a witness will give before you ever ask a question, and you must not ask questions that will hurt your cause. Most of all, you must control yourself. Do not permit yourself the folly of enjoying some personal thrill at your client's expense. You do not have to prove your skill to your client. If he or she didn't think you were the best, you wouldn't be trying his or her lawsuit.

Most Important: Believe Your Ears and Eyes

What could be more critical to Cross-examination than knowing precisely what the witness has testified on Direct in order that you might cross-examine the actual testimony? You must, therefore, carefully listen to the witness's words, watch the witness's demeanor on the stand, and believe it as it actually is, as the witness actually transmits that testimony and demeanor. *Do not interpose your concept or interpretation for the witness's own words or acts.* Believe and accept only that which you actually hear and see. And believe in yourself. That is what you actually heard. That is what you actually saw.

There is a great art to listening and reading so that you actually hear or see what has occurred. Studies show that people actually apprehend and comprehend only a portion of what was actually said. The art of listening requires that you not close your mind and not put your own meaning to that which is being transmitted by the witness. Do not have a half-open mind to receive only half of what you hear or see. Try to follow what you are perceiving and get the meaning that is being transmitted, with all its own nuances, its own intendment, and even its own imperfections. For example, what is being written on these pages is intended exactly as it is written. Not one word is being put down idly or carelessly; each word is here because the author believes that it is necessary to convey the meaning intended. While you might have put your thoughts on paper differently, in order to understand what the author is saying, you must accept his words as he gives them, and attempt to assimilate that meaning as it is given.

When a witness is saying something, he or she must be using his or her own, chosen words for a purpose. Psychologists and psychiatrists often quote Freud as saying there are no such things as accidents, not even with words. So when witnesses are saying something, when they are testifying, they are conveying meaning even in their choice of words. Listen to the exact words they are using; try to understand and flow along with them. Cross-examine based on what they *actually* said, not on what you believe or assume they said.

A great deal of meaning is transmitted by the witness through his or her demeanor on the stand, through facial expressions, through anger that is too intense, through laughs and smiles, through hesitations, and through recitation by rote. These must be received by the cross-examiner as they are actually transmitted, giving an understanding of what the witness is saying thereby, and thus be used to modify or frame the Cross-examination of that witness. You must believe your ears and eyes, you must accept what they pick up from the witness, and you must work from that material, for that, and only that, is direct evidence. *Your interpretation of what was said is not direct evidence.*

This, of course, does not mean that your mind must cease functioning, that you need not attempt to translate what the witness says into your own thoughts, that you need not think beyond what the witness says. Your first task, however, which is quintessential to using your own thoughts to decipher what the witness said, is to know exactly what the witness *did* say. You will find suggestions in the following text as to how to capture the exact testimony on paper as it is being given, and how you can simultaneously begin to frame, on paper, your own reaction to that testimony, your contrapuntal questions.

Nail Down the Answers

Many a cross-examiner, knowing all the rules, the pitfalls, and the tenets of Cross-examination, still permits a trapped witness to walk out of the trap unscathed. This is not because the witness was so crafty, but because the examiner was too lethargic and casual to bother flushing out the witness. It is not unusual for a cross-examiner to take a piece of information, perhaps a Deposition or grand jury minutes, in which the witness made a prior inconsistent statement under oath, hold the document in hand, even show it to the witness, casually refer to something contained in the document, then sit down, pleased in his or her own mind that it was a complete and exhausting examination.

Be cautioned: It is not enough for the cross-examiner to be satisfied that he uncovered inconsistency. That inconsistency must be brought home to the attention of the jury, clearly and precisely. You are shaping the pieces of the mosaic *for the jury,* and they must be shaped with precision. It may be that the jury need not know exactly what you are going to do with the pieces of the mosaic until summation, but the jury must know exactly what the pieces of the mosaic are. They must know all of its nuances, meanings, and boundaries. Therefore, when you have a witness on the ropes, finish him off, nail down your point, and form that part of the mosaic fully and completely before the jury or the trier of fact, with no mistakes about it. It is worthless just to mention something in passing and sit down without being careful that the point is fully formed, fully shaped, and fully understood by the trier of fact.

This doesn't mean that the jury has to sit up and applaud. The mosaic should only be assembled completely at summation. But be careful. Because you understand a point, because you read a report that makes a witness a liar, don't *assume* that the jury knows it too. Get the point before the jury; get it out there clearly and on the record, so that it will be there for you to remind them of it later. If the witness is a liar, make sure the jury knows it; read the report to them, make the witness testify that two opposites are true, and make the witness admit he made three different statements, even if he insists they are all true.

With all of these points in mind, with the concept of what Cross-examination is and what it isn't, let's proceed to the preparation that must be made in order to effectively cross-examine at trial.

And remember, no one said it was easy.

John Nicholas Iannuzzi

PART I

Cross-Examination of Witnesses

1.

The Scope of Cross-Examination

1.01 Limitless, Except

The scope of Cross-examination of an Adverse Witness is wholly unlimited, except that the questions asked must be relevant, material, and proper.

1.02 Relevant Cross-Examination

Relevant Cross-examination means simply that the thrust of the inquiry must relate to an issue of the trial at hand; it must have a nexus, a connection to the trial. A line of inquiry is not necessarily relevant, however, merely because it has some abstruse, strained connection to one of the parties or the subject matter at issue. Nor is an inquiry irrelevant merely because it is not directed at the *specific* subject matter of the trial.

To be relevant, Cross-examination of an Adverse Witness must be directed either toward that witness's (1) general knowledge, (2) specific knowledge of the particular event, or (3) the witness's personal character and integrity. These three cardinal target areas of Cross-examination are discussed more fully later in this chapter.

One can easily imagine that some of the inquiry relating to an Adverse Witness's personal character and integrity, his background, his possible criminal past, and his prior immoral or vicious acts would in no way be connected either to the principal parties of the litigation or the trial issues. Yet such inquiry is significant and relevant because it permits the jury to better gauge the credibility and truthfulness of the witness. Since the witness is testifying in connection with some aspect of the issues at trial, anything which bears upon that witness's credibility, which thus permits the jury to better assess some of the evidence in the case, is relevant to the trial. Thus, an inquiry as to a witness's criminal past while living in California five years prior to a trial arising from a contract action brought in Pennsylvania might be highly relevant. Yet, an inquiry in the same contract action, as to the route the witness took to get to the Pennsylvania courthouse that very morning, might be totally irrelevant.

Relevant Cross-examination, therefore, can be defined as an inquiry into one of the three cardinal target areas which, in some fashion, bear upon the Adverse Witness's:

1. general knowledge;
2. specific knowledge of the particular event; or
3. personal integrity or character.

1.03 Material Cross-Examination

Merely because a question falls into one of Cross-examination's three relevant cardinal target areas, however, does not guarantee that the trial court will permit the inquiry. The inquiry must also be *material*.

Materiality can be defined as something significant to an issue of the trial. For instance, an inquiry into the area of an Adverse Witness's general knowledge of rocks and geological matters would more than likely be totally *immaterial* to his testimony as a witness to a traffic accident. Such geological inquiry might be material, however, if it were to reveal to the jury that the witness's general intelligence is low and his capacity to recall impaired. Such revelation, however, might more appropriately be drawn out by questions relating to the subject matter at issue, rather than questions seeking totally unconnected information.

Thus, materiality sharpens the focus of relevant inquiries further, and requires that relevant issues be of some material significance to the issues on trial. If an inquiry, even though relevant to an issue at trial, shall, in no fashion, add to the jury's capacity to decide the issues, or give the jury a better view of the credibility of the witness, it may be considered immaterial by the trial judge. *Therefore, remember that not every relevant piece of information is sufficiently significant to be material.*

1.04 Proper Cross-Examination

Proper Cross-examination is easier to define than either relevant or material Cross-examination; it is that which is permitted by law, by the rules of evidence. Thus, an inquiry may be both relevant and material to a trial issue, but the trial court will still not permit the inquiry because it violates some rule of evidence, such as hearsay.

Therefore, I urge the cross-examiner to know the law thoroughly: not only the substantive law, but particularly the rules of evidence, the procedural law. In my view, a complete Trial Advocate cannot possibly be formed from an attorney who does not know the law, is not conversant with the very latest decisions, and does not read the law constantly.

Without knowledge of the direction in which to travel, of the new trails that have been blazed on the outer edges of the law, the cross-examiner might completely miss his destination, might even be traveling along an old, outmoded road no longer leading anywhere, and thus lose the entire trial. A cross-examiner might have the most harmful evidence with which to actually destroy an Adverse Witness, but, if she is not aware of the proper and approved legal method of bringing that evidence before the jury, it will do her client—and, therefore, herself—no good whatever.

In the following chapters, I discuss the proper methods of cross-examining witnesses, including some of the applicable procedural laws. Read these chapters carefully so that this information shall become knowledge stored in your head, which, together with the evidence in hand, shall at some future time be used before a jury when it may do some good.

1.05 The Cardinal Target Areas of Cross-Examination

As stated previously, Cross-examination is the trial attorney's most significant tool with which to subject the testimony of an Adverse Witness to searing heat and to hone that testimony down to an unadorned, unembellished fact. To do this, the cross-examiner must attack testimony in the three cardinal target areas: the general capacity of the witness; the witness's specific knowledge of the particular event; and the witness's personal integrity and character.

1.06 General Capacity of the Witness

Naturally, general knowledge refers to the witness's capacity to know, to understand, to observe, and to remember; that is, the witness's general capacity to be a recording and recounting agent. This capacity is revealed during even the most fundamental questioning, through the witness's capacity to hear and understand your questions; to respond with basic common intelligence; and his or her capacity to describe events, to gauge distances, and to be consistent.

A jury can observe the witness's demeanor on the stand, his basic reliability, at the same time as you are inquiring into other matters. In other words, you do not have to devise an I.Q. test as preliminary Cross-examination to permit the jury a view of the witness's general intelligence. While you are examining a witness, either on preliminary matters or essential facts, you should, at the same time, be drawing the witness out in the area of his or her general intelligence. If the jury sees and hears a witness whose story about an event is perfectly and consistently recited time after time, yet, in every other area except the story of the event at issue, the witness is floundering, confused, and incapable of speaking with accuracy or intelligence, that jury will get the idea that the witness has merely been rehearsed, but is generally a person they—the jury—would never rely upon even for common traffic directions. Therefore, try to draw the witness out; make him think before the jury; and pose questions that do not permit mere recitation, but require actual thinking and answers to your questions, instead of practiced responses to anticipated inquiries.

1.07 Specific Knowledge of the Particular Event

In addition to drawing out the general intelligence of the witness, the specifics of the event or the occurrence about which the witness testifies should be probed. Despite the fact that the witness may have superior intelligence and retentive capacity, if the witness was not in a position to see or hear what he or she has described, if the witness could not possibly have been able to perceive the events described, then all the intelligence and wisdom in the world should not permit the witness to withdraw from the witness stand unscathed.

Your Cross-examination may be long or short, depending on the particular case and witness. Where you perceive a gross and glaring error or inconsistency, this might, by itself, render the witness's testimony ludicrous and patently false. Thus, bringing this error or inconsistency directly to the jury's attention might be all that the cross-examiner needs to do to discredit the witness totally. *I quickly suggest here, however, that, ordinarily, Cross-examination is not that dramatic or absolute.*

Where the witness's story is inconsistent and inaccurate in more subtle ways, Cross-examination will obviously have to be longer and more subtle, setting factual traps into which the witness, hopefully, shall fall. The ultimate result should be a display of inaccuracy, inconsistency, and unreliability, which prevents the jury from totally accepting the witness's version of what occurred. A chink in every witness's armor reduces your Adversary's army to a disarmed mob.

1.08 Personal Character and Integrity of the Witness

Even though a witness is intelligent and was potentially in the perfect position to have seen or heard what has been described, he or she may be discredited as a person of questionable character or an interested witness, one who has an ulterior motive to effect a result favorable to the party on whose behalf he or she has testified. This does not mean that a mere attack upon a witness because he or she may be living in unsolemnized union, or because the witness once was convicted of a crime, or once had a disagreement with the party against whom the witness testifies, shall, *ipso facto,* totally discount the witness's testimony in the eyes of the jury. Indeed, such fact might accomplish precisely that. On the other hand, even a prostitute, a criminal, a drunk, or a person who delves in any sort of behavior that might be considered antisocial could have a truthful or lucid moment, which, if believed by a jury, could be your unstringing. Thus, your Cross-examination must be channeled toward meaningful, telling targets which are relevant, material, and significant to the issue on trial, and not merely an abstract exercise in Cross-examination.

1.09 Control the Examination

Controlling your witness as indicated in my Opening Statement is quintessential. For without such control, a garrulous witness will bombard you with his adverse version of the event at every opportunity. For instance, you could ask:

> Q: The reason you were at the window, looking out into the street, was to watch your son cross safely, correct?
>
> A: At first, *but then I turned and saw the car come through the light.*

Your question has been answered, of course, but the witness has added a gratuitous remark (italics) intended to and which does hurt your position. You have two choices: ignore it and go on or discipline the witness.

Ignoring the gratuitous remark:

Q: But your initial reason to be at the window was to watch the street—that is where your attention was, watching your son cross the street, was it not?

A: Only at first; *when he got to the other side, I looked and saw the car go through the light.*

By ignoring the gratuitous statement, by permitting the witness, with impunity, to lard on the hurt, you are teaching the witness that you are permissive and shall suffer such injury with impunity.

NOTE: "What is not corrected, is taught."

In the previous instance, your brains are being beaten out by the gratuitous remarks of the witness who is doing it purposely. Rather than having ignored the nonresponsive answer, it would have been better to undertake remedial action immediately, turning to the court and saying:

CROSS-EXAMINER: Your Honor, I object to the answer as not being responsive to the question. I ask that the answer be stricken and the witness instructed to answer the question only and not make gratuitous remarks.

THE COURT: The answer will be stricken. Please answer only the questions asked. Mr. Adversary will have an opportunity on redirect examination to bring out any other factors relating to your observations. Proceed.

You must undertake to discipline the witness, to curtail the witness taking liberal potshots at your client as many times as necessary to force the witness to answer the questions asked. *You must be in control!* Of course, your questions have to be properly couched and framed so that you do not unartfully seek the wrong answer. Also, the court must properly direct the witness to respond to the questions only. In other words, the court must back you up in controlling the witness. Where the court fails to require the witness to answer only the questions asked, there are other courses, which I discuss later, that must be taken.

REMINDER: You are not on your feet to show the jury or the court how clever, cute, or correct you are. Your client's ultimate concern in the facts of the case is the polestar you follow.

2.

Analyzing the Case on Trial

2.01 Cross-Examination Is Formulated Long Before Trial

The cross-examiner cannot wait until after the Adverse Witnesses have testified on Direct examination to begin formulating a plan of attack.

It is far too late at that point!

The plan for cross-examining a witness must be initiated long before either party or any witnesses reach a courtroom. The plan of attack must start with counsel's initial analysis of the case, of the issues to be tried; followed by an analysis of your Adversary's, as well as your client's, goals; and, finally, an analysis of what witnesses your Adversary shall necessarily have to rely upon in order to reach his or her goal.

True, it is not possible to formulate a finished, precise script of Cross-examination questions for a specific Adverse Witness long before trial. In the ordinary instance, only after a particular witness testifies are you aware of his or her exact testimonial words. However, it is possible, by careful and thorough pre-trial gathering of material, evidence, factual explorations, and witnesses's prior statements, in advance of trial, to formulate a fairly accurate picture of the path your Adversary's case must take and the facts to which your Adversary's witnesses must testify. Concomitantly, as a result of this advance knowledge, you shall be able to begin to erect formidable defenses to protect your client and to shape the Cross-examination by which to tear apart your Adversary's case.

2.02 Assembling Cross-Examination Materials

In order to best analyze your Adversary's case, you must put yourself in his or her shoes, think of what proofs he or she shall be required to offer, what elements of law he or she must prove, what witnesses he or she must necessarily bring forward, and to what facts those witnesses must testify in order to establish the Adversary case. Once you have analyzed what your Adversary must prove, the basic facts about which the Adverse Witnesses must testify, you shall, *ipso facto,* be able to determine both the defense posture you must assume, and what you must try to prevent your Adversary from proving. This anticipated defense posture shall be the mold in which you must form your defense and Cross-examination.

2.03 Knowledge of the Law

In addition to the analysis of both sides of the case that you anticipate shall come to trial, you must also research and familiarize yourself with the law, both procedural and substantive, relative to the specific questions that have arisen or shall arise relative to that case, particularly singular or unique issues.

> NOTE: *Don't delude yourself by thinking I'm a Trial Advocate, not a law person. There is no way that you can be a brilliant Trial Advocate without, at the same time, being a law Advocate. Indeed, the most important tool of the trial lawyer is knowledge of the law.*

While the trial Advocate may never write a brief or argue an appeal, in order to properly represent a client, the trial lawyer must necessarily be "up" on the latest appeal court developments in both the substantive and procedural law, to ensure that the thrust of Cross-examination—the entire direction of the case—be guided away from paths abandoned or outmoded by the latest appeal court decisions.

The lazy or arrogant Advocate, just having read the above, has already said to himself or herself, I am "up" on the law. If it is not your habit to continually read the latest decisions, either in slip opinion, or, at least, in advance sheets from federal and state reports, how do you know that you are "up"? Perhaps three weeks ago, or last week, a case was decided on a matter similar to the one you are preparing for trial, and an issue on all fours (or perhaps threes) with the one you are presently trying was redefined. If you do not read the advance sheets, in a few months perhaps, you will eventually "discover" the new decision after the concentric ripples reach further and further out from the stone in the pond (the decision); but what happens between the time of the decision and the time that you "discover" the new holding? How many clients shall be poorly served, how many pleadings shall be incorrectly drawn or answered, and how many questions on Cross-examination which should have been asked, won't be because you didn't know and weren't really up on the latest cases?

Stare decisis, our common law system of refining the law through appellate review, is a vital, living system because it is ever-changing, ever-improving, and held back from perfection only by the lack of philosophical and theoretical imagination of its participants. Indeed, had lawyers been too timid or unwilling to joust on the outer perimeters of the law, seeking to push into new areas and to modify decisions no longer viable because the conditions which existed at the time of those decisions had changed, as one appellate judge once wrote, our law would be no different now than at the time of the Plantagenet. Thus, the trial lawyer who does not keep up with the latest cases and decisions is guilty of malpractice, for he or she can not truly and properly represent his or her client's interests. Examples of the need to be aware of the ever-expanding body of law are, for instance, the issue formerly raised by an injury to a pregnant woman. At one time, the woman could recover for injuries sustained to herself but not to the child, even if it was later born deformed as a result of negligence, because at the time of the injury the child was not a being *in esse.*

As a result of advances in medical science and follow-up legal trail blazing, the law has come to recognize that a child in the womb is *in esse* long before it actually reaches full term. If a child can be plucked from its injured mother's womb and remain alive by medical supports, is it not a being *in esse,* independent of its mother? The mere fact that it must grow and mature further is no more a reason for its being considered nonexistent, than it would be to consider a child of two years of age not a human being because it is dependent on its parents. Going further, if a child is a genetically complete human being immediately upon conception, with a full complement of genes, its sex, eye and hair coloring already determined, its height and weight potential fixed forever, needing thereafter only shelter and nourishment from its mother to continue in existence (do we, the already born, not need continued shelter and nourishment to live?) then is not the child *en ventre sa mere* a being *in esse* immediately upon conception?

It is not necessary here to delineate the latest law on the subject matter of recovery for injury to an unborn child. However, the implications for a trial lawyer representing such a pregnant woman are obvious; how can you develop evidence, through Direct and Cross-examination, to support your client's claim for damages without knowing the current state of the law on the subject? How can you properly cross-examine the medical witnesses, to lead them into the necessary avenues and cul-de-sacs to develop the true proportions of your case, to uncover the facts which might develop a proper record for an appeal that will unlock further doors in the evolution of the law, unless you know what the law currently holds on your subject?

In the criminal field, an example of the need to be "up" on the law might be a claim, on behalf of a defendant, of a violation of constitutional protection from illegal search and seizure. Let's say you make a motion to suppress certain physical evidence, an illegal pistol, found on the person of your client. You, the judge, and the prosecutor know that if the weapon is suppressed, the prosecutor has no other evidence against your client and the case must be dismissed. Thus, the suppression hearing is the essence of the case against your client.

During the hearing, the prosecutor develops, upon his examination of the arresting police officer, almost as an aside, that the area in which the arrest was made was a high-crime area; that the police officer felt some concern for his own safety. During your Cross-examination of the officer, you inquire about all the facts concerning probable cause that you believe are significant. You do not bother, however, to inquire into the high-crime portion of the officer's testimony and are not aware that current decisions have held that certain extenuating circumstances might raise a nonpermissive search into a permissive search. Examples of such extenuating circumstances are a high-crime area and a perception of endangered personal safety on the part of the policeman, or circumstances like furtiveness, resistance, and flight.

Surely, many trial lawyers familiar with civil or criminal matters have said to themselves, "That's kid stuff." It might be kid stuff now, to you. That's because you know these particular factors. But they wouldn't be kid stuff if you weren't familiar with them; they weren't kid stuff when the cases permitting such recovery in the civil law, and such searches in the criminal law, were just decided. It wasn't even kid stuff for six to nine months after the decisions appeared in the advance sheets, that time before the osmosis effect of the decisions made them so widely known that even the legal laggards became aware of them and took their holdings into account. And it wasn't kid stuff—and it still isn't—to the people who did not make a financial recovery, to the people who went to jail because their lawyers didn't know that kid stuff.

By the way, I can't tell what tomorrow's "kid stuff" will be, nor can you, until I read my slip opinions and advance sheets.

CAUTION: Advance sheets are ordinarily three months behind the actual date of decision. In that hiatus, the law may have been changed again.

I suggest you subscribe to or regularly read a library's copy of slip opinions of the highest appeal courts within your jurisdiction or area of practice.

Remember, the law a lawyer must know is not yesterday's law, or last month's law; it's today's law.

2.04 Physical Investigation

In addition to analyzing the issues to be tried and researching the applicable law, the trial attorney must conduct a physical investigation of whatever real evidence might exist in the case: the scene of the accident, the place of occurrence of a crime, the physical documents, or whatever other tangible evidence may play a part in the forthcoming trial.

Being completely familiar with all the physical evidence which might possibly relate to the issues on trial, however remotely, pays amazing dividends to the trial lawyer, giving greater insight into the true character of the case, forearming the cross-examiner against attacks from quarters not anticipated, from witnesses whose testimony may raise issues brought forth for the first time during the trial. That little extra time and work spent during investigation before trial on seemingly unimportant details arms the cross-examiner to protect the client from attack from almost any direction in mid-trial. It also gives the trial attorney greater confidence and self-assurance that a hidden trap shall not be sprung to unhorse him or her in mid-trial.

If you are using an investigator, rather than investigating for yourself, be sure that the person you use is one who is reliable, thorough, and who, as you know from past experience, submits reports—preferably written—which are on the same wavelength as your understanding of reality. This ensures that you get the true and full picture of the entire fabric of the case necessary to do a complete, professional job for your client.

2.05 Photographs Should Be Obtained

Photographs of the scene, aerial photographs of the land, comparative photographs of size, graphs, charts, and any visual aids which give you a complete picture of the case should also be obtained and held in readiness so that you may confront any Adverse Witness with physical evidence of his inaccuracy or deviation from actual facts. As a picture is worth a thousand words, so too is a picture or other pieces of real evidence worth a thousand questions of an Adverse Witness who has misrepresented the facts, is inaccurate, or whose description of physical condition is actually inaccurate.

Being familiar with the physical realities about which the testimony shall, or even may, revolve puts the cross-examiner in a far stronger position to know and understand a surprise witness's testimony which suddenly reveals a new or unanticipated tactic of your Adversary, permitting the cross-examiner to probe the weakness of that testimony and tactic. Had the cross-examiner not taken the time to physically inspect and familiarize himself or herself totally with all aspects of the case, a witness, purposely or accidentally, might mislead the jury or fact finder by making incorrect or untrue statements which could escape the unknowing (when you don't know a fact, read this as unprepared) cross-examiner. As a result, the facts shall not be presented properly to the jury, and the outcome of the case and your client's cause shall turn on errors.

2.06 Rebuttal: Another Reason to Prepare for the Unknown

Some of you may think that in this day and age of enlightenment and full disclosure by way of witness lists, Depositions, and Discovery that there is no such thing as a surprise witness. Wrong!

First of all, in criminal cases, despite exceptional jurisdictions (Florida permits some Depositions in criminal cases) and high-profile Hollywood-like judicial settings, witness lists, full disclosure, and Depositions are the exception, the very rare exception, rather than the rule. In all federal cases—and the Federal Rules of Evidence are slowly evolving into a "national" standard Rules of Evidence—and in the majority of state cases, there is no such thing as Depositions in criminal cases, nor is there even any requirement for disclosure of a witness's prior Grand Jury testimony or of statements made by a witness to law enforcement until *after* the witness takes the stand and testifies (see 18 U.S.C. 3500 and your local disclosure statute). Totally at the option of the generous prosecutor, you may have such "Jencks" or Rosario, or whatever it is denominated, material the night before the witness takes the stand.

So the only way you can pre-trial prepare for such evolution on the spot, and put yourself in the educated position to interpret and analyze this last moment disclosure of significant witness information that certainly shall affect your Cross-examination, is to be fully aware—by way of pre-trial investigation—of all the physical evidence, the scene, the setting, and the circumstances of the case, in order to be able to move in any direction the disclosure and the soon-to-follow witness's testimony takes you.

Moreover, although there may be more generous witness lists and disclosure in civil cases, don't you Advocates who toil in the civil vineyards gloat with relief and be complacent because of the lack of necessity to anticipate surprise moves by your Adversary. There's always rebuttal.

If you are handling the defense case, and your Adversary feels that witnesses or evidence that you have put forth in your case requires a response or rebuttal, you may very well be facing undisclosed witnesses whose testimony is new, unexplored by way of Deposition. The only way to prepare for the unknown is to be prepared for anything, to know as much as you can about everything, so that nothing is the unknown.

2.07 Interviewing Witnesses

In addition to all the investigation of the physical evidence, photographs, documents, graphs, etc., described in the previous paragraphs, it is also essential to personally interview the witnesses who shall testify at the forthcoming trial.

Just as an aside, in criminal cases, interviewing prosecution witnesses may have the untoward effect of causing the prosecutor to attempt to intimidate defense counsel with the accusation that such interviews are an attempt to interfere with or are tantamount to an obstruction of justice. Therefore, be cautious to propriety, have another person with you, record the interview, and go forward to interview every witness who is willing to speak with you.

It is suggested that personal interviews, rather than telephone interviews, be utilized, as people have a greater tendency, when not confronted by a live interviewer, to be evasive, or to deny knowledge of the events so as not to be bothered having to testify, and, in general, to thwart the efforts of the interviewer to obtain a statement.

2.08 Write Out the Statement In Front of the Witness

When interviewing, you should always write out the statement being given by the witness—even a statement negative to your cause—and have the witness sign the same. Obviously, this must be done in front of the witness, so as to have the witness read the statement and sign it. There are several reasons why you should not write out an anticipated statement in advance. First, it may not turn out that the statement you wrote mirrors the witness's actual recollection of events. Second, the witness's reading of a preprepared statement shall turn your interview into a reading session. As a result, you will lose the flavor of the witness. You want to talk to the witness, feel him or her out for where his or her sentiments, if any, lie, for their viewpoint, their animosity or friendliness to your cause, and then write out the statement as you hear what they say.

2.09 Have the Witness Sign the Statement

As you shall learn in future chapters of this book, there are four "prior inconsistent statements" that may be used to challenge a witness's testimony. The second in order of importance is a document in the handwriting of or signed by the witness. Thus, to have the witness sign the interview statement is to create a prior statement which may very well become a prior inconsistent statement, depending on the longevity or fickleness of the particular witness's memory. In the event that the witness's testimony comports with the pre-trial interview statement, there is no inconsistency. However, variations occur in such a variety of ways and so often that a signed statement should be obtained on every occasion and with every witness possible.

2.10 Proving That the Witness Read the Statement Before Signing

In writing out an interview statement of a witness to, or a participant in, the events at issue in a particular case, the statement should be handwritten by the interviewer during the interview, and then read by the witness. When the witness has finished reading the statement, ask the witness to sign it. If the witness refuses, you still have the interview, your notes, and a very good idea what the witness may testify to at trial. Notice I say what the witness *may* testify to at trial. The very purpose of having the interview is to get an idea of what may come. The very purpose of having the statement signed is for future possible use as a prior inconsistent statement.

When writing out this memorialization of your interview with the possible trial witness, a good practice is to make occasional, intentional mistakes in the writing of the document. Don't be concerned that you may have to cross out your mistakes. In fact, *you actually want* the crossings out to appear in the document. During the reading of the said document by the witness—assuming the witness agrees to sign the same—have the witness initial the xxx'd out errors. By having the witness initial the document in various places where errors were made and crossed out, you have gone a long way to eliminate a future claim by the witness whose testimony may change adversely to your cause, that the witness did not read the entire document before signing it, but merely signed it at its foot, in compliance with your demand for signature.

Each page of a multipage document should be signed at the bottom of each page by the witness. Thus, the witness shall sign and initial not only the mistakes or crossings out on each page of the document, but you should ask the witness to sign the bottom of each page of the document.

To have a more complete handwriting sample and proof that the witness truly signed the entire document, ask the witness to write the following:

"I have read the above two pages and they are true."

Then have the witness sign his or her name and write in the date at the end of the handwritten statement about having read the document. You have now gone a long way to ensure that the witness cannot make a claim of having only signed the document at the bottom without reading it.

2.11 Negative Statements Are Equally Important

I've prepared you for the witness who gives you a statement and refuses to sign it. Now I want you to be prepared for a witness who makes a statement that is totally adverse to your case or totally negative because the witness claims not to know anything about the events. It is equally important, when interviewing such witnesses who profess adverse or no knowledge of the events, to obtain a written version of their statement. Why, you ask? Why would you want a totally adverse statement or a statement in which the potential witness declares that he or she has no information that can assist you in your case? The reason is simple: to eliminate any fluctuation in that witness's testimony at trial. If he or she gives you an adverse statement and his or her trial testimony varies, you have a prior inconsistent statement to show that the witness has told other versions of the facts on other occasions, thus undermining the reliability of the witness.

In the instance where the witness has declared that he or she knows nothing of the events of the case, by taking a statement of his or her ignorance, you are ensuring against that witness having a sudden flash of recollection, particularly if that flash favors your Adversary. Negative statements such as one that clearly sets forth that the witness's adverse position or one that shows that the witness is incapable of testifying, give you a solid position vis-à-vis that witness. You are eliminating your Adversary's capacity to mold that witness's testimony otherwise, to miraculously refresh that witness's recollection and use the witness against you in an unexpected fashion.

There are some who may counsel against the recordation of an Adverse Witness's statement because the same may have to be turned over to your Adversary. First of all, if you found that witness, as a result of your investigation into the case, it is likely that your Adversary also found that witness. You aren't giving your Adversary much of a find. Your Adversary already knows what that testimony is likely to be. You haven't changed it or added a single morsel of information to the Adverse Witness's testimony. You only recorded it. It is truly amazing how a witness's testimony changes each time he or she gives it. You are likely to have created your own prior inconsistent statement when you recorded the witness's recollection. It is likely to vary somewhat upon repetition at trial. Unless you intend to call the witness you have interviewed and who gave you a less than favorable recollection of the facts, and unless you know your Adversary intends to call or is going to use that same witness, there appears to be no obligation created by the Rules of Evidence to turn over to your Adversary statements of persons who are not intended to be called by either side.

2.12 Obtain Official Records and Reports

The cross-examiner, in preparing his case, should obtain every official report or document which has bearing on the issues in the case: i.e., hospital reports, weather reports, statistical analyses, studies, economic evaluations, and so on. These documents, just as the physical examination of evidence and the interviewing of witnesses, may often be superfluous, but the superfluity shall only be determined in hindsight when the trial is over. It is far better to have extra arrows in your quiver which may not have to be used, than to reach back into the quiver to draw an arrow and find nothing there but air.

2.13 Prepare Your Case in Every Respect

It may ultimately turn out that you do not use each and every item that you have investigated. However, the fact that you are totally familiar with the case can, in no fashion, hurt. In fact, such familiarity with the case will stand you in good stead when your Adversary presents a witness you have not anticipated or for whom you have not specifically prepared. Your total readiness shall put you in a position to know and understand everything that your Adversary may put forward and all that any Adverse Witness may testify to, and that puts you in a position from which you can cross-examine with strength.

2.14 Use Electronic Technology to Store and Retrieve Evidence

Computers and electronic gadgets that are so much a part of modern life can in no fashion substitute for an Advocate's hard work, investigation, interviewing, or analysis of evidence. You have come a long way, studied long and hard, passed the bar, and proven that you have high intelligence. Computers are made of plastic and glass, have no intelligence; except what you put into them. They cannot do your work for you. However, computer technology can and should be used to store and sort the information that you have uncovered.

2.15 Create a File for Each Witness and Each Subject

Witnesses

Create a computer file for each witness. Into that file input each piece of information that you uncover concerning the witness, the participation, or lack thereof, of that witness in the events, and the testimony that the witness may or may not be able to give from the witness stand. Scan into your computer a copy of the witness's statement that you took at the interview. In that file, begin to prepare a tentative script for the upcoming Cross-examination that you anticipate. With each new twist in the case and with each new piece of information, you may want to add to or modify your evolving script. Move around the segments of the script for better dramatic presentation to the jury. You do not have to wait, indeed, you should not wait for the trial to begin the script of Cross-examination for each witness. (More on this in later chapters.) However, at this point, let it suffice to say that computers have made it far easier to store and retrieve information, to formulate strategy, and, therefore, to begin to plan the downfall of the Adverse Witness.

Make a list of witnesses with their addresses and phone numbers. Print a hard copy of this witness list and add the list to your trial book to be updated on an as-needed basis so that you won't have to waste any time finding or contacting witnesses.

Subjects

As you begin to uncover information, make an investigation file under a directory of the case on your computer. In this investigation file, input subjects that you think may have some bearing on the case. As your investigation proceeds, add to each subject whatever information you uncover, developing or refining the information as you go along. Sort the information alphabetically to form an index. Print a hard copy of your index for your trial book. Add to the factual subject information, any names, addresses, or phone numbers that may be significant in following up on the subject matter. Add the names of experts that you might want to contact to unravel some of the aspects of the subject, i.e., engineers, handwriting analysts, actuaries, psychologists, doctors, and the like. Add these experts to your witness subdirectory with their addresses and phone numbers.

Research

Begin to research the case, inputting the names of cases that shall have a particular impact on the case and salient language from the case that you may want to have ready for the court when needed. Copy over to this file any standard language or citations that may ordinarily play a part in the type case at hand, whether this relates to picking of the jury, conduct of the trial, examination of witnesses, or judge's charge. You will soon see that the computer can be a superb assistant, ready to provide you with an up-to-date picture of the case, to stand ready to provide you with an accurate picture of the state of the case. But remember, the computer is only an assistant. It can produce nothing except a quick retrieval of information that you have uncovered. You are the Advocate.

3.

Pre-Trial Discovery

3.01 Physical Evidence

As mentioned Chapter 2, to totally analyze the case to be tried from the point of view of your Adversary and yourself and understand all the issues which must be developed or which you shall face at trial, you must obtain all of the physical materials available: documents, statements, and official reports, which are potential ammunition to attack those witnesses offered against your client and yourself.

3.02 Discovery by Court Order

In pre-trial preparation, it is helpful to explore with your Adversary the avenue of voluntary disclosure of documents and statements under her control. Of course, this is a two-way avenue and you must be prepared to reciprocate in voluntarily turning over such documents or information to your Adversary. In a criminal case, the defendant and the defense counsel are constitutionally protected from turning over certain types of evidence, i.e., the equivalent of testimonial evidence from the defendant which might normally be required in a civil case.

In practical terms, perhaps because of the lack of *quid pro quo,* Discovery material supplied by the prosecutor in a criminal case is minimal and selective. Courts often require prosecutors to turn over only the documents that the prosecutor, by the strictest interpretation of statute, deems are necessary to disclose.

Regardless of the type of case and the generosity of your Adversary, if you believe that there are more documents or Discovery that you are entitled to receive, do not hesitate to apply to the motion part of the court for the additional information, by way of a demand for a Bill of Particulars, a request for Discovery, or both, to obtain such reports, physical evidence, photographs, witness statements, tape recordings, and the like.

Since a motion to the court for additional particulars or discovery is by far the simplest method of having your Adversary involuntarily turn over materials, such a motion should be employed in every case without exception. The judge may not give you all that you demand, but that should not deter the trial lawyer from attempting to obtain the broadest discovery possible. You should include in such motion an application to have a physical inspection and examination of any implements, vehicles, photographs, products, or any other physical items or devices involved in the case. In this way you or your experts can see, feel, touch, analyze, or just stand back and look at that item or device which may be the pivotal point around which the issue of the trial may revolve.

After receiving documents and discovery, if you determine from the revealed information that there are other items that you believe should have been turned over, do not hesitate to make yet another Application to the court.

> NOTE: *It may be redundant at this juncture to suggest to the thorough trial lawyer that it is beneficial to have more information on hand that he or she can use, rather than to have one iota less than ultimately needed at the trial. At the risk of such repetition, I suggest that the preliminary minutes spent in preparation are far more beneficial than hours of last minute, frenzied panic.*

Since there are a variety of means available to both the Plaintiff, Prosecution, and Defendant, it would be foolish in the extreme for a trial lawyer not to exert himself or herself in the cool calm of his or her office, to obtain the discoverable facts in the case, rather than subject his or her client to the rigors of trial by the seat of the lawyer's pants or skirt.

Naturally, a busy trial lawyer does not have the luxury of working one case at a time to its completion. Indeed, it is not unusual that while an Advocate is working on a totally different matter, she continues to ferret out the pieces that shall ultimately compose the entire evidentiary fabric of a different case. However, by the time the Advocate is ready to sit down for the final trial preparation, her trial book should contain every scrap of information available for the trial. If it does, the final hours before the trial may be spent in substantial theory-of-the-case preparation rather than in investigation.

More importantly, with all the facts and potential evidence at hand, the Advocate shall not labor to formulate a half-baked theory of the case, or formulate a less than complete Cross-examination to support that theory, based on partial evidence.

To sum up, you should be completely familiar with all the real, physical evidence that might possibly exist in the case so that, in standing back and overviewing that evidence, the trial lawyer can intelligently determine which facts are material, relevant, and proper evidence, which are not, and which, therefore, need not be included in the preparation.

3.03 Obtain Witness Statements

I have already mentioned that witness statements should be obtained. Certainly, obtain every witness statement available, and try to find those witnesses who have not already made statements and have them make one as well, so that you will have prior statements available, if necessary, for use against those witnesses on Cross-examination. You will see in Chapter 4 that you can serve a Notice to Depose (also known as a Notice to Examine Before Trial) a non-party witness in order to reduce the witness's statement to a transcript under oath. The Deposition then serves not only as a discovery device—arming the Advocate with information—but *eo instante* becomes a potential prior inconsistent statement under oath for Cross-examination purposes when that witness testifies.

In yet another later chapter I explain why there is no weapon more effective in a cross-examiner's arsenal than a prior inconsistent statement, whether under oath, in writing, or oral, made by the very witness who is testifying against your client. I should note that it is relatively difficult to discover prior statements of potential witnesses not reduced to oath or writing. Your Adversary will hardly tell you if her potential witness made prior oral statements to her or her investigator. Additionally, it is nearly impossible to have a court-ordered divulgence of something not reduced to writing, which exists only in the mind of an attorney or her staff. Occasionally, however, during a Deposition, or even during trial, sworn testimony concerning a prior oral statement may be divulged. Occasionally, too, you or your investigator may interview a person who shall reveal to you that he or she heard a potential witness make a prior inconsistent oral statement. Gather all of these statements and input them into your computer, notes, and Trial Book.

3.04 Criminal Case Discovery

In criminal cases, amazingly, where the stakes involved are not dollars and insurance policies, but rather lives, liberty, and years in jail, there is far less discovery available than in a civil case. Not only is it difficult to ascertain pre-trial whether prosecution witnesses have made prior statements, whether oral or written, but Defense Counsel may find it difficult to discover even the names or the number of witnesses the Prosecutor intends to have testify against your client. As aforesaid, this nondisclosure by a prosecutor may exist, in part, as a direct official reaction to the constitutional privilege of the defendant in a criminal case not to be required to turn over any personal testimony or statements to his prosecutor.

This official lack of generosity may also result from the fact that prosecutors may be imbued with the altruistic notion that they are involved in protecting the commonweal, everyday citizens, from the depredations of criminals. While this is theoretically a noble concept, prosecutors may fail to realize that Defense Counsel, by the same laws and authority as the prosecution, is protecting the rights of members and citizens of the same commonweal. Both, from different sides of the table, undertake to enforce the law and constitution. Official disregard, evasion, or mere lip service to the constitutional provisions enacted by legislatures or decided upon by appellate courts can hardly be considered a preservation of the legal system. It should be academic that it is no skin off a prosecutor's nose to grant a fair trial to a citizen accused of a crime, giving that defendant every pre-trial and trial benefit and protection prescribed by law, only coming down with vigor upon the guilty defendant after conviction.

Additionally, part of the breakdown of blind justice enforcing the law with an impartial hand may result from the fact that the vast majority of judges are former prosecutors who may in some fashion maintain or extend while on the bench their "noble" perception of the need for them to personally overreach to protect the citizens from what they might consider a too-liberal system. Since the system and the law are synonymous, it is difficult to understand whence this righteous propensity flows, or how it can be perceived that curtailment of some citizen's rights, when defendants, is preserving the system. This role perception results far less frequently in places such as England, where barristers may act as prosecutors in one case, and in their very next case, act as defense counsel. The lack of a locked-in role may result in a clearer view of the Advocate's even-minded participation in the system.

However, merely because the road to fair trial may be difficult, it does not mean that it must not be pursued or tried. Some cases decided by the United States Supreme Court and Circuit Courts of Appeal have formed steps in the right direction toward more expanded Discovery, including, where appropriate, the names of witnesses who shall be presented at the trial. By the same token, it has been rightly determined that when there are extenuating circumstances, such as the possibility of intimidation or threats to the actual witnesses, the names and addresses of such witnesses need not be made available to defense counsel. Not surprisingly, the court before whom the motion is made for the Discovery of the names and addresses of witnesses in a criminal case is often advised by a zealous prosecutor that indeed there is a possibility of just such threats or intimidation to thwart the attempted discovery.

The only consolation I can offer, in the situation where there shall be resistance to your attempt to discover everything about the oncoming trial, is that cross-examiners lose 100 percent of the discovery motions they never make. Therefore, you have only to gain by making the motion, by attempting to get the discovery, by attempting to fully prepare yourself with all of the facts, which will then give you the platform from which to operate when you are facing the witnesses against you.

3.05 Utilize the Discovery

Naturally, once you have the desired Discovery, names of witnesses, or authority granted by the court to inspect, copy, or have certain items or things tested that are relevant to the case, do not hesitate, thereafter, to avail yourself of this information and to personally, or through experts, have the pieces of evidence developed. In the circumstance where you have the names of witnesses who may be called during the upcoming trial, it is incumbent upon counsel to have those witnesses interviewed for the purposes of a positive or negative statement for use during the trial.

3.06 Depositions and Interrogatories

In addition to application to the court for permission or authority to obtain particulars or discovery, trial counsel should also obtain Depositions or interrogatories which, as aforesaid, shall generate both knowledge and information as well as a potential prior statement under oath of the prospective witness. Also aforesaid, it is truly amazing how the recollections of witnesses vary during the pendency of the proceedings. Thus, the more prior statements that you have on hand, the more ammunition you have for Cross-examination. If the witness made an initial statement at or near the scene of the event, and is thereafter interviewed by your investigator and later deposed under oath, or fills out written interrogatories, you have more opportunity to test the recollection and credibility of the witness and perhaps develop a prior inconsistent statement which can be used with tremendous effect at the trial. Therefore, it is highly advantageous to depose or have interrogatories of as many witnesses or parties as may be available to you.

3.07 Pre-Trial Hearings in the Criminal Case

As previously stated, in the criminal sphere, the rules and decisions are far less liberal in permitting discovery than in the civil area. However, there is one phase of the procedure in criminal cases which is broader in the criminal field than in the civil, and this is pre-trial, preliminary hearings. As this is such a significant area, the following paragraphs shall cover this subject more fully.

3.08 Preliminary Hearings

A preliminary hearing in a criminal matter to determine whether or not there is sufficient evidence to hold your client answerable to the charges proffered by the prosecutor is an excellent opportunity to get your initial understanding of the skeleton of the case that will ultimately be presented against you. Additionally, the preliminary hearing is an ideal opportunity to face the witness who will eventually be the trial witness, or some of them, against your client, and to determine, face to face, the kind of witness, his or her strengths, intelligence, and capacity to observe, and your capacity to cross-examine successfully. Further, depending upon the ability of the cross-examiner and the latitude permitted by the court, you shall also be in excellent position to develop information which will be most helpful and usable on the Cross-examination of the same witness or witnesses during subsequent hearings relative to suppression of evidence, voluntariness of confessions, minimization of impermissible intrusions via electronic surveillance, etc.

Thus, I recommend never waiving a preliminary hearing despite the fact that the hearing might seem perfunctory, pro forma, or whatever other phrase might indicate that the hearing is not worth the effort on the part of defense counsel. I differ on that point because you can never tell in advance what information might be obtained, what strange twists might be involved in the testimony of the witness. Also, the opportunity of facing the witness and getting a feel for the kind of witness that you will ultimately be facing during the trial is beneficial and should not be waived, except for significant and substantial reasons.

It should be noted that a preliminary hearing has been constitutionally provided to insulate a defendant from the police authority by the interposition of a neutral magistrate. Courts have determined that a Grand Jury is just such a neutral, insulating authority. As such, if a defendant is indicted by a Grand Jury before the preliminary hearing is conducted, such Grand Jury consideration is a substitute for the preliminary hearing. As the Grand Jury is a secret proceeding, however, where neither defendant nor defense counsel participate—except if the defendant wishes to testify—prosecutors make every effort to indict before the date of preliminary hearing, thus obviating the necessity for a preliminary hearing, and thus eliminating the participation of defense counsel and the exposing of witnesses to preliminary Cross-examination or interrogation. Indeed, many prosecutors would prefer to have initial charges procedurally dismissed, which is not an on-the-merits determination, preferring to present the case to the Grand Jury—thus protecting potential witnesses from the searing fire of Cross-examination at the preliminary hearing.

3.09 Pre-Trial Hearings on Motions

As indicated in the previous paragraphs, there are secondary pre-trial hearings involved in criminal cases such as hearings to determine whether certain evidence should be suppressed, or to determine the voluntariness of an alleged confession, the propriety of a corporeal lineup, or the propriety of the minimization of electronic surveillance. All of these pre-trial hearings necessarily involve witnesses who will ultimately testify at the trial. Each and every opportunity to familiarize yourself with the witnesses against you, their style of speech, their physical characteristics in testifying is only a further step in being better prepared to attack those witnesses before the trial jury. Thus, there is a triple purpose to be achieved in each and every examination of a witness: (1) to thrash out the issue of the instant hearing, (2) to draw out testimony from your Adverse Witness which will ultimately be useful at a full-scale trial of the issue, and (3) to familiarize yourself with the witness to prepare for Cross-examination at trial.

The aforementioned is not indicated for the purpose of having the defense counsel waste the time of the court. Obviously, the court is not going to sit idly by and have you waste its time. However, you certainly can legitimately develop issues at the preliminary hearing or pre-trial hearing and still be effecting the additional purpose of familiarizing yourself with subsequent issues or preparing yourself for the Cross-examination of the witness by gaining insight into the witness's mental agility or capacity to recollect and respond to questions.

Now that you have fully investigated the case and have undertaken all manners and methods of pre-trial discovery, you are prepared to proceed to the next adjourned date.

3.10 Pre-Trial Hearing: Limited Purpose

I do not want to give any cross-examiner the impression that a judge is going to let you run rough shod over the prosecution in a criminal case, using the limited purpose pre-trial hearing as a discovery device. That is not the purpose of the hearing and that is not what you should expect. The pre-trial hearing is limited in scope to determining if the defendant was subjected to overly suggestive identification procedures, or had evidence or other items seized in violation of the constitutional proscription against unreasonable search and seizure, or gave a statement without having been first properly admonished concerning the rights available to that individual. The issues involved in these hearings are quite limited in scope. Ordinarily, the judge is not going to permit you to expand such a limited purpose hearing into a full-fledged discovery bath.

Notwithstanding, you certainly can, while conducting the Cross-examination of the witnesses at the hearings, familiarize yourself with those witnesses, their capacity, manner of testifying, their quickness, hostility, etc. For this very reason, the prosecution ordinarily limits the exposure of lay witnesses, where possible, providing only police personnel as witnesses at the pre-trial hearing. Since the acts proscribed are all those emanating from impermissible official police conduct, such presentation is perfectly proper—except in those instances where lay witnesses, let's say in identification procedures, add more to the hearing than the plain vanilla denials of the police personnel. However, to keep you from unnecessary anticipation, don't hold your breath waiting for a court to require lay witnesses to appear.

3.11 Method of Examination at a Pre-Trial Hearing

The method of examination at a pre-trial hearing is precisely the same as that for a trial, as covered in the ensuing chapters of this book. The examination is limited to the scope of the proceeding, as is any Cross-examination, and the same methods and techniques used at trial are used at pre-trial hearings, including the exploration of the witnesses' capacity, credibility, etc. You may be somewhat more curtailed in the use of those devices where, as aforesaid, you are facing police personnel. However, to whatever extent they are implicated in the hearing, you, the cross-examiner, are free to use all Cross-examination techniques in examining witnesses at the pre-trial hearing.

4.

Depositions: Cross-Examination of a Different Color

4.01 What Is a Deposition?

In previous chapters I have spoken of the benefits of taking Depositions of every potential witness who is subject to your notice. In this chapter, I shall explain what a Deposition is, how you obtain the attendance of witnesses, how you conduct a Deposition, and the significant difference between examining a witness at Deposition and examining a witness at trial.

For starters, a Deposition, also called an Examination Before Trial (E.B.T.) is just that, an examination of a witness before trial. It is a discovery device, one of the weapons in the Trial Advocate's armormentorium, utilized to determine the true facts of an issue for future use at a trial. The examination is not a physical examination. After all, we are doctors of law, not doctors of medicine. Rather, the Deposition is a pre-trial interrogation or questioning of a witness, under certain limitations of scope and rules of evidence (see Rules 26 and 30, Federal Rules of Civil Procedure), concerning the witness's knowledge of the facts of a particular matter or incident. Before testifying at the Deposition, which is usually conducted in an attorney's office, the witness must be sworn under oath, usually by the private reporter (stenotypist) who is there to record the testimony. The testimony is thereafter reduced to print, then submitted to the witness for his or her reading and any corrections the witness may deem necessary. Then the Deposition must be signed, notarized, and returned to the party who "took" or conducted the Deposition for possible later use at trial.

4.02 Videotaping a Deposition

Within recent times and the development of economically priced video cameras and equipment, and under the stricture of Rule 30 F.R.Civ.P., which provides that a Deposition may be memorialized by "sound, sound-and-visual, or stenographic means," videotaped Depositions are becoming more frequent. Using the video camera to record the Deposition is a far more effective means of recording the true essence of the testimony, as it permits a jury, if the Deposition is ultimately presented to a jury, or yourself for reviewing purpose, to better evaluate the testimony of the witness by observing the actual demeanor, facial expressions, body reactions, and intonations of the witness.

4.03 Audiotaping a Deposition

Rule 30 also permits audiotaping of a Deposition, which, of course, is somewhat more effective than a mere typed transcript of a Deposition, but less effective than the videotaped Deposition.

4.04 Telephone Deposition

The use of a conference telephone hookup between distant locales is another practical method of conducting a Deposition. Such arrangement can certainly be more convenient to all concerned, may save substantial time and cost of travel, hotel accommodations, etc., and may be more acceptable to the witness to be deposed (the Adverse Witness may feel more comfortable in the familiar surroundings of your Adversary's office, speaking into a telephone rather than looking into the cold, steely eyes of your litigation face).

A telephone Deposition, one where the examiner and the subject of the examination are not in the same location, is the exception rather than the rule, although the rules specifically permit such. Therefore, it is important to obtain the prior agreement of your Adversary to set up a telephone Deposition.

4.05 Comfortable Deposition

You say you may not want the witness to be comfortable? You prefer to keep the witness off balance and leery. Perhaps you do for Deposition purposes, perhaps you do not. Perhaps you shall be able to exact more information out of the comfortable witness than you can out of one who you put on guard by your severe demeanor. More about the method of attack in a few paragraphs.

4.06 Notice Must Contain the Recording Method

In the main, prior court order is not necessary to take any of the aforementioned Depositions during which you utilize other than a stenotypist to record the Deposition. However, your notice to take the Deposition must specify the particular method you intend to use during the taking of the Deposition. This notice provides your Adversary with the opportunity to object to such manner of recording the Deposition. Of course, any party to the Deposition may arrange for a stenographic transcript of the Deposition to be made from the original tape or video recording.

4.07 What Cross-Examination and a Deposition Have in Common

There are many rules and provisions for the taking and making of a Deposition which I shall not cover in this book. Here we are involved with the method of Cross-examination, questioning of an Adverse Witness, rather than the nuts and bolts of a Deposition. Be advised at the outset that a Deposition is pure Cross-examination for the Advocate "taking" the Deposition [if you are conducting or "taking" the Deposition, your Adversary is "defending" the Deposition]. Initially, you may not perceive of a Deposition being taken under Cross-examination conditions. After all, a Deposition is often rather informal; it is not conducted in a courtroom setting. Most Depositions are conducted in a lawyer's office or in a room set aside for that specific purpose in a courthouse. Ordinarily, there is no judge or other court official presiding.

Another aspect that *facially* distinguishes a Deposition from trial Cross-examination in a courtroom is that the examination of the Adverse Witness by the Advocate taking the Deposition—for our discussion's purposes, yourself—does not follow the Direct examination of that witness by your Adversary. Direct examination and then Cross-examination may be the order or rule ordinarily employed in the courtroom. At the Deposition, however, you who have noticed the Deposition of the witness, you who are taking the Deposition, you are the first person to examine the noticed witness. Logically, until now, you may have considered the examination of a witness you are deposing to be Direct examination because you were the first Advocate to question the witness. However, the order of the examination is not controlling. The essence of the examination controls. At a Deposition, the Advocate taking the examination is examining an Adverse Witness, uncovering facts from a witness who is clearly not friendly or under your control. If the witness were cooperative and interested in helping you uncover the facts, you would not have had to notice a Deposition of that witness in the first place.

4.08 It Really Is Cross-Examination

Most individuals in the legal profession, judges and experienced lawyers alike, may not, at first blush, have considered the examination conducted at a Deposition of an adverse party or an Adverse Witness to be pure Cross-examination. As previously noted, that is a formalistic misperception because the attorney who noticed the Deposition is the first one to examine. However, the mere order of proceeding does not change the fact that the witness who you examine at a Deposition is, unquestionably, not *your* witness, not a friendly witness, but is either an adverse party or Adverse Witness who is not readily amenable to you, and from whom you have to resort to a Deposition to obtain information not readily available to you.

As Direct examination is the nonleading questioning of a friendly witness, one available to you on an informal basis, prepared by you, and presented by you at trial, the circumstance where you examine an Adverse Witness or party through procedural notice to obtain information that such witness or party may possess, and reluctantly discloses to you, is obviously, quite different, and is, simply, testimony that is obtained by Cross-examination. Another indication of the taking Advocate being a cross-examiner at the Deposition is the fact that the defending Advocate, your Adversary, if he or she participates at all, questions after you, for the purpose of rehabilitating the witness *after* you complete your examination.

4.09 The Benefits of the Deposition on Later Cross-Examination

During the taking of a Deposition, not only can you gain significant factual knowledge of the incident that is the subject of the litigation, but equally important, you can gain insight into the witness's manner and makeup, antagonism to your cause, intelligence, and the pace of their answers, all of which shall assist you in fashioning your trial attack, which in turn shall greatly influence the script you put together for Cross-examination at trial. In addition, you can also set testimonial traps for the witness, which traps you should not spring on the witness until the actual Cross-examination during the trial. Thus, the taking of Depositions is a hand-in-glove aspect of Cross-examination at trial.

4.10 The Importance of the Deposition

Looking at a Deposition from the point of view that it sets the stage for the trial and permits you to obtain information not only about the facts of the case but also about the Adverse Witness you later have to cross-examine at trial, every Advocate, even those who have never conducted a Deposition, should realize quite clearly, that a Deposition, where you examine an Adverse Witness or party for the specific purpose of discovering or uncovering information that witness or party possesses, is very important to the outcome of the upcoming trial. As previously said, it is nothing less than Cross-Examination.

4.11 Cross-Examination of a Different Color

Now that you know that a Deposition conducted by you, taken by you, to use our term of art, utilizing your skills as a cross-examiner, is so important to your upcoming trial, perhaps you view a Deposition in a new light, with new and heightened significance. You should. I want to point out clearly at this point that the terms and modalities discussed previously, such as Direct Examination and Cross-Examination, are covered in far greater detail in the ensuing chapters dedicated specifically to those very tools and techniques. The reason that a chapter on Depositions is included at this juncture of the book is to delineate that a Deposition is a *pre-trial Discovery Device* not a trial discipline. Yet, because it shares in the use of the basic trial tools, particularly Cross-Examination, an explanation of the similarities and dissimilarities is required at this early stage. For more details as to the method of Cross-Examination employed during a Deposition and the Direct Examination that may subsequently come in to play by the *"Defending"* Advocate during the Deposition, you should refer to the chapters where those subjects are covered later in this book. In other words, this chapter should be read in conjunction with the other later chapters on Cross-Examination and Direct Examination for a complete picture of the methods of examination.

4.12 In What Cases Are Depositions Available?

As Depositions are a Discovery Device, they are available in practically every civil case, both Federal and State, and are not available in practically any criminal case. There are a few jurisdictions which permit Depositions in criminal cases. But, in the main, the Device is not available in criminal matters.

4.13 Other Discovery Devices Available in Place of a Deposition

In addition to Depositions, there are others Discovery Devices used in place and stead of Depositions, such as Written Interrogatories and Letters Rogatory. However, these are only available in such cases where Depositions are available. In other words, where Depositions are unavailable, for example, in most criminal cases, the other Discovery devices are equally unavailable. Since this is not a book on Discovery, let it suffice that Interrogatories and Letters Rogatory are the printed equivalent of the oral examination conducted at a Deposition. These variations on the Deposition theme are available, in the types of cases where Depositions are available, meaning, in practically every civil case and practically no criminal case.

4.14 Should I Depose?

While the device of Deposition may be available to you, you must consider whether, in fact, you want to depose a particular witness. The determination is a balancing of whether your need to take the Deposition and to gather information is outweighed by other factors.

Some of those *other* factors are that by your deposing a witness you require that witness be prepared by your Adversary early on. If it weren't for the Deposition, the witness might not be prepared or have the facts set in stone so early on. Moreover, the witness shall not have the benefit of the Deposition transcript to study for trial as an actor studies a script. In addition, you may lose some of the anxiety and diffidence the witness may experience in facing *you* for the first time. In the informality of the Deposition, the witness might get to realize that you are not really as bad as he or she thought you would be, and he or she shall be more relaxed, and therefore more able to parry your thrusts at the trial.

How else do you get the information you need for trial? The answer is by other Discovery devices and Notices to produce. Ordinary Discovery rules and devices that require an Adversary to turn over documents, expert reports, handwritten notes, etc. do quite well in obtaining a substantial overview of the case without resort to Deposition; so do interrogatories and letters rogatory. In other words, those devices that obtain the information you require and at the same time continue the Adverse Witness's anticipation of the ultimate confrontation with you with dread and trepidation. You can also obtain information directly from the witness by having an investigator interview, or at least try to interview, the witness. An investigator's report, rather than subjecting the witness to Cross-Examination too early by Deposition, may serve your purpose quite as well, perhaps better, than a Deposition, as you are prepared by the information obtained, but the witness does not become familiar and comfortable with your Cross-Examination until the actual moment of truth. If the information is not available except by way of Deposition, you have no choice.

Thus, the rule is to depose if you must, but only if you must.

4.15 Who Can Be Deposed?

The simple answer to that question is: practically anyone who has any knowledge of the facts of a particular matter or incident. You can depose the Adverse Party, anyone connected with the adverse party, anyone who was witness to the event, or anyone who has knowledge of the event, whether they are friendly or unknown to your Adversary. You can even depose your Adversary. Oh, what a joyous thought that is. To corner that evasive creature that is your Adversary and skewer he or she with your questions. That is a consummation devoutly to be wished. But, of course, you can only depose your Adversary in connection with fact matters that relate to the incident, not to matters of work product or investigation in preparation for trial.

It is obvious that you have a very broad range of persons who can be deposed.

With all of that good, fallow ground available to you, it would be foolish, indeed, not to obtain every grain of information relating to the case, in advance of trial, to be fully aware of the entire fabric of the case, to be fully armed with facts, to fully analyze the case, and to fully be prepared to do battle. However, depose with a caution to not give away, indirectly, more through conducting the Deposition than you might otherwise obtain through other, less invasive Discovery devices. In other words, don't depose for the sake of Deposition. Depose if you can't obtain the information through other Discovery devices.

4.16 How to Decide Which Witnesses to Depose

I have previously discussed that one of your major preliminary undertakings in preparing for trial is to analyze the entire case, to determine what are the basic issues, both factual and legal, then to determine, what your Adversary must have in order to carry his or her end of the case. Assume for the moment that you are Plaintiff's counsel. Which witnesses does your defense Adversary need to counter the Plaintiff's case? Assume you are Defense Advocate. What information must your Adversary put together to fulfill the burden of proof in this case? In other words, you must determine who the witnesses are who your Adversary shall need to support the adverse claim. When you have completed this task, this list of potential witnesses your Adversary may require to prove his or her case shall, *ipso facto,* be a list of the potential individuals to be deposed. Do you have to depose each and every one of those witnesses? "No!" While some trial Advocates might say, "Yes, you only have to depose the witnesses for whom you want to be prepared," I do not totally agree with that sanguinary concept. Yes, it is my view that you should not depose witnesses about whom you can discover information and get a good line on their potential testimony through the use of other Discovery devices.

Remember, your total purpose in obtaining information about a potential witness and his or her knowledge of the facts is to prepare a Cross-Examination script, in order to tear his or her credibility apart when he or she takes the stand at trial. If you can prepare the Cross-Examination script completely, to your total satisfaction, without the necessity of the Deposition, do so. However, if you need any information you deem significant in order to be fully prepared for Cross-Examination at trial, information which you cannot otherwise obtain, then, by all means, depose.

In every jurisdiction, Federal and State, there are rules of practice and procedure, both civil and criminal, which list the persons or types of persons who can be deposed in your case. Your local rules may require you to apply to the court for permission to depose nonparty witnesses. This is not such a terrible burden in order to put yourself in a position to be prepared and to show your client just how right he or she was in choosing you as their

Advocate. However, by making such motions, you are also giving your Adversary a glimpse at the hand you intend to play, by indicating who you think are the witnesses who may give you trouble. Thus, and again, only make such a showing when you cannot obtain the information you need for trial by other discovery devices, and you deem it essential to undertake the Depositions. Ordinarily, if there is some overwhelming reason to depose a person who happens to fall outside the categories permitted by your local rules or the category of a nonparty witness, you are still free to apply to the court for permission to depose that person.

4.17 How to Initiate the Deposition—The Notice

As aforesaid, in every jurisdiction, Federal and State, there are rules of procedure and practice which prescribe the method of undertaking Depositions. These rules shall also ordinarily prescribe the form for a Notice to Take a Deposition. Most often, a printed, blank Notice to Take Deposition may be obtained from the local stationer. Or, if you have a computer and are industrious, you should input a blank, standard form of a Notice to Depose to be used on occasions when you wish to undertake a Deposition. Simply make up the Notice with the caption of the case, the name of the witness to be deposed, and the date, time, and location at which you wish to conduct the Deposition, listing thereon whatever documents you wish that witness to bring to the Deposition in order to fully examine the facts and facets of the issues.

In addition, if you intend to take the Deposition by recording onto videotape or audiotape, or any method other than ordinary stenographic transcription, that information should also be included on the Notice.

If you should wish to undertake a Deposition telephonically, not only should you make that desire clear on the Notice, you should also discuss and secure the acquiescence of your Adversary to the method. Telephonic Depositions, although seemingly innocuous, are the most radical of the Depositions. All others Depositions are "normal" in every aspect of their procedure, except for the recording device to be used. On the other hand, the telephonic Deposition is one where the participants may be separated by hundreds of miles, are not face to face, and the exhibits are not readily transferable from hand to hand. This requires that copies be provided for both ends of the Deposition. If you really think about it, this is quite a different kind of Deposition. For these reasons, you really have to clear this type of Deposition in advance with your

Adversary or with a judge based on exigent circumstances. However, as a suggestion concerning a telephonic Deposition might save both you and your Adversary time, travel, and trouble as well as provide both your clients with a greater comfort level your Adversary might surprise you and agree to your suggestion.

4.18 The Where and When of the Notice to Take Deposition

Where Do I Notice the Deposition to Take Place?

You are free to Notice the Deposition to be conducted at your office or the conveniently located office of another attorney in the jurisdiction of the witness to be deposed or at the local courthouse. Naturally, it is far more convenient for the Deposition to be conducted in your office with your staff, equipment, and familiar surroundings available. You won't have to travel anywhere to conduct the Deposition. More importantly, however, it is psychologically advantageous for you to conduct the Deposition at your office. Your Adversary and the witness shall be on unfamiliar ground and this may tend to cause them to be less comfortable. Disadvantage and discomfort are buzzwords that are heartwarming to the cross-examiner. It tends to diminish the Adverse Witness's confidence, thus making the witness more susceptible to you and less able to parry your thrusts.

Does that mean that you can have your way with the witness merely because you conduct the Deposition in your office? Obviously, not. But it is more, rather than less, advantageous to have the witness less comfortable and somewhat ill at ease.

Your Adversary is probably aware of the comfort/discomfort advantage vis-à-vis taking Depositions. Thus, in order to have the Deposition at your office, you better be the first party to send out a Notice. The reason for this is practical. Ordinarily, when your Adversary receives the first Notice of Deposition, he or she may very well set up counter Depositions of your client or your witnesses at the same time and place as the first arriving Notice. This is done, as aforesaid, for purely practical reasons, so that neither you nor your Adversary have to carve out two separate days to take Depositions in this case. In addition, the Reporter costs money just to attend a Deposition. Cost, always a factor, is kept down by having the same Reporter take all the Depositions in the same place on the same day; the setup fee for the Reporter to be shared by the parties participating in the Deposition. Ordinarily, each party pays the Reporter for the Depositions of the Adverse Witnesses they conduct.

Noticing the Deposition for the Courthouse

Of course, if you or your Adversary has noticed a Deposition to take place at his or her office, the local rules ordinarily permit either you or your Adversary to change the place of Deposition to the courthouse. At the courthouse, neither of you shall have the home court advantage. If your Adversary Notices the Depositions at his or her office, and the game of one-up-person-ship is important to you, you can change the situs of the Deposition to the courthouse. Significantly, in addition to one-up-person-ship, there is a legitimate, salutary reason to conduct the Deposition at the courthouse—rulings.

As aforesaid, the Deposition is conducted without a judge or official presiding. Not uncommonly during the Deposition you or your Adversary may object to some part of the Deposition, or some questions during the Deposition. To resolve any potential objections and to proceed forward with a Deposition that may be log jammed by objection, you may need a ruling by a judge. In every courthouse, no matter how large or small, there is always an Ex-Parte Judge, sometimes called the Miscellaneous Judge, whose function it is for the particular day, week, or month (in small court settings, for the year) to resolve miscellaneous matters that arise, including, but not limited to, rulings on objections at Depositions.

Naturally, if you are in your office or your Adversary's office and the need for a ruling arises, the Deposition either has to be terminated temporarily, while you, your Adversary, the Reporter, and the witness travel to the courthouse for a ruling on the objection. Either that or the objection may be preserved for later ruling. While preserving the objection may permit the Deposition to continue, you may have been forestalled from the main thrust of your examination by such objection. Thus, the objection, even the preservation of the objection, may forestall the main thrust of where you were going with this witness. Thus, Deposition at the courthouse may not be such a bad idea after all. Ordinarily, however, Deposition can be conducted either in your office or your Adversary's office without untoward event.

> NOTE: *Naturally, if your Adversary sends out the first Notice for Deposition, your Adversary, who may have also read this book, shall Notice the Deposition at his or her office. Mail early is good advice for Christmas cards and Notice to Take Deposition.*

When to Notice the Deposition to Take Place

You can select any day that is convenient for you. If your Adversary has an objection or a conflict with the day you select, you shall thereafter set a mutually convenient date. It is better to conduct the Depositions early. It is also beneficial to have a fairly good idea of what the case is about and to have gathered a substantial amount of the evidence before conducting the Depositions. Somewhere between immediately and at the end of your trial preparation is a date when it would be beneficial to conduct the Deposition so as to be armed with yet more information to conduct future investigation and preparation. You will have to play the when-to-take-a-Deposition question by ear. Remembering however, that the first Notice to Take Deposition usually selects the situs of the Deposition.

4.19 The Examination

Now we get to the nitty-gritty of the examination. What questions should I ask?

One of the differences between Cross-Examination at trial and the conduct of a Cross-Examination at Deposition is the frequency of the questions. At trial, the judge may give you latitude to explore the underpinnings of a witness and to dig into the background of the witness in an attempt to undermine the credibility of the witness before the trier of fact.

Such is the purpose of trial Cross-Examination.

Not so, the examination you employ at a Deposition. Remember, a Deposition is still a discovery device, despite the fact that you, the taker of the Deposition, are cross-examining. There is no jury present, no trier of fact, and the undermining of credibility has no role whatsoever to play at the Deposition. Thus, what might be considered clever and undercutting Cross-Examination for trial is objectionable and repetitive during Deposition.

4.20   General and Specific Questions

Some practitioners hold that a question can be asked only once during the Deposition, and another question to the same effect, in different words, might very well bring an objection of repetitive from your Adversary. You might be well served, therefore, to ask the witness questions that call for a generalized description of the event. Then, with that outline in mind, home in closer, using the generalized description as a guide, to ask "different" questions about specific facts relating to the general description of the event.

Often, you can take the witness step-by-step or yard-by-yard as to where his or her hands were on the steering wheel and his or her feet on the pedals, as he or she neared the intersection, attempted to apply the brakes, or stood when he or she observed the event. However, this is best explored *after* you have a generalized description of the event.

For example, in the case of an automobile accident, where the witness at the Deposition is the Adverse party, the driver of the vehicle, you might ask:

> Q: Ms. Witness, were you driving your car on Main Street on the 15th of April, last?
>
> A: Yes.
>
> Q: And as you approached the intersection of Main and Randolph Street were you involved in an accident?
>
> A: Yes.
>
> Q: What occurred at that time and place?
>
> A: I was driving along Main Street and as I approached Randolph, the light was green. It was still green as I entered the intersection. In the middle, the light turned yellow. The other car immediately zoomed out in front of me, and we had a collision.
>
> Q: As you were fifty yards from Randolph, what speed were you traveling?
>
> A: About twenty-five, thirty, no more like twenty-five miles an hour.
>
> Q: And as you were that fifty yards from Randolph, where were your hands?
>
> A: On the wheel, the steering wheel.
>
> Q: And, as you were fifty yards away from Randolph, where were your feet?
>
> A: My right foot was on the gas pedal, my left foot, well, it was, I guess, on the floor.

Q: What was the color of the traffic control signal when you were fifty yards from Randolph?

A: Green.

Q: Were you looking at the traffic control signal or were you looking straight ahead when you were fifty yards from Randolph?

A: I guess I alternated.

Q: As you were thirty yards from Randolph . . .
etc, etc. etc.

I'm sure you could ask a myriad of specific questions after the witness has given you the generalized description above, none of them being repetitive. Do you want to ask such questions and so many questions? That's up to you, and is more easily decided when you are in a hands-on position facing the witness. In some cases, perhaps yes. In other cases, perhaps no. I cannot give you a pat answer that will work in all circumstances. You have to decide that while up close and personal with the witness and the situation.

4.21 Good Guy/Bad Guy

You might wonder, during the Deposition should I be hard on the witness, digging at the witness, as I might in court, or do I try to be pleasant and amiable?

That depends.

As each Cross-Examination in the trial setting is different, depending on the witness, so each Deposition may also be different. For example, you cannot cross-examine at trial a grandmotherly type bystander to an accident the same as you would a police officer who was involved in battering down a door and arresting a Defendant in a criminal case. Nor can you cross-examine a young, teenage girl in the same fashion that you might examine a cooperating witness who was involved in a heinous crime with a Defendant against whom that witness now testifies.

You must temper your Cross-Examination by consideration of the specific attributes of the witness, taking into account age, frailty, mental toughness or quickness, or the lack thereof, circumstances which shall permit you to avoid offending the trier of the fact with a pugnacity where mildness would be more appropriate, and offending with acidity, where a friendly mien might be more effective.

4.22 Usual Stipulations

Often, either your Adversary or the Reporter who is to record the Deposition as well as administer an oath to the witness asks the participating attorneys whether they agree to the "usual" stipulations. And often by rote, the attorneys agree that the usual stipulations shall apply.

Unfortunately, such ready agreement to who-knows-what is rather improvident since it is hard to understand what "usual" stipulations are and because some of the usual stipulations may be inappropriate. It is better to know what the Reporter or the other side means by usual stipulations.

One of those "usuals" is to the effect that objections are to be reserved for the trial court. This apparently is intended to preserve objections until you are in front of a judge, thus eliminating the necessity to stop the proceedings to seek a ruling by a judge at the courthouse when you reach an impasse. Unfortunately, Rule 32 indicates quite clearly that objections, unless they are spread specifically on the record, are deemed to have been waived. Thus, reserving objections does not really mean *reserving* interposing the word "objection" until you get to court, at trial or otherwise.

Moreover, as the purposes and subject matter of the Deposition have been clearly set forth in the notice to take Deposition, one of the objections that should never be reserved is to matters that are clearly irrelevant, immaterial, beyond the scope of the stated subject of the Deposition. Thus, an agreement as to usual stipulations is something that should be specifically explored as to what your Adversary considers usual and, in addition, what the reporter has intended if he or she has asked about the usual stipulations. If you agree, after knowing what is intended by the usual stipulations, then by all means enter such stipulation.

4.23 Objections

Rule 32 is quite explicit that objections that are not preserved are waived, even objections as to the form of the question. Thus, while *rulings* on objections may be reserved for later decision by the Court, *objections* must not be reserved for a later time. They must be made at the moment the objectionable question or act occurs. While the Federal Rules only govern during Federal litigation and litigation in those jurisdictions that have adopted the Federal Rules (which jurisdictions are increasing slowly but surely) those rules are a safe benchmark as to the controls in place during the handling of

Depositions. Thus, while you defend the Deposition, you might decide *not* to direct your witness not to answer the question or questions posed by your Adversary in order to permit the Deposition to continue. Yet, you must be careful to specify any objection that you have, and the basis therefor, else your Adversary may opt at trial to advise the court at trial that you have, by your silence during the Deposition, waived any such objections.

4.24 Directing the Witness Not to Answer

One other subject to be covered here, because of the frequency of its occurrence, is whether during the course of the Deposition, whether you are taking or defending the Deposition, you may direct your witness not to answer your Adversary's question and what to do about such a direction if your Adversary directs his or her witness not to answer your question.

These concerns are addressed in Rule 30, subsection (c), which indicates that after an objection, the Deposition shall proceed. Implicit in such direction, the Deposition is to continue after an objection is spread fully upon the record. Subsection (d) (1) of Rule 30 appears to provide the only three grounds upon which the directive not to answer may be given: to claim a privilege against disclosure; to enforce a court directive as to the scope of discovery; and, to enable the objectant to move to curtail impermissible acts by an Adverse party or Adversary.

However, as aforesaid, if your mutual understanding of the scope and breadth of the discovery on which you now embarked is vitally violated, I believe that you may direct your witness not to answer. However, that directive should be merely the beginning of a curative or limiting application—if the conduct to which you object doesn't cease immediately—to formally curtail such conduct.

5.

On-Trial Discovery

5.01 Discovery: A Continuing Task

In previous chapters, pre-trial discovery and further refining of the issues for the forthcoming trial were the subjects of discussion. The trial Advocate must, however, constantly continue to add to the storehouse of information and knowledge that he or she has of the issues at hand. This continuing compilation and analysis of information continues even after the trial begins and continues throughout the trial. This is particularly so in the criminal case where prior statements that a witness may have made, prior sworn testimony taken at a Grand Jury hearing, are required to be turned over only *after* the witness has taken the stand and testified in chief. Often, a Prosecutor, in an attempt at fairness, turns that material over to Defense Counsel after jury selection or the night before the witness takes the stand. In any of the above situations, your obtaining of material for Cross-examination is a continuum even after the trial begins.

5.02 Analyzing the Materials Turned Over

Where your Adversary turns over materials relative to the case, or where your subpoenas are complied with only at the point that the particular witness is in the midst of testifying, obviously you must find sufficient time wherever it can be spared, whether it be during a recess the court allows specifically for that purpose, during a luncheon break, at night after the first trial day, or whenever, to analyze each and every bit of that information, not only from the point of view of discovering further aspects of the facts of the case, but also to determine whether or not the witness or other witnesses, have previously made statements that contradict the trial testimony.

In the situation where you have been provided prior statements and materials in advance of the witness's Direct testimony, thus not having the benefit of having heard the anticipated witness's actual Direct when studying the pre-trial material, you should make careful notes of the salient points of the witness's pre-trial statements, retaining these notes in your trial book or computer for comparison with the later, Direct testimony on trial.

For example, if your Adversary turns over to you an interview that a police officer conducted of a witness who is about to testify at the trial, you should have a fairly educated guess as to what the witness's testimony shall be on the trial. You should make a detailed written analysis of the contents of the police officer's report, so that at the point of the Direct, you shall be able to compare the statement or information turned over against the Direct, and perhaps be able to glean prior inconsistencies made to the police officer. The subject of analyzing and recording the prior inconsistent statements is discussed more fully in later chapters.

5.03 Analyzing Statements Turned Over during Trial

Now that your Adversary has turned over material to you which contains, among other things, references to a witness who is about to take the stand, you must read the said documents carefully, not only for any prior written statements that the witness may have made in his or her own hand, or statements that the witness made to third parties, which have been signed or sworn to by the witness, but also for prior oral statements made to third persons which have been memorialized by those third persons, regardless of whether the witness signed the statements or not.

You must be particularly alert for prior statements made orally to third persons which have not been reduced to a verbatim memorialization by that third person, but have merely been summarized as part of a report by that third person, which report is then included in an official file. For example, the witness who has just testified, or is about to testify, may have made prior statements under a variety of circumstances: he or she may have made a statement to a police officer at the scene of an accident or event; he or she may have made a statement to a district attorney or a police officer during a later interview in a criminal case; he or she may have made a statement to an in-take nurse or other hospital official; the witness may have been interviewed by his or her employer concerning the event; or, the witness may have made a statement to another official not in direct connection with the case, i.e., an interview by a Probation Officer or a Social Worker; all of which statements may have been included in the written notes of that official or person. All of these statements, whatever form they take, may be ammunition for your Cross-examination. Unfortunately, however, you may not have the opportunity to have heard the testimony in chief of the witness at the time you read the prior statements, and are, therefore, unsure whether there are any inconsistencies—*yet*. Therefore, the careful Advocate must make a conscious, preferably written, detailed analysis of the prior statements observations, or remarks by the anticipated witness, storing this information in his or her trial book or computer in anticipation of that witness's testimony. After hearing the Direct, you will be able to quickly refer back to the prior statement(s) and be in a position directly to attack the witness with any prior inconsistency, or lay the proper foundation for later calling to the stand on your own case, the third person who recorded that witness's prior inconsistent statement.

For example, the official police file of the case indicates that the witness who has just testified gave a prior statement to a police officer who has recorded the statement in his notes which are part of the official file of the case. The Officer has recorded that the witness told him that at the moment that shots were fired, he looked up from his workbench through the front window of his store and saw the movement of someone running, but was unable to get a good look at the fleeing person's face.

You make a note of such a report, adding it to the information in your trial book.

Later, that witness is called by your Adversary and testifies that indeed he did look up from his workbench, and did see a fleeing person, and *that fleeing person just happens to be your client, the defendant whom he recognized and is able to identify in court.*

You shall be able, because of your careful preparation, to immediately retrieve from your notes the prior statement made to the police officer, locate the physical statement turned over to you by your Adversary, and incorporate that inconsistency into your Cross-examination.

You will learn, later in this book, that you can not attack the witness directly with the report written out by the police officer after interviewing the witness. This is because the report is the police officer's recordation and is, technically, the report of a third party—*not this witness*—in which the witness's statement is merely recorded. Therefore, you must know how to lay the appropriate foundation for the calling, on your case, of the police officer to whom the statement was made in order that the police officer may testify about the prior inconsistent statement and in order that you bring before the jury facts upon which they may evaluate the truthfulness, credibility, and quality of the witness's trial testimony.

A basic lesson that you must learn as a trial Advocate is that all things do not happen automatically; you must have the patience to build your entire case a piece at a time. At the moment, as we are talking about analysis of evidence as an ongoing necessity during trial, suffice it to note that had you not combed through all of the reports made, whether they seemed relevant or not at the time you were reading them, you would be unaware that the witness had, in fact, previously given statements immediately after the event took place, which are contradictory and inconsistent with his or her present trial testimony. In short, you must read and make notes of *everything* turned over to you, not only for the obvious, but for the total content which may ultimately only become useful after the witnesses begin to testify and after the evidence is put before the jury by your Adversary.

5.04 Analyzing Prior Testimony

In addition to official reports and information contained in official files, in a civil case you may have a Deposition that was taken of the witness. In a criminal case, the Prosecutor may, just before or after the witness has testified, turn over Grand Jury testimony of the witness. In the case of the Deposition, you should have already prepared an analysis of the Deposition testimony. The same goes for Grand Jury testimony that was turned over to you last night, prior to the direct. In the case of the Grand Jury testimony that is turned over *immediately before or just after* the witness testifies, you must immediately ask the court for a few minutes continuance to read the material and familiarize yourself with its contents. Then you must, on the spot, compare that prior testimony with the Direct testimony that the witness just gave (which Direct you will have recorded in your Trial Book) and be able to utilize the prior testimony by fitting it into the fabric of your Cross-examination for use as prior inconsistent statements made under oath.

For a detailed explanation on how to record the Direct testimony and how to analyze and use prior inconsistent statements under oath, see later chapters on those specific subjects.

5.05 Analyzing Prior Criminal History

In addition to the statements that a witness may have made or the prior testimony that the witness may have given, you may find that a Prosecutor and, rarely, a civil Adversary, just prior to the witness testifying, may give you evidence of a prior criminal history of the witness. This must be analyzed too.

The mere fact that a witness may have previously been arrested or convicted of various crimes does not, in and of itself, cause the automatic and total destruction of said witness. The crimes of which the witness may have been convicted may be insignificant in the face of the type of case you are trying or the type of testimony that the witness is giving. For example, a witness who had been arrested and convicted of a minor crime 15 or 20 years ago, who has thereafter lead an exemplary life, being industrious, and hardworking; who is a fruitful member of the community, with children he has put through college by sheer dint of his manual labor, could hardly be attacked by you as an incorrigible criminal based on such past criminal history, particularly where he is a disinterested witness whose testimony is substantially corroborated by other facts in the case. In fact, you would be far better off never to mention the prior criminal history, lest the jury resent your tactic which attempts to demean the witness on the basis of an insignificant past criminal history, particularly where that individual has manifested obvious rehabilitation by an exemplary life.

Not every criminal history or background is going to be cannon fodder for your Cross-examination. Indeed, you will often be better off not to mention the criminal background where it serves no purpose in your Cross-examination and may only serve to antagonize the jury against you or your client's position, i.e., a disinterested bystander witness in a civil accident case had a Youthful Offender determination twenty years ago. Is such a criminal background really significant in this circumstance? It would seem not. However, where you have a witness who is actually an incorrigible and continual criminal, who has been continually arrested or convicted of crimes, and who has manifested throughout his life a propensity for antisocial behavior, such information may very well be the basis upon which to discredit the witness in the eyes of the jury; and, though he may testify to having been in a perfect position from which to observe the entire incident, the jury may disbelieve such witness as being an incredible, untrustworthy, unreliable human being, whose testimony they would not adopt or accept against your client.

For a detailed outline of the methods and use of such prior criminal history on Cross-examination, see Chapter 12, infra.

5.06 Analyzing Immoral or Vicious Acts

Additionally, although a person may not have been convicted of prior crimes, you may determine that the witness, nonetheless, may have led a life which is a manifestation of activities indicating to the jury an unreliability, incredibility, and a loathsome, unacceptable manner of existence, which would create in the minds of the jury the fact that the witness is not to be relied upon. For instance, although the witness may never have been convicted of such as a crime, you might have a woman who is a prostitute, who has lead a life of total disrepute; or, you may have a man who is a drunkard and ne'er-do-well, who fails and refuses to support his family, who has never worked, and who has no gainful employment; you may have an individual who is a drug addict, or a person whose means of existence is such that the community would look upon him or her with disfavor or disgust. These factors *may be* significant in the minds of the jury, just as they might be significant to anyone who would be presented with this individual in everyday life and be told certain facts by that individual.

The evaluation of the witness is ultimately up to the jury—not you—and the witness's background must be presented so the jury can make a total evaluation of the witness. The issue is would this information presented to a jury or to an ordinary person meeting this witness in daily life cause the jury to hesitate in relying, wholly or partially, upon the witness's testimony and recitation of facts, or would his or her past experience cause the jury to hesitate, doubt, or question the witness's reliability? These are questions that you have to weigh on an individual case basis, determining if such background might make a difference to the jury or would your presentation of this information cause resentment against you in the jury. There is no fast rule in these situations. You must evaluate and make a determination in each individual situation.

5.07 Subpoena Power

In gathering information for trial, you do not have, in every situation, to sit and rely solely upon the largess of your Adversary. The subpoena is an extremely effective weapon or method by which to obtain information you need. You should subpoena for trial all documents and records relating to the case that you have been unable to obtain to the point of trial, whether police reports, hospital records, official files of governmental agencies, files from businesses, personal records, etc.

Be sure that your subpoena is complete and specific, since the person, business, or agency receiving the same—particularly if it is a governmental agency—may receive many such subpoenas each day and its function is not to provide you with as much information as possible, but merely to satisfy that which is specifically requested in your subpoena.

The subpoena should be served with sufficient prior notice so that the material requested can be compiled by the person or entity which maintains that information and forwarded to the court in sufficient time for the beginning of the trial. Once the information is in the court, even during the picking of the jury, you will then be permitted to peruse the same, and familiarize yourself with its content so that you are prepared, at the moment the trial begins, with the information contained in it.

Another reason for you to be clear and specific as to the information that you require by subpoena, and to provide sufficient time for the person or entity to comply with the said subpoena, is in the event that the person or entity applies to the court to quash the subpoena, you want to be in a position to justify the subpoena, and the reasonableness of that request contained therein, to the court.

Now that you have analyzed all the information available from investigation and information turned over to you or subpoenaed to the moment the trial, it is now time to begin the actual trial.

6.

Rules of Evidence

6.01 You Have to Know the Rules

Every trial, federal or state, civil or criminal, requires the Trial Advocate to invoke and be guided by Rules of Evidence. A trial cannot take place and an Advocate cannot function without knowing these rules.

The Rules of Evidence form a significant and essential component of proper Cross-examination. Therefore, at this juncture, in order that you begin to comprehend some of the rules that limit or inhibit your freedom of movement in examining a witness—whether on Direct or Cross-examination—as well as some of the tools that you can utilize on that Cross-examination, a short dissertation on the more significant rules is appropriate.

In Part IV there shall be more discussion of other rules and tools that you must know for Cross-examination purposes. For now, however, the discussion of the Rules, particularly the proscription against hearsay, shall be brief.

6.02 The Rules Are the Cross-Examiner's Bible

Although this is a book on Cross-examination, in order to be a true Trial Advocate, a compleat Cross-examiner, it is essential that you be a master of the Rules of Evidence. The rules must be your bible, your code of conduct. You cannot function or cross-examine without them.

Until recently, the task of knowing the rules was complicated by the fact that each state had its own peculiar Rules of Evidence, and the federal courts had yet another and different set of Rules of Evidence. The formidable task of knowing multiple sets of rules for the same evidentiary problem has been somewhat simplified since the adoption of the Federal Rules of Evidence (FRE), originally enacted in 1973. Since their inception, the FRE have been adopted in more than 30 states as the standard rules of evidence. This trend is moving inexorably toward a future where a unified set of Rules of Evidence, on both a federal and a state level, will be in place throughout the United States.

As long as the Rules of Evidence are of such significance to your future as a Trial Advocate, it would be better if you knew them verbatim—each word and each comma of each section. However, it shall do you no good whatsoever to know merely words and empty phrases verbatim without knowing in your mind, in your gut, the essence, concept, and the theory of evidence.

6.03 The Evidentiary Essence

A trial is not a mini-recreation of real life. The way that people conduct and manage their personal and business affairs in the lay world is not at all like the precise, codified fashion in which life in the well of the courtroom is conducted. Trials are their own existence. The purpose of the Rules of Evidence is to ensure that a trial is conducted in a certain, very controlled environment where no testimony and no fact or piece of documentary or physical evidence is admitted into that trial unless it is as precise and antiseptic, as free from undue prejudice, and as reliable as the savants throughout legal time could have made it. In short, the Rules of Evidence are intended to preserve and maintain the integrity and reliability of evidence, in antiseptic fashion, so that a trial can become a pure exercise in weighing sheer, unadulterated fact.

> *NOTE: All evidence is prejudicial; it is intended to be such. Each side in an adversarial contest submits evidence that shall indeed negatively impact, affect, and prejudice the other side. Thus, the Rules of Evidence do not protect a party and counsel from prejudice, only from undue, improperly, contaminated prejudice (evidence).*

In order for testimony to be allowed, there are rules that govern the content of that testimony. For example:

The rule against hearsay is intended to proscribe from the consideration of the jury testimony that cannot be chastened before a jury by a cross-examiner. If a witness were permitted to testify about an out-of-court statement made by a third person, the cross-examiner would be impeded from cross-examining that statement, since the person testifying, when asked what the statement meant and why it was made, could continually hide behind the phrase, "I don't know, I didn't say it. I'm just telling you what I heard." Thus, the rule relating to hearsay requires that a Declarant, the person who makes a factual statement or assertion, must make such statement in the courtroom, subject to being cross-examined, or the hearsay statement cannot be allowed into evidence.

The use of prior inconsistent statements to impeach a witness's credibility is governed by certain rules that require different foundations be established before such inconsistency can be used against an Adverse Witness. A prior statement taken under oath, such as a Deposition or Grand Jury testimony, because of its greater reliability can be used the most readily and the most easily, and therefore requires the least foundation. A statement in the handwriting of a witness or signed by a witness on some prior occasion is somewhat less reliable than one taken under oath and, therefore, requires somewhat stricter evidentiary scrutiny. Statements that were made and testified to by third persons require the most stringent scrutiny because the reliability of such statements is far more suspect and vulnerable than one taken under oath or in the handwriting of the testifying witness.

In order to secure the integrity of documentary or physical evidence, the rules governing the introduction of such evidence require that a basic foundation need be established before that document or piece of physical evidence can be admitted or received.

All these precautions are intended to be sure that the evidence at trial is not irrelevant, immaterial, or extraneous, so that the trial does not become contaminated with a separate trial within a trial to determine a collateral issue about a witness or a piece of evidence.

From these examples, you should get the perception that not only do the Rules of Evidence govern the integrity and precision of trial evidence, but that you are not going to be able to participate in a trial without knowing the rules precisely.

6.04 The Federal Rules of Evidence (FRE)

The Federal Rules of Evidence and, in the main, the rules of all those jurisdictions that have adopted the FRE are divided into 11 Articles.

1. General provisions
2. Judicial Notice
3. Presumptions
4. Relevance
5. Privileges

6. Witnesses

7. Opinions and expert testimony

8. Hearsay

9. Authentication

10. Best evidence

11. Miscellany

The above list is the entirety of the Rules of Evidence by which trials are conducted. The Rules, therefore, are not so overwhelming an amount of words, facts, and knowledge that they cannot be known with great particularity by every Trial Advocate.

To make it even more simple for the Advocate, and, therefore, less forgivable not to be totally aware of the meaning and essence of each rule, is the fact that some of the articles are of lesser significance and importance to the average trial, whereas others are of great significance.

For example, rules 1, 2, 3, 5, 9, and 11 are lesser used and lesser referred to rules than are numbers 4, 6, 7, 8, and 10.

We shall cover many of these Rules, where applicable, in other sections and chapters of this book. Here we shall concentrate on the one most important to our purposes at the moment—the rule relative to Hearsay.

6.05 Hearsay—Enfant Terrible

Because it is the most used and abused evidence, the rule controlling hearsay is the centerpiece of any Rules of Evidence.

Let us first explore what hearsay is. I should add, parenthetically, that the definition of Hearsay in the FRE is flawed. FRE 801 says that "Hearsay is a statement other than one made by the Declarant (witness) while testifying at the trial or hearing, offered in evidence to prove the truth of the matter asserted."

There's an awful lot to that seemingly simple definition. Let us explore the Rule and the essence further.

The Declarant

The first component of hearsay is the Declarant. Here is where the drafters of the FRE were in error. For our purposes the person who makes an original, *out-of-court* statement or assertion is the Declarant. I repeat: The person who made the original *out-of-court* assertion of fact—not necessarily the witness on the stand—is the Declarant.

The Witness

The second component of hearsay is the person who takes the stand at trial, called the witness—not necessarily, the Declarant—who testifies of hearsay about the out of court statement or assertion of another person (the Declarant).

Offered for the Truth of the Assertion

As the third component, there's the present trial testimony concerning an out of court statement of a person other than the testifying witness, is offered for the purpose of proving the truth of that out of court statement or assertion.

> NOTE: *Where the Witness and the Declarant are the same person, there ordinarily is no hearsay, as a witness can be examined about his/her own prior Declaration (statement).*
>
> NOTE: *The word* ordinarily *is most important in the foregoing sentence, because the statement of a Declarant, even though he/she is also the Witness* may *nevertheless be hearsay. See below.*

6.06 Why the FRE Definition of Hearsay Is Incorrect

Rule 801 confuses the Declarant and Witness. As delineated above, the Declarant is the one who makes the out of court statement. The Witness is the one who testifies about the Declaration of another. If the Declarant and Witness are the same person, there ordinarily is no hearsay, because the person who made the original statement is also the trial witness and can be cross-examined about the statement.

When the FRE definition indicates that "hearsay is a statement other than one made by the *Declarant while testifying*" it unnecessarily creates confusion be referring to the witness at trial as the Declarant. Hearsay arises only where the witness and the Declarant are different people. Where the Declarant is the same person as the trial witness, there is ordinarily no hearsay whatever. Thus the text of the FRE when referring to the "Declarant while testifying" makes no sense whatever vis a vis the proscription against hearsay.

For our purposes, if you refer to the person who testifies at trial as the Witness, and the person who made the out of court statement as the Declarant, such proper respect for distinctions shall easily clarify the rule for you.

6.07 An Assertion Need Not Be Verbal

Yes, that's right, an assertion need not be verbal, yet may, nevertheless, be hearsay.

An assertion is a proffer of fact, a laying out of details in a certain order to establish reality. Notice, the words "declaration" or "statement" of facts has purposely been avoided. An assertion is more than both of those words. Declaration and statement imply spoken word. Assertion is both more and yet less; it is an indication of fact about something, whether in words or by other means. For example, a person was not at the scene of an intersection collision at the moment it occurred. This person turned a corner moments after the event and sees and hears two drivers, now out of their cars, arguing as to whose fault caused the accident. At trial, this non-firsthand person is called to the stand and asked who was the driver of car #1. Wordlessly, the witness points to the Plaintiff or Defendant. Although not a single word is spoken by the witness, her pointing out the person who was the driver of vehicle #1 is classic hearsay!

Why?

Because, first of all, the person on the stand has made an *assertion*—an indication of the existence of a certain set of "facts"—in this instance, about the happening of the accident. Second, and most significantly, the assertion is NOT of something from the actual perception of the testifying witness, but is merely a repetition by that witness of certain assertions made by others during the overheard argument. Third, this assertion is being offered to establish a certain truth about the accident, i.e., that the person at whom the witness pointed was, in fact, the driver of car #1. Since the witness did NOT actually perceive the accident, but is merely repeating the assertions she overheard during the argument, the repetition of that assertion at trial, though nonverbal, is hearsay.

Let's go through that again. The testifying witness is not a firsthand witness who actually saw the accident or who even saw who was driving the cars. Remember that the two drivers were outside their cars arguing when the witness first arrived. When the witness is called to the stand, the witness is asked:

Q: Who was driving car #1?

A: (The witness wordlessly points to the defendant.)

At that point, if you were the Advocate for the defendant, you must stand up and object to the hearsay.

6.08 A Witness's Own Prior Statement As Hearsay

It was mentioned previously that a Witness's own out-of-court statement or declaration might actually be hearsay. You might counter that definition by asking if the declarant (of the out-of-court statement) is also the witness, and could be cross-examined about her own prior statement, why is it hearsay? This conundrum is presented so you understand the essence of hearsay and the rule proscribing hearsay, so that, while on your feet, during trial, you will be ready to pounce on real hearsay.

What's really essential in the entire mix of hearsay/nonhearsay testimony is that in order for a statement or declaration not to be hearsay, *the witness must testify in court and make a PRESENT declaration* about which he or she can be cross-examined. For example, if a witness were an author who wrote a book about a particular subject, and takes the stand, not to offer *present testimony,* but rather to be shown her own book and to introduce portions of that text, the witness would be testifying to hearsay contained in her *own* book.

The reason is, for trial purposes, it is essential that the witness on the stand testify in detail *in front of the jury* concerning his/her own statement or declaration so that the trier of fact (the jury) can hear the live witness give live testimony about which he or she can then be cross-examined.

Since the content of the author's book was not testified to before the jury and merely presented in book fashion—albeit a book written by the witness—the book is a written, out-of-court declaration, and is hearsay.

Thus, an out-of-court declaration, when offered for its truth through a trial witness (even a former declaration of the currently testifying witness), is hearsay and is not admissible at trial *because the witness did not testify in front of the jury about that subject matter.*

If, on the other hand, the author of the book is called to the stand, is asked questions about the subject matter, and testifies, even in the verbatim words that are in the book she authored, the testimony is heard by the jury and is not hearsay. It is Direct testimony, evidence-in-chief, that has been presented directly to the jury and is subject to Cross-examination.

The abstruse example just mentioned is merely an exercise to make you think of the different aspects of the rule that proscribes hearsay.

> NOTE: *If the text of the author/witness's book is consistent with her trial testimony, the book cannot then be introduced to further support her testimony for yet another Rule of Evidence: The proscription against bolstering. For more on this subject, see the chapter that discusses prior* **consistent** *statements.*

6.09 The Reason Hearsay Is Forbidden

Sure, some of the foregoing material may be somewhat confusing. It is far better that you become confused now, when you can explore Rules, study and understand them, than it might be in a courtroom, standing in front of the jury.

Let's explore why this thing called hearsay is so *verboten* in trial courts. In days of yore, juries were composed of landholders in the shire. If selected as jurors to settle a dispute, they would go about, talk to folks who were involved in the dispute or to neighbors who knew some of the facts, then get together with the other jurors, discuss the matter, and reach a verdict. As it was unknown what facts the various jurors uncovered on their own, therefore, relied upon to make their determination, rules to standardize the evidence to be considered at dispute resolution proceedings (trials) evolved.

6.10 The Cardinal Rules of Trial

The three cardinal rules relating to a trial witness are:

1. a fact witness must appear in person;
2. must testify in open court, before the jurors, to the facts within that witness's knowledge;
3. and must be subject to Cross-examination.

While a witness may appear in person before the jury, if that witness testifies to (or offers nonverbal) assertions of another person (the original Declarant), the witness *cannot effectively be cross-examined about the assertion of that other person.* Therein lies both the "rub" and the basis of the rule against hearsay. The non-firsthand witness who appears personally in court to testify about what someone else said out of court *cannot be cross-examined about that statement of another person.*

Let's go back to our example of the non-first-hand witness who was asked about the driver of car #1 and who pointed to the defendant. This witness did not see or in any way perceive with her own senses that the defendant was actually the driver of car #1. The witness is merely repeating information that she picked up while listening to the argument between the two drivers. The witness, therefore, cannot be cross-examined about the truth or falsity of her own perceptions about the defendant's driving of car #1 because the witness never saw the defendant drive the car. The witness is merely repeating an assertion heard and is not the person to be cross-examined about who was actually driving car #1. The one who made the original assertion, the one whose statement the present witness merely repeats, is the only one who can be cross-examined about the truth or falsity of the statement or assertion. For that reason, the repeater, the non-firsthand witness, is not permitted by the Rules of Evidence to testify to such a statement intended to prove the truth of the assertion. The original assertor (Declarant) must be called or the Advocate intending to prove such fact forfeits the opportunity to present the statement.

6.11 When Hearsay Is Permitted

What? We went all through that, and now you say hearsay *is* permitted? Actually, hearsay is never permitted. But you will often hear or read decisions in which it is said that hearsay is permitted under certain exceptions to the hearsay rule. Without getting into a discussion of semantics, those exceptions take the Declaration (assertion) *out* of the hearsay rule. Thus, what is permitted in evidence is not hearsay.

For example, a case not long ago decided in the Federal Court of Appeals, Second Circuit, involved a man who went to India on vacation. Just before returning, the defendant testified on his own behalf at trial that someone he met in India asked the Defendant to take a wedding suit back to a relative who was about to be married in the United States. The defendant testified that he was told that the relative, who was a livery taxi driver, would meet the defendant at the airport and drive the defendant to Manhattan. Upon the defendant's going through Customs at Kennedy Airport, the suit was found to contain narcotics, and the defendant was arrested. The defendant told his story to the Customs agents. He attempted, in cooperation with the Customs agents, to make a controlled delivery of the suit to the relative/taxi driver waiting at the airport. The delivery was made and the relative was apprehended and interviewed by the agents. He denied that he was getting married and that he was going to give the defendant a ride to Manhattan. The carrier of the suit, not the relative, was arrested.

At trial, the defendant, in addition to testifying, attempted to introduce through a government agent that upon a second interview, the un-arrested relative admitted to an interviewing agent that he was, in fact, soon to marry and that he was, in fact, a livery car driver. This statement was intended to show the innocent frame of mind of the Defendant in carrying the suit at the request of someone in India. The trial court ruled that such out-of-court statement made by the (now unavailable) relative to an agent, elicited at trial through the interviewing agent, was impermissible hearsay.

The Court of Appeals disagreed. While, indeed, the Declaration of the relative during the second interview was an out of court assertion elicited at trial from a person *other* than the Declarant, the statement was not hearsay as it WAS NOT OFFERED FOR ITS TRUTH.

Rather, the Appeal court held, the defense offered the statement to show the *state of mind* of the Defendant in carrying the suit to the United States—regardless of whether the statement was true or false. The statement was sought not to show the truth thereof, but to show the lack of intent, the innocent motive, of the defendant, regardless of whether the statement was true or false when made to the agent. Thus, the statement as used was approved for use at trial by the Second Circuit not because it was hearsay, but exactly because it was not hearsay; it was NOT offered to prove the truth of the matter asserted.

6.12 Other Uses That Eliminate Hearsay

Under the hearsay rule of the FRE, Rule 801(d), there are many assertions not originally made by the witness on the stand that are offered for the truth of the assertion and are admitted into evidence under certain and particular circumstances. These particular types of statements may be introduced in evidence although the person testifying to them is not the Declarant because, from eons of human experience, such statements are reliable, are ordinarily not made under circumstances where they can be falsified and, therefore, are NOT hearsay because such statements can be accepted as factual. Some of the more frequently seen statements that fall within this category follow. There are others with which you should be familiar. For these, see the text of Article 8, FRE in its entirety.

Statement of a Party Opponent

First of all, this sort of declaration is called an Admission, rather than a statement. When you see the word Admission, it relates ONLY to the Declaration of a Party. A witness cannot make an Admission. A witness's declaration is called a statement. Only a Party makes an *Admission.*

The very fact that a party is just that, a party, and therefore is deeply involved in the lawsuit, available for explanation or clarification, is the reason that the declaration of that Party (an Admission), in either an individual or a representative capacity, is admissible in evidence *whether the said* Party takes the witness stand or not.

> NOTE: *Any confession of a Defendant in a criminal case is an Admission introduced, ordinarily, by a detective or some other witness. It is admissible without the Defendant/Party taking the stand because it is an Admission.*
>
> NOTE: *There is no difficulty whatsoever using either an Admission or a Statement for impeachment purpose during Cross-examination if the person making that statement takes the stand (see use of inconsistent statement section, infra).*

Statement Made in the Presence of a Party

Following right behind an Admission of a Party as an assertion introducible in evidence, regardless of whether or not the Party takes the stand, is a statement made by a third person *in the presence of that party*. Because of the prominent role played by a Party in a litigation, this declaration is not considered hearsay and is admissible in evidence whether or not the Party becomes a witness in the litigation.

Because human experience has come to realize that a statement made of or about the subject of the litigation, in the presence (and awareness) *of a Party,* would not ordinarily be permitted to stand *unchallenged,* a statement that impacts negatively against the litigation, *uncorrected or unchallenged by* the Party in whose presence the declaration was *made,* is admissible as a *tacit admission.* Remember, we're talking about a Party here. The statement had to be made in the presence of a Party, not a witness. Thus, an adverse statement, made in the presence of a Party, *unchallenged,* is considered to be a tacit acknowledgment of the content of the statement by a Party, and *is not hearsay.* It is an Admission by Silence.

Statement of a Party's Co-Conspirator

Since a conspiracy is likened to a partnership, each person found to be a partner is deemed the agent of all other partners (co-conspirators). And, as in any partnership, each partner is responsible for and bound by the acts and words of all other partners. Thus, theory goes, the statement or admission of any person found to be a partner/co-conspirator is admissible in the same fashion as if it were the direct Admission of each of the other partners/ co-conspirators. That is, a statement made by a person's partner is deemed an Admission made by an authorized agent, and thus is considered the direct Admission of the party. The Admission of a Party is not considered hearsay for the reasons set forth at length above and is admitted in evidence whether the specific party takes the witness stand or not.

However, *before such statement may be used,* the party(ies) *against* whom the statement is offered must be shown to be a member(s) of the partnership (conspiracy), fully familiar with the purpose and aim of the conspiracy. Once this status of partnership is established, however, the statement of any co-conspirator becomes the Admission of and binding upon any other co-conspirator/party regardless of whether those other partners take the witness stand.

> NOTE: *The determination of whether or not a party is a member of a particular conspiracy is considered a question of law, not a question of fact. Thus, the determination of whether or not a party is a member of a conspiracy is currently decided by the judge as a Matter of Law, not by the jury as a Question of Fact.*

Excited Utterance—Present Sense Impression

An excited utterance is a declaration that, in human experience, has been made with reflex action at or near the scene of an incident, or in response to the happening of an incident, at a moment before the person, party, or witness uttering the declaration has the opportunity to think and fabricate. These declarations ordinarily describe an event or condition while the Declarant was actually perceiving or reacting to the event, or immediately thereafter. Thus, a witness who, immediately after the happening of an accident, overwrought by emotion and concern and running about screaming that someone who just walked backward into a plate glass window is bleeding and needs help, is making an excited utterance. This statement, depending on its spontaneity and closeness in time to the event, could be admitted in evidence even by a third person/witness who heard the statement as it was being screamed about precisely because it was an excited utterance, and because of its emotional spontaneity, not considered hearsay.

Prior Inconsistent Statements

Prior Inconsistent Statements have been mentioned previously and shall be discussed at length in later chapters. These are different from those statements or declarations discussed immediately above in that they are hearsay but are nevertheless permitted to be utilized at trial *to affect credibility,* not to be introduced in evidence.

> NOTE: *When introduced to affect credibility, a prior inconsistent statement is NOT evidence-in-chief. It is not introduced to assert the truth of the statement, but is being used to affect credibility, to show the jury that the witness may be unreliable as that witness had previously made another and different statement concerning the case.*

For a complete discussion concerning the four different kinds of prior inconsistent statements, their use, and the foundations necessary for each different category of inconsistency, see the specific chapter relating to the type of prior inconsistency, infra.

Prior Consistent Declarations

Unlike prior inconsistent statements, a prior *consistent* statement CANNOT be admitted into evidence or utilized in any way during trial, not because it is hearsay—a consistent statement is ordinarily one that has been previously testified to by the witness on the stand—but because such a statement violates yet another rule *of evidence.*

Prior consistent statements cannot be used by the party offering a witness because such prior consistent statements do not add anything factual to the case, but merely tends to repeat, therefore, *bolster* the testimony of the witness/prior declarant. For the aforementioned reason, i.e., that a prior consistent statement is a repetition of the same statement the witness makes directly from the witness stand, adding nothing factual to the proceedings, it is considered superfluous and cumulative. After all, a person saying something once, twice, or five times is still the same person making the same declaration. Repetition does not make it more true, nor more cross-examinable.

Neither party can utilize a prior consistent statement except when the witness's testimony has been attacked as a *recent fabrication.*

Recent fabrication, as a term or art, means that as the time for trial drew nigh the witness has changed or fabricated his or her testimony to accommodate the position of one of the parties. Not every Cross-examination, even a scathing, ripping Cross-examination of a witness, is an attack of recent fabrication. Such an attack of testimony is a specific attack on the witness as having changed his or her testimony within recent time to assist the party on whose behalf the witness is presented. See the following example.

Q: The light at the intersection that you saw was actually green for the defendant, wasn't it?

A: No, it wasn't.

Q: The testimony you're giving now isn't what actually happened, is it?

A: Yes, it is.

Q: You've changed your testimony specifically to assist the plaintiff, haven't you?

A: Of course, not.

Q: Haven't you been meeting with Mr. Plaintiff on a regular basis during recent months?

A: That's not unusual. He's my brother-in-law.

Q: You've changed your testimony about the facts of this case for the purposes of assisting your brother-in-law and sister in their law suit?

A: No, that's not true.

The above is an example of a Cross-examination which attacks the witness as having recently fabricated his or her testimony. In such case, a prior *consistent* statement can be utilized on Re-Direct examination and would not be considered *bolstering* because it is used solely for the purpose of showing that the current testimony of the witness is NOT a recent fabrication but is exactly what the witness had previously said on an occasion prior to the alleged time of fabrication.

> NOTE: *Just as when dealing with prior inconsistent statements, the use of the prior* consistent *statement, when utilized as described here, is NOT being introduced into evidence, but is merely utilized to affect credibility, to show that the prior statement was, in fact, previously made and, thus, that the testimony is* not *a recent fabrication. While, hearsay, the prior consistent statement can be used for the sole purpose of showing that the testimony has not been recently fabricated. The prior consistency is, ordinarily, not introduced in evidence.*

Declaration against Penal Interest

A prior declaration by a party or a witness that is adverse to that person's own penal interest, that is, that admits something that would put that person at risk or jeopardy vis-à-vis the penal law, is considered a declaration against penal interest. There is also a concomitant declaration against economic interests which would impact negatively against a person's economic interests that may also qualify as an exception to the proscription against hearsay. The reason that the preceding indicated declarations against penal and economic interest are considered exceptions to the rule against hearsay and therefore might be utilized at trial whether or not the party or witness takes the stand is that, in ordinary human experience, such statements are not made by persons unless they are true. People do not ordinarily say things adverse to themselves for fun, in jest, or to amuse an audience. Humans may have a tendency to boast and puff, but not to deprecate themselves. Thus, negative statements about oneself that affect one's penal or economic interest carry the human implication or indicia of reliability of the truth of such statement.

Exceptions Where Witness Is Unavailable

Where a witness is unavailable, certain declarations of that witness may be used as a substitute for current testimony, where those declarations are clothed in reliability. Not *every* prior statement of an unavailable witness can be admitted. It must pass other qualifying criteria. There are several bases for a court to declare a witness unavailable: inability to be present due to death or then-existing mental or physical illness; inability of the proponent of the statement to procure the declarant's attendance by process or other reasonable means; refusal of the Declarant to testify under color of legal privilege (Fifth Amendment); refusal of the Declarant to testify despite court order; or inability of the Declarant to recall the subject matter of the declaration. Under this category, Depositions and prior testimony both under oath qualify as the sort of prior statements that, if available, are admissible in the absence or unavailability of the witness.

There Is More to the Rules Than This

This is just a smattering of what is involved in the Rules of Evidence. There are other rules and other exceptions to the rules. These should be studied so that the Advocate is familiar with all of them, knows when to use them, and knows how to counter his or her Adversary's attempt to use them. They may seem difficult, confusing, and too numerous to master, but they're not. As indicated earlier, there are certain rules that are more significant, and when you master the essence of these rules, the real meaning and purpose of the rules, you will be well on your way to being able to understand and use them easily. Start absorbing the essences. The trial is at hand. We're about to pick the jury.

PART II

Controlling the Cross-Examined Witness

7.

To Control the Witness, First Control the Question

7.01 Cross-Examiner, Control

Control! Control! Control! That is the beginning, the middle, and the end of Cross-examination.

After investigation and research uncovers all the materials that you intend to employ in your Cross-examination have been analyzed, after the Cross-examination script has been prepared in the calm, cool atmosphere of your office or library, when you are in court, the Adverse Witness in the witness chair, you rise to your feet to cross-examine. Your task is very simple. You must control everything that happens, like an absolute monarch, which, for the moment, you are. You must control the witness, control the question, control the flow, and control the subject matter. But, most of all, and most importantly, you must control yourself.

7.02 The Question Is the Key

Newton's theory that for every action there is an equal and opposite reaction is firmly applicable to Cross-examination. Your questions directly control the return response of the witness. For example, ask about weather. The witness responds about weather. Ask about a broken leg, the witness responds about a broken leg. You control the subject matter, the pace, everything. Now use that control.

The method by which you control the Adverse Witness, therefore, to contain the hurt she may inflict on your case and your client, to compel her to answer questions in a manner you desire and about the subject you desire, you must ask very measured and calculated questions. This does not mean that, every time you ask a question in a certain, carefully couched way, the witness will respond with the desired answer. But, without doubt, your questions, in the first instance, give direction and substance to the examination. Thus, it is your choice to ask questions about the subject matter you wish to ask and have the witness restricted to that subject.

7.03 Not Only What You Ask, But the Way You Ask

Not only must you, by your questions, control the subject matter you wish to probe, you must also limit the boundaries in which you permit the Adverse Witness to roam with his answer. Let's use an analogy. If you had a horse in a three-acre field, the horse might stay within the boundaries you selected for him and yet, because of the room you provided, elude being caught and tied for a substantial period of time. If you place the same horse in a 12'×12' box stall, you permit it very little room in which to elude you at the moment you wish to put a halter and lead line on it. In both situations, the horse is free to move about comfortably and safely within the parameters that you have selected for it, but in the latter situation, you have far more substantially controlled the horse; there is much less chance for it to elude you in the smaller area you've permitted him.

The same applies to the witness you cross-examine. Not only must you control the subject matter, but additionally, your inquiry concerning that subject matter must be put forward in such a limited fashion and your question formed with such restricted wording that the witness is quite restricted in the answers he or she may give. For example, if you ask the witness to "Tell the jury about the weather on January 5, 1995," the witness is free to tell that jury anything about any aspect of the weather. He could testify about the bitter cold, the wet, or the wind, begin anywhere, and describe any aspect of the weather he pleases. It was you who opened the door to any sort of general answer concerning the weather on January 5, 1995, by couching the question in the general fashion you did. You might better have asked questions concerning that day's weather as follows:

Q: On the evening of January 5, 1995, it was raining, was it not?

A: Yes.

Q: And it was quite cold, was it not?

A: Yes, it was.

Q: The streets were *not* covered with snow though, were they?

A: No.

Q: Nor were they covered with ice?

A: No.

Q: By the time you were driving east across Canal Street, the rain had pretty much stopped, had it not?

A: Yes.

Q: It had not stopped completely, though, had it?

A: No.

Q: Would it be fair to say it was only a drizzle at the time you were going east on Canal Street?

A: I guess so.

Q: Please don't guess, Mr. Witness, just tell the court and jury whether it's a fact that it was just drizzling when you were driving east on Canal Street on the evening of January 5, 1995.

A: It was drizzling.

This pattern of questions was purposely chosen to limit the witness's responses about the weather of January 5, 1995. The example also points out the fact that, often, to better restrict the witness's answers, rather than asking one general question, you may have to ask many small questions to safely get to the point at which you wish to arrive. By so doing, however, at least you arrive at your destination by means of transportation *you* choose, not that which the witness chooses.

You can not be lazy! If it is too much trouble for you to ask all the questions necessary to get where you're going safely, to ask the questions that shall result in answers that are not going to blow you out of the water, then the subject matter about which you are asking must not be significant enough to warrant the effort. If that be so, don't ask about it at all. If, however, the subject matter is worth exploring, if the question is worth asking, then it is worth being asked correctly.

7.04 The Cardinal Rule—Control the Question

To be sure that the witness does not give you an answer you do not wish, you must break the subject of inquiry down into its basic ingredients, asking only as much of the subject in one question that can be answered in a simple and direct answer. Thus, if you want to control the answer, you must first control the question. For instance, you can ask the witness to describe an individual he says he saw on a particular occasion as follows:

> Q: Mr. Witness, please describe the man you say you saw on the morning of March fifteenth.
>
> A: He was kind of tall, about six feet, and had blond hair and looked very much like your client there. In fact, he had the same bushy eyebrows your client has. That's why I've said your client is the man I saw.

You asked a blanket question, and you deserved to be inundated with that blanket answer. The way to have avoided the witness giving you that unwanted answer was to have controlled the space in which he could have meandered with his answer. This should have been done by strict attention to, and control of, your questions. For instance, to explore a previous description given by a witness, you might do it as follows:

> Q: Right after the incident, you spoke to Police Officer Rigby and described this person you saw as being of medium height, is that correct?
>
> A: Yes.
>
> Q: Would you consider my size to be medium height?
>
> A: Just about, maybe a little taller.
>
> Q: When you say a little taller, do you mean an inch or so?
>
> A: Yes.

CROSS-EXAMINER: May the record show, Your Honor, that my height is 5′ 10″.

THE COURT: Very well, the record will so reflect.

> Q: And, at that time, you also described this person as having blond hair, is that correct?
>
> A: Yes.
>
> Q: In fact, you described that blond hair as short and curly; almost kinky, isn't that correct?
>
> A: I don't remember that.

(*Authors Note:* Your client here does NOT have blond kinky hair.)

Q: You do remember being interviewed by Police Officer Rigby a short while after the incident occurred?

A: Yes.

Q: And that police officer asked you questions, did he not?

A: Yes.

Q: And you responded to those questions?

A: Yes.

Q: And at the time you told the police officer whatever you told him, you were describing what you had seen that very night, were you not?

A: Yes.

Q: And the reason you were describing what you had seen was to give the police officer accurate information so that he might investigate that incident, isn't that correct?

A: Yes.

Q: And isn't it a fact that you told the police officer at that time that the person who was involved in this incident had blond hair, very short, curly, very kinky hair?

A: I don't believe I did.

In the above example, by several precise, smaller questions, rather than one broad general question, the cross-examiner has prevented the witness from making gratuitous remarks or adding unwanted information to the answer.

> NOTE: *The last part of the above Cross-examination, as to a prior a statement made to a police officer, is the requisite method for laying the foundation needed to ultimately call Police Officer Rigby to testify that the witness did, in fact, make a prior inconsistent statement, in which the witness described the perpetrator as having short, blond, kinky hair. (See Chapter 14.)*

A few more examples of controlling the witness's answers by controlling your own questions are appropriate here. For instance, you could ask a witness to describe an incident which occurred, or you could provide a description of the incident yourself in your questions, requiring the witness only to affirm or negate your description. See the wrong method that follows.

Q: What occurred when you were attacked?

A: I was walking towards the door of the bar. I was just reaching for the handle of the door when I felt a tremendous blow on the back of my head. I turned and your client, the defendant there (pointing), was behind me, with two other men, and a pool cue in his hand. I fell to the floor unconscious. I woke up in the hospital.

In this example, the witness repeated the same story he told on Direct testimony. And by your question, you have just helped him to sink his hook further into your client. A witness should rarely be asked to repeat his Direct testimony. (See Exceptions, Chapter 9.) Rather, the witness's testimony should be attacked in piecemeal fashion with short-ranged questions that do not permit the witness to empty his guns at your client.

The above subject matter might better have been explored as follows:

Q: Now you say that just before you were struck in the head with this terrible blow, you were walking toward the door of the bar, is that correct?

A: Yes.

Q: You reached the door just before you were hit, correct?

A: That's right. That's right.

Q: You were just reaching for the doorknob, is that correct?

A: Yes.

Q: Now up to this point you hadn't seen the defendant behind you, had you?

YOUR ADVERSARY: Objection, Your Honor, at what point?

THE COURT: Yes, sustained as to form.

Q: Up to the point that you reached the door and were reaching for the door handle, you hadn't seen the defendant behind you, had you?

A: I saw him as soon as I was hit. I turned around.

Q: The question is: *before* you were hit, you didn't see anyone behind you, did you?

A: Before? No.

Q: You saw someone behind you, whoever it was, only after you received the blow on the head, isn't that correct?

A: (Pause) Yes.

Q: In fact, before you received this blow, you were facing toward the door and the street, weren't you?

A: Well, sort of facing the street, sort of facing in, you know.

Q: You weren't walking sideways, were you?

A: No.

Q: Before you were hit, you were walking normally toward the door, weren't you?

A: Yes.

Q: And you were walking toward and facing the door when you reached for the doorknob, weren't you?

A: Yes.

Q: And it was then that you received this blow, isn't that correct?

A: Yes.

Q: The very first thing you even knew about an attack that night was when you were hit on the head, correct?

A: Yes.

Q: And this blow was a terrible blow, wasn't it?

A: Well . . .

Q: Didn't you describe this very blow to the jury and previously to the police officer as being a terrible blow on the back of your head?

A: Yes.

Q: And it was that, wasn't it, a terrible blow on your head?

A: Yes.

Q: You've already testified that as a result of this blow, this terrible blow, you became unconscious, correct?

A: I saw him, I saw that guy (pointing to the defendant).

Q: As a matter of fact, the next thing you know, after this terrible blow, is that you woke up in a hospital, correct?

A: (no response.)

Basically, in both the above examinations, you have asked the witness for the same information; that is, what he saw at the time of the alleged attack. Yet there is certainly a substantial difference in the way the witness describes and the jury hears those two versions of the incident. The first is in the witness's own words—whatever words the witness chose. The second version is in *your* words—whatever words you have chosen for your questions, permitting the witness only enough room to affirm or deny. And, whether the witness affirms or denies your question, he shall not be in a position by that one affirmance or denial to damage you so severely that you cannot correct your course, keep going, and still emerge in a strong position. For example, let me change a significant answer that the witness gave in the previous example. Suppose, for instance, that the witness had answered as follows:

Q: You saw someone behind you, whoever it was, only after you received the blow on the head, isn't that correct?

A: At the same time as I got hit, I saw him (pointing to your defendant). At the same time.

Remember, an Adverse Witness has been called to the stand to hurt your client and sometimes a witness goes to extremes to do that. Be prepared for just such an eventuality. And part of that preparation is to limit the amount of hurt by limiting your question. You must unflinchingly continue the examination as follows:

Q: At the time you were walking up to the door, you hadn't already been hit, had you?

A: No.

Q: Anybody curse at you, spit at you while you were walking?

A: No.

Q: Anybody threaten to beat you up, tell you to get the hell out of the bar?

A: No.

Q: So as you were walking up to the front door, you were doing so only because you wanted to, not because anyone made you, correct?

A: That's right.

Q: And you weren't suspicious of anything that had happened up to that point, because nothing had happened, right?

A: (hesitantly) Right.

Q: And when you got to the door, you reached for the doorknob to go out, right?

A: Yes.

Q: And at that point, when you were reaching for the doorknob to go out, you were facing the door, weren't you?

A: Maybe not facing the door completely.

Q: You weren't standing facing the bar, reaching backwards over your shoulder to open this door, were you?

A: No.

Q: You were going out of a bar normally, opening the door in a normal fashion, weren't you?

A: Yes.

Notice that the witness is not voluntarily being cooperative, he is looking for any opportunity to hurt you, and you must avoid that pernicious desire by limiting the scope of the questions *you allow him to answer*. If you permit the witness to blurt out his answer in one narrative, you would, thereafter, become involved in an argument with him as to whether or not he really meant what he said he saw. By breaking the questions into palatable pieces—palatable for you, for your purposes—you can control the direction in which to take the next answers. You, at the same time, with the same question, preserve your opportunity to lead the witness back carefully over material, change course, and even abandon a fruitless line of small inquiries without giving up the ship.

When you ask a question that courts the long narrative answer and you receive it, you cannot abandon the Cross-examination without abandoning your client. The difference between the sample examinations, relative to the happening of the incident in the bar, is twofold. In the first, a blanket question was asked, and you would receive any answer that the witness wants to give. Naturally, if that witness is testifying against you, the answer that he is going to give you is not going to be beneficial to your client if the witness can help it. In the second, although the examination is much longer, it is direct and to the point, but more, it does not permit the witness to answer anything that he pleases. You are in control of the flow, you are playing the witness, directing him, curtailing him, containing him, and in short, controlling him.

7.05 Litigator or Real-Estate Closer

To be an effective cross-examiner, you must get into the habit of breaking the subject matter down into bits and pieces where you provide the information, permitting the witness to respond with direct, simple answers. The lazy man's approach, the blanket question that asks for blanket answers because the fragmented bits-and-pieces examination is too long or too tedious, will result in your being inundated by answers that you do not appreciate or desire, which are not helpful to your client's cause. If you are too lazy to ask all the questions necessary to control the witness, if it is too much trouble to break the questions down into palatable pieces, don't bother to cross-examine; pack up your bag, go home, and handle real-estate closings.

8.

The Best Control of the Witness: Compel Yes or No Answers

8.01 Compelling Yes or No Answers

The best of all methods to control the Adverse Witness is to pose questions which require either a yes or no answer. In this way, the cross-examiner supplies all the information the witness and the jury hears, permitting the witness only to answer in the affirmative or in the negative. By posing such questions, the cross-examiner totally controls the information which is put forth before the jury, and no gratuitous remarks, no damaging information, or misinformation which is unnecessary and undesirable can be blurted out or gratuitously provided by the witness.

There are two steps to take in order to obtain the desired yes or no answers. The first step is that you must ask simple questions that can, in fact, be answered yes or no. The second step is to request that the witness advise you when he or she cannot answer the question in yes or no fashion so that you can rephrase the question. In other words, do not permit the witness to answer the question if he says it cannot be answered yes or no. Ask the witness to advise you of his or her inability to so answer the question, so that you may rephrase and ask the question in different form.

8.02 Your Adversary May Attempt to Curtail Yes and No Answers

If, at the beginning of your Cross-examination, you tell the witness you want he or she to give yes or no answers, almost automatically, your Adversary or the court may attempt to curtail your demand for such answers on the ground that not all questions can be answered yes or no. And they would be right in quoting this old bromide. The bromide is the result of hordes of inept cross-examiners in the past, who have indicated that they wanted yes or no answers, then went ahead to ask questions which clearly did not lend themselves to yes or no answers. In order to be entitled to yes or no answers, the cross-examiner must carefully formulate questions the answers to which are appropriately either yes or no. Demanding yes or no answers can not be an empty crutch by the inept cross-examiner to support otherwise poorly crafted questions that cannot be answered in that fashion. In order to get yes or no answers, you must be entitled to them. Either you formulate questions that clearly lend themselves to yes or no answers, or no amount of demanding or wishing is going to result in your getting such answers.

8.03 Your Adversary's Motives

Your Adversary's motives for not wanting to permit you to compel yes or no answers from the witness are another story. Your Adversary doesn't want *you* to supply all the information that the jury hears, thus eliminating the witness's opportunity to purposely damage your case by blurting out gratuitous information before the jury, or to eliminate the witness's opportunity to repeat, time and time again, your Adversary's version of the case. Thus, in an attempt to stop your demand for yes or no answers, your Adversary may advise the court that not all questions can be answered yes or no, that the witness may not be able to answer questions in such limited fashion, and the witness should be permitted to give full answers to the questions. Your Adversary is right; your attempt to curtail and control the witness shall be subverted, and you are going to be inundated with whatever answer your Adversary has rehearsed the witness to give—unless you are alert and react properly under the above conditions.

8.04 What to Do?

First, it is arrant nonsense that you should not be permitted to compel witnesses to give yes or no answers *if you ask the appropriate question.*

The problem is that most cross-examiners do not pose proper questions which can, in fact, be answered in a yes or no fashion. Thus, the first discipline to be mastered by the cross-examiner desiring yes or no answers is to ask questions which strictly lend themselves to such answers. Again, this may seem simplistic, but if you sit in on various trials in your local court-house, you shall see that it is apparently not so easy to control witnesses by containing them to yes or no answers. The solution to this dilemma, which has long plagued cross-examiners, is not simple. It is not easy, normal, or natural to get only yes or no answers. But you shall be able to do it if you are willing to work at it. It shall only happen by dint of studied and hard work.

The unquestionable first step on the road to compelling the witness to the yes or no answer is to craft questions which are answerable by yes or no. In other words, as previously stated, it is you, the cross-examiner, who is to-tally responsible for the questioning of the witness, the area of questioning, the actual wording of the question, and every other aspect of what questions are asked of the witness. If you ask a question which has a very limited scope, and which can, in fact, be answered yes or no, there is no basis what-soever for your Adversary to claim that such a question cannot be answered in a yes or no fashion.

8.05 Where the Problems Arise

The greatest number of problems in this area arise when the cross-examiner intends to ask a question which he or she ardently desires to have answered yes or no. But in the actual asking, the question is not asked in simple enough form; the question does not lend itself to be answered "yes" or "no." At the end of the nonsimple question, when the witness attempts to give a full answer to the question actually articulated, the cross-examiner at-tempts to cut off the answer and demands that the witness answer yes or no. To this the Adversary leaps up, objects, the court sustains, and the witness is permitted to give a full and complete answer to the question you shouldn't have asked. The fault, as Shakespeare said, is not in your stars, or the Adver-sary, or the court, but in yourself. You have asked a question that cannot be answered yes or no. And, therefore, you are not justified in demanding that the question be answered yes or no.

8.06 The Right Stuff

When a question is properly couched, actually lending itself to a yes or no answer, the witness's response does not have to be cut off, nor the aid of the courts invoked to require the witness to answer properly. The answer should flow naturally from the question. It is when the cross-examiner asks an un-artful question that does not lend itself to yes or no, and the witness pro-ceeds to give a full answer, that the cross-examiner has to cut off, curtail, and demand that the answer be yes or no. It is in just such an instance that the court and your Adversary will resist your attempting to hack the answer you want from the question you never really asked. The best thing for you to do is to rephrase your questions and to ask proper questions which lend themselves to yes or no. For example:

Q: At the time of the accident, traffic on Main Street was rather light wasn't it?

A: Not really.

CROSS-EXAMINER: Your Honor, I'll ask the court to direct the witness to answer that question yes or no.

YOUR ADVERSARY: Objection, Your Honor. Not every question can be answered yes or no. Certainly not that one. The witness should be per-mitted to give a full answer.

THE COURT: Mr. Witness, if you can answer that question yes or no, please do so. If you feel that you cannot, then you may explain fully.

(*Author's Note:* Is there any doubt what the next words of the wit-ness will be?)

A: I cannot answer that yes or no.

THE COURT: Very well. Answer it as you wish.

A: The traffic wasn't bumper to bumper, but there were a number of cars on the road. Specifically, particularly there was a car in front of me which blocked me for a moment. But that car moved over and then I was in a position to observe your client directly in front of me. Three car lengths ahead of me . . .

It might seem that the question *"at the time of the accident, traffic on Main Street was rather light"* is simple. However, that which followed by your Adversary and the court was not unreasonable. And, you, by your ques-tion, have given the Adverse Witness an opportunity to bury you a little deeper. The information might better have been elicited in the following fashion, with a more beneficial result:

Q: At the time that you say you observed other vehicles, particularly that of my client, were there other vehicles on the road?

A: Yes.

Q: This road was and is a public highway in the State of New York, correct?

A: Yes.

Q: And there were various lanes of traffic going in each direction, were there not?

A: Yes.

Q: And at the time of the accident, there were other vehicles on the road besides yours and my client's?

A: Yes.

Q: And these other cars were traveling in the same direction as yourself and my client?

A: Yes.

Q: At the time just prior to the observations that you said you made, were there vehicles behind your car?

A: Yes.

Q: You noticed these vehicles behind your car, did you not?

A: Yes.

Q: Did you observe them through your rearview mirror, or had you turned around in order to see them?

A: I observed them through the rearview mirror.

Q: So that you were driving carefully, observing not only what was ahead of you but behind you, is that correct?

A: Yes.

Q: And at the time, just prior to the observation that you said you made, in addition to the car of my client, there were vehicles ahead of you on the road, isn't that correct?

A: Well, there were other vehicles but . . .

CROSS-EXAMINER: Your Honor, I object to the answer going any further and ask that Your Honor direct the witness to answer only the question asked and not give gratuitous remarks.

YOUR ADVERSARY: Your Honor, I object; not every question can be answered yes or no, and I think that the witness should be provided an opportunity to give full and complete answers to the questions asked.

CROSS-EXAMINER: Your Honor, the question was simply whether there were vehicles other than the defendant's and witness's vehicle on the road. This question is subject to a yes or no answer. If my Adversary wishes the witness to answer other questions and give further information, he can have a redirect examination on this subject.

THE COURT: While not every question can be answered yes or no, I think that question can be. The cross-examiner has asked merely whether or not there were other vehicles on the road ahead of this witness's vehicle, other than the defendant's. Answer that just yes or no. You can inquire, Mr. Adversary on redirect examination, if there is further information you wish the witness to bring out.

Q: Were there other vehicles on the road ahead of yourself, other than the vehicle of my client, prior to your making the observations?

A: Yes.

Naturally, some people reading the above can think that the court could just as easily have permitted the witness to give a full and complete answer at that point, and that is true. I cannot specify simply, and in every case, a situation where the court will act favorably to your contention that a question can be answered yes or no. However, I can assure you that the carefully crafted question, the simpler question, the one that does not permit a wide range of possibilities for answers, is the one that will more than likely pass muster on the yes or no test. The secret in containing the witness is simply that you must not try to travel by yards, asking questions that, in an attempt to move directly, quickly toward your desired goal, permit a wide range of information, permitting, therefore, the witness to give a wide-ranging answer. Thus, you must be prepared to move slowly, in measured cadence, asking questions which you can control, which do not require more of an answer than you are willing to have the witness make.

8.07 Ask the Witness to Advise You if He or She Cannot Answer Yes or No

At the outset of your Cross-examination, alert the court and the witness that you intend to pose questions that can be answered in a yes or no fashion, as follows:

> CROSS-EXAMINER: Mr. Witness, I am about to ask you various questions which, hopefully, you shall be able to answer yes or no. In the event that you cannot answer these questions yes or no, please advise me of that, so that I can rephrase the question, all right?
>
> A: Yes.

Now you have set the stage and laid a foundation for asking questions which can appropriately be answered in a yes or no fashion. In the event that the witness believes a question cannot be answered in a yes or no fashion, rather than giving a free ranging, gratuitous answer, the witness should properly state to you that the question cannot be so answered. Neither the court nor your Adversary should object to your requesting a yes or no response—*provided you actually follow up with questions that lend themselves to be so answered.* Having laid your foundation, if you properly formulate your questions, making them crisp, lean, and simple, and the witness, nevertheless, attempts to respond with gratuitous information, attempting to bury you, you can properly ask the court to admonish the witness, to direct the witness to answer the question asked, and not give gratuitous remarks. In other words, you have properly set the stage for the answers that you want, and are perfectly justified in demanding the witness answer the question asked—*again, assuming that you follow up with properly couched questions.*

> CAUTION: *Do not permit your Cross-examination to become sloppy, casual, or without discipline. The instant the witness advises you that the question cannot be answered yes or no, ask another question. Do not lose the initiative.*

Do not let the witness formulate his or her own question, or select the question to answer. The same restriction applies to your Adversary and the judge. It is your Cross-examination. You select the questions. Pose another question that you feel can be answered yes or no. Keep at it. It's hard work, but it's worth it.

Q: Were you alone on the stairway at that time?

A: I cannot answer that question yes or no.

Q: Very well. When you first exited the apartment and entered the stairwell was anyone else with you?

A: No.

Q: And there were several flights of steps going down, correct?

A: Yes.

Q: You were on the fourth floor?

A: Yes.

Q: As you were walking down was there anyone walking down on the same flight of steps as yourself?

A: No.

Or perhaps you might have asked:

Q: Was the work on the bank's main computer to compile monthly interest done by anyone other than yourself?

A: I can't answer that yes or no.

Q: All right. There were several different functions and tasks that were done on that computer, correct?

A: Yes.

Q: And you accomplished one of them, correct?

A: Yes.

Q: Other people may have used the same computer for different functions or for different clients, correct?

A: Right.

Q: Were you the only one who computed the monthly interest amounts for this particular client?

A: Yes, I was the only one.

Thus, the two steps necessary in attempting to contain the witness, in order to ensure that the witness's answers shall be yes or no, are:

1. ask the simple question that can be answered yes or no; and
2. where the question cannot be so answered, have the witness advise you of that, and then ask a question that can be answered yes or no.

8.08 Old Chestnuts Die Hard

The old chestnut that is constantly thrown at you in a courtroom, or in other treatises, to prove that all questions cannot be answered yes or no, is the question "Have you stopped beating your wife?" The classic objection is that neither a yes nor a no answer could fully explain to the jury that the man is not married and thus has never beaten his wife. Under those circumstances, naturally, the judge must permit the witness to fully answer the loaded question, which, actually, does not lend itself to a yes or no answer. The obvious fault in this cited classic example is not with the witness, your Adversary, or the judge. It is with the question. That question does, in fact, presume two circumstances which may or may not be in evidence: (a) that the man is married, and (b) that he had, in the past, beaten his wife. If you ask a question of that sort, artlessly, then you deserve to be inundated. Perhaps, to get at the same information, the cross-examiner might have better asked:

Q: Are you married?

A: Yes.

Q: Have you ever struck her or hit your wife in the face or about the body with your hands or any object for any reason whatever?

A: Yes.

Q: Have you struck your wife in such fashion within the last two months?

A: Yes.

Q: So this is an activity which has continued right into the recent past, isn't it?

A: Yes.

In this example, you have obtained all the information that was required from the original question, "Have you stopped beating your wife?" The only difference is that, in order to be answered, the question had to be broken down into several pieces that could properly be answered by yes or no.

9.

Controlling a Witness

9.01 Controlling the Questions

To illustrate the art of controlling a witness by controlling the question, I provide herewith an excerpt of a Cross-examination by prominent New York Trial Attorney Jay Goldberg examining Salvatore "Sammy The Bull" Gravano, self-confessed Underboss of the Gambino Crime Family to now imprisoned for life, John Gotti. This Cross-examination took place during an actual trial in a Federal District Court in New York City.

In this trial Mr. Goldberg represented an individual named Gambino—not the one for whom the reputed crime family was named. Mr. Gravano is the witness.

By Mr. Goldberg:

Q: Sir, you told us when you were arrested on December 11, 1990, you were charged with committing or participating in the commission of three murders, is that right?

A: Yes.

Q: You told us that as you understood it, if you were convicted for those three murders—for the participation in those three murders you could have spent the rest of your life in jail, is that right?

A: Yes.

Q: You were 46 then?

A: Yes.

Q: With life expectancy, you could have spent 25, 30 years in jail, is that right?

A: Yes.

Q: Okay. Now, you have not pleaded guilty, as you sit here now, to three murders, but to having participated in the killing of 19 human beings. Is that correct?

A: Yes, 19 murders.

Q: 19 people? Is that right?

A: Yes.

Q: And you actually face, as you sit here, less punishment than when you were charged with killing three people. Is that right? Is that what I understand, yes or no?

A: Yes.

Q: Am I right about that?

A: I said yes.

Q: In other words Mr. Gravano, you face 20 years in jail—maximum 20 years in jail for taking the lives of 19 human beings and you said yes. Isn't that right?

A: Yes.

Q: But I don't recall, and perhaps I missed it. I didn't hear if Mr. Mearns (the prosecutor) had asked you whether there was a low end, a minimum period of time that the learned sentencing judge, if he saw fit, would be authorized under this plea agreement to grant you, do you remember anything like that having been put to you?

A: No.

Q: As a matter of fact, under the agreement that you worked out with the government, you replaced an exposure of three life sentences for the three murders with a possibility, if luck be with you, for 19 murders, doing no additional time? Is that so, zero on the low end, isn't that a true statement?

A: The judge isn't bound by the guidelines.

Q: Does the plea agreement not permit the judge, be he so inclined, because you haven't been sentenced yet, to impose a probationary period, a zero term of incarceration?

A: Yes.

Q: Have you not said within the last several weeks that, if luck be with you, that you could be on the street by Christmas, have you said that?

A: I don't think I said if luck be with me.

Q: Forget the luck. If fate be with you, you hope to be with us again as early as the Christmas season, have you said that?

A: I believe I wasn't asked that way, but . . .

Q: Well, I will ask you, given the festive mood of Christmas, is it your hope, as you sit here, that by Christmas you will one day be free, that's your hope, isn't that so?

A: My hope is to be free one day, yes.

Q: Yes, and you have said as recently as the last two weeks, you made reference to the month of December as your hoped for goal of freedom, is that so, for these 19 homicides?

A: I think that's what a lawyer presented.

Q: And what did you say in response to what the lawyer said?

A: Yes, I hope to be out at the earliest possible date.

NOTE: *Notice that controlling the witness is not just a textbook exercise. Here you see a sample of real-life Cross-examination, in a real life, high profile case, being utilized by an extremely capable Trial Advocate, with the precise type of control discussed in Chapter 8.*

Notice that Mr. Goldberg asks a question in which he provides all the information he wishes revealed—thus containing the area in which Mr. Gravano's answer might ramble—asking Mr. Gravano merely to affirm or deny the proposition contained in the question. Additionally, Mr. Goldberg goes very little step by very little step, patiently undermining the posture of Mr. Gravano as a credible witness.

Q: Let me see how I understand this. When you called the government or the F.B.I. on October 24, 1990, you were sitting in a prison which Mr. Mearns refers to as the MCC, the Metropolitan Correctional Center, right?

A: Yes.

Q: Facing this prospect of three life sentences without parole, correct?

A: I don't believe so. I think it is just one sentence of life without parole.

Q: I mean one life without parole. Is that right, one life sentence without parole?

A: I believe that's what the sentence would have been.

Q: And you picked up the phone and you called the government. Is that right, or the F.B.I.?

A: Yes.

Q: Did you make that call because you had some conversion, some change of direction in the way in which you had lived your life? Is that why you picked up that telephone?

A: No.

Q: Okay. You picked up that phone to try to work a deal for yourself. Is that true?

A: I guess you could put it that way.

Q: Because when you went down on October 24, you met an F.B.I. agent, I think you told us several F.B.I. agents, and the United States Attorney himself, Mr. Maloney. Is that correct?

A: Yes.

Q: And you talked to them about the possibility that you wanted to come clean with your life of crime. Is that correct?

A: I believe I said something to the effect that I was turning my back on my life and I was changing direction.

Q: Let me see if I understand this. You were turning—give that to me one more time, I missed it?

A: I was turning my back on my life, my lifestyle, and I was changing my direction.

Q: Changing direction, that was October 24, 1990, is that right, and you told that to Mr. Maloney? Is that right.

A: I believe that's the date.

Q: Did you tell Mr. Maloney that, despite the statement that you made to him that you wanted to turn your back on your other life, you were going to go back to the MCC and commit further extortionate credit collections, did you tell that to him?

A: No.

Q: But there is no question that after you left Mr. Maloney's office, when you told him that you wanted to turn your back on your former life, you uttered those words, intending for him to believe that you could now be trusted to turn your back on your former life, isn't that so, that is why you uttered those words to him, isn't that true?

A: No.

Q: When you said to Mr. Maloney, I am here because I want to turn my back on my former life you conveyed to him, did you not, the fact of your intention to change your way of life; isn't that a fair statement?

A: I don't know if that is what was running through my head at this particular point.

Q: As a matter of fact, despite what you said to Mr. Maloney, for the next few weeks after you went back to the MCC you proceeded to arrange collections, or extortionate credit collections between October 24, 1991, and November 8, 1991, when you left the MCC, isn't that true?

A: No.

Q: That is not true?

A: No.

Q: *(At this point, Mr. Goldberg, as he stands before the witness, reaches for a trial transcript from another trial at which Mr. Gravano testified.)* Do you recall being asked this question at page 4232? This is Gravano Cross in the 4,000 numbers, 4232. Do you recall this question having been asked you—*(Mr. Goldberg is thumbing through the pages as he looks at the witness)*—the shylocking business you were involved in continued right up until the time that you were arrested, correct?

A: Yes.

Q: In fact you even continued it there while you were in the MCC, did you not?

A: Yes.

Q: Are you saying here that you didn't continue engaging in shylocking right up until the day you left the MCC? Are you saying that?

A: What I am saying is—

Q: Are you saying, is that yes or no?

A: What I am saying is I didn't stop it.

Q: Wait a minute.

A: It would be a complete and total tip-off to the street to stop it. It was being run while I was in prison for months, and when I cooperated I didn't go back in and tell people on the street: Stop the shylocking, I cooperated.

Q: Mr. Gravano, until I reached for a transcript, I recall the question on the floor had been, did you, sir, not after leaving Mr. Maloney's office on October 24, 1991, until November 8, 1991, when you left the prison, you left the MCC, did you not continue to engage in loan sharking, you said no. Isn't that right?

A: I just answered you, it is, yes.

There is more to this excellent Cross-examination by Mr. Goldberg in the supplement section at the back of this book, where you can read the more complete texts of superior Cross-examinations by excellent attorneys.

10.

Enlisting the Court's Aid to Control the Witness

10.01 The Vengeful Witness

As indicated in previous chapters, the essence of Cross-examination is control. The cross-examiner must control the questions he asks; he must control the witness; and he must control the answers received from the witness. Often, a witness will sit in the witness chair and purposely, vengefully, attempt to undermine and thwart your efforts to cross-examine. Understand right from the get-go that all witnesses proffered by your Adversary are intended to hurt your client's position. At this juncture, however, I am going to talk not about the ordinary adverse testimony you should anticipate from a witness you are about to cross-examine. Rather, I want to discuss a witness who purposely attempts to inundate you with gratuitous remarks, who wishes to turn his or her answer to the question into some harmful comment which is actually not responsive, but is definitely more harmful to your client. I want to talk about the witness to whom you might pose a question, and the witness tangentially answers your question by a comment which springboards into a spear aimed directly at your client's heart.

When this occurs you must exert effort, right at the outset of such hostile action, to bring that witness under control, to discipline the witness, to punish or humiliate him or her, until you have the witness submit to your will. To do this, you should not hesitate to enlist the aid of the court to curtail the witness's nonresponsive, hostile thrusts. The witness I am talking about may not be overtly, physically antagonistic to you or your client. But, the answers that are given and the gratuitous remarks that are added to the answers make you certain that the witness is purposely going out of his or her way to sink you with every answer. See the following example.

Q: Mrs. Witness, as you were walking on 86th Street, you weren't paying total attention to the cars traveling along Park Avenue, were you?

A: No, not totally. But I was watching the cars, and I saw your client's car coming west on 86th Street very fast, and then I saw the light change, and I saw him go through the light, and I saw him hit the plaintiff.

NOTE: Everything after the word NO is gratuitous, obviously nonresponsive to the question, and is so loaded against you as to be intentional and purposeful. You must act immediately to curtail that sort of gratuity.

CROSS-EXAMINER: Your Honor, I move to strike the witness's answer as not being responsive to the question, and ask the court to direct the witness to answer only the questions asked and not make gratuitous remarks.

THE COURT: Yes, Mrs. Witness, please only answer the questions asked, and don't volunteer information not called for by the question.

Perhaps the Adverse Witness is not attempting to be totally antagonistic. Perhaps she is merely garrulous, unfamiliar with the formality and ritual of the courtroom. If that be the case, your efforts to curtail her unresponsive answers shall be easily successful. Let us continue with this examination to find out.

Q: Mrs. Witness, you weren't paying total attention to the cars in the street as you were walking on 86th Street, were you?

A: Not to all the cars. But I saw your client go through the light and hit the plaintiff.

This continuation of gratuitous information, not responsive to the question, is indicative of the fact that your efforts, even the court's effort, to discipline the witness have fallen on deaf ears. You could ignore the witness's obvious efforts to be harmful, and continue the examination blithely, as if the comments were totally inconsequential.

Although I've indicated that it is sometimes possible to ignore the antagonistic witness and the nonresponsive, nonessential answer he or she has given, it is not a recommended practice. Permitting the witness to be nonresponsive to your questions and give gratuitous remarks without you cutting the witness short immediately, even though the area of interrogation is nonessential, is to permit the witness to answer questions in a certain fashion, which apparently is approved by your permissiveness. Later in the examination, if you attempt to bring the witness back into your control on essential matters, your belated attempt to control the witness shall highlight the harm the witness is doing by the fuss you make over that particular portion of the testimony. Additionally, you are in a weak position to ask the court to require the witness to be responsive to your questions when, to that point, you haven't bothered, because you had been permissive or lethargic. Thus, the better practice is to control every witness to the fullest extent possible, constantly, without exception. Let us continue the above examination:

CROSS-EXAMINER: Your Honor, I move again to have the witness's answer stricken as not responsive to the limited question "whether this witness was paying attention to the cars on 86th Street." I ask that the gratuitous remarks of the witness be stricken, and that Your Honor again direct the witness to properly respond to questions asked.

THE COURT: Mrs. Witness, we have certain rules of evidence, and you must answer the questions that are asked, not give whatever answer you please. Now please listen to the questions and give the answers to those questions only and don't add gratuitous remarks. This will save us all time.

Q: It was about 5:30 P.M. when you were on 86th Street and Park Avenue, wasn't it?

A: Yes.

Q: It was a normal weekday night in New York, wasn't it?

A: Yes.

Q: In other words, traffic was normally heavy on that evening on Park Avenue at 86th Street at 5:30 P.M. rush hour, isn't that right?

A: Yes.

Q: And that means that there were many cars going in both the east and west direction on 86th Street, right?

A: Yes.

Q: And there were many cars going north-south on Park Avenue as well, right?

A: Yes.

Notice that the focus of the cross-examiner's questions has been shifted substantially from the previous questions about the actual event where the witness was trying to bury the cross-examiner. The reason for this shift is to craft questions to less essential questions which more readily lend themselves to yes/no answers, to show the witness can answer questions without gratuitous remarks, thus to emphasize the witness's antagonistic purpose to the jury if she again gives inundating answers filled with gratuitous remarks when the cross-examiner returns to the previous subject area. If the witness begins again to add gratuitous remarks to every answer relating to the actual happening of the accident, the jury shall, hopefully, notice the overreaching and the antagonism in the witness's attitude, and this may result in the jury discounting the obvious harm the witness was purposely trying to inject against your client. Another result of making the overreaching of the witness more obvious is that the witness may become self-consciously aware of her appearance of hostility before the jury and may be compelled to be more restrained in answering the questions in order that she does not appear to be trying to overkill your client.

Q: You were walking on 86th Street at the time, were you not?

A: Yes.

Q: And you had just crossed Park Avenue, walking in an easterly direction, right?

A: Right.

Q: You had completely crossed Park Avenue, and were on the easterly Park Avenue sidewalk when the accident occurred, correct?

A: Yes.

Q: And, the accident, when it occurred, involved cars traveling westbound on 86th Street, correct?

A: I could see the corner though.

(The witness, knowing how and where the accident happened, now senses where your questions are going and begins to resist.)

CROSS-EXAMINER: Your Honor, I move that the answer be stricken as not responsive, and ask for your direction again, that the witness respond only to the questions asked.

THE COURT: Yes, once again, Mrs. Witness, please just answer the questions.

(If the witness's tactic begins to annoy the judge, so much the better, as the jury will pick up that signal.)

Q: The accident, when it occurred, involved cars traveling west-bound, isn't that correct?

A: Yes.

Q: And the accident actually happened at the northeast corner of 86th Street and Park Avenue, did it not?

A: Yes.

Q: By the way, when you crossed Park Avenue, you crossed from the southwest to the southeast corner, right?

A: (Thinks) Yes.

Q: And as you crossed, traffic which had been proceeding north on Park Avenue, approached you from your right side as you crossed in the easterly direction, right?

A: I guess.

Q: That is correct, is it not?

A: Yes.

Q: And as you crossed the street, were you watching the traffic as it approached you on your right, to be sure it came to stop at the crosswalk?

A: No, I wasn't looking at the cars that were stopping.

Q: Were you looking straight ahead at the curb you were approaching?

A: I was looking all around.

Q: So, as you crossed Park Avenue, you were looking to your left, away from the traffic approaching you on your right, and away from the curb you were just about to step on, and you were looking to your left, toward the opposite corner, is that what you are telling this jury?

A: I'm telling them I was looking around.

Q: At the point of the looking around, the accident hadn't happened yet, had it?

A: No.

Q: In fact, the accident didn't happen until after you had already stepped onto the sidewalk, and were walking east on 86th Street, isn't that what you've already testified?

A: I didn't go too far from the corner—

CROSS-EXAMINER: Your Honor, I ask that that answer also be stricken as not responsive.

THE COURT: No, I'll allow that answer.

Q: However far you went, when you stepped up on the sidewalk, you were facing east, were you not?

A: Correct.

Q: Had anything happened on the street, in the intersection, before the accident, that attracted your attention as you stepped onto the sidewalk and were headed along 86th Street, east of Park Avenue?

A: I wasn't far east, as I've already said.

Q: However far east you were, even an inch, had anything happened in that intersection prior to your stepping onto the curb?

A: Not that I noticed.

NOTE: Every question is couched carefully with the cross-examiner providing all the information he wishes the jury to hear, requiring only a yes or a no. This method of inquiry must become your second nature.

Q: And what you first noticed in reference to the accident, was the sudden squeal of tires as the cars braked, isn't that right?

A: It was about simultaneous.

Q: What you saw as you walked east on 86th street and the squeal of brakes were about simultaneous, is that what you're saying?

A: Right.

Q: Actually, the squeal attracted your attention first, then the seeing, right?

A: It was about simultaneous.

NOTE: *The last three questions may be posed as such, with you making an assumption, asking the witness if that is true or not. If your Adversary were to rise, asking the court to advise the jury that it is not the question, just the answer that is evidence, let him. Your purpose is to formulate these questions before the jury, causing the jury to think of the absurdity of what the witness is describing.*

Q: It was the squeal of tires that made you turn your attention very quickly to see what was happening on the corner, was it not?

A: I guess so.

Q: Whenever you turned to look to your left, at whatever you looked, you turned very quickly, did you not?

A: Yes.

Q: Is it your testimony that you looked very quickly to your left, though nothing had occurred, and the brakes and the squealing tires occurred only after you turned your head quickly, is that your testimony?

A: (hesitant) I guess.

Q: Don't guess, Mrs. Witness. Isn't exactly what happened that you heard the squeal of brakes first, then turned quickly?

A: Very quickly.

Q: However quickly it was only after the brakes squealed that you turned, not before, correct?

A: I guess so.

THE COURT: Please don't guess, Ma'am.

Q: Isn't that exactly right, you heard the squeal, then you turned?

A: I saw what happened, that's all I know.

CROSS-EXAMINER: Your Honor, I ask that the witness's answer be stricken and that the witness be directed to answer the question posed.

THE COURT: (somewhat unhappy). Yes, please just answer the question. Repeat the question, Mr. Cross-examiner.

CROSS-EXAMINER: May the reporter read the last question to the witness?

NOTE: *Since the question you have already asked has passed judicial muster, it is better to have the Reporter read the approved question than to rephrase another.*

The reporter reads the same question aloud to the witness.

Q: You may answer that, Ma'am.

A: Yes.

10.02 The Court May Not Always Help

While it is very pleasant to have a judge who may understand the rules of evidence, and may enforce them with equanimity, very often you will run into the situation where the court will not aid you in your quest, will not require the witness to answer the questions as posed, and will leave you to flounder in the inundation that the witness gives you. In such case, you must attempt, as was done in the foregoing example, to take a different tack, approach the facts from a different angle, control your questions as strictly as you can, and try to push the witness into the corner that you want. All you can do is try, adhering to the principles of control.

10.03 Be Resolute

In the ordinary instance, if proper, controlled questions are asked, the court will be hard pressed not to require the witness to answer properly. Be resolute, firm, and do not tire. You must insist on the witness answering the questions, and each time that he or she does not, you must move to have the answer stricken. You can not have a faint heart and be a litigator. That does not mean you have to be obstreperous, difficult, crude, rude, or anything of the sort. You need only verbalize your applications and objections for the record. Remember, the record need only be complete, it need not be accomplished in a cantankerous manner. Indeed, it is ordinarily better not to be cantankerous in front of the jury, or to disrespect the court or your Adversary, or the witness, in any fashion.

If the motion for the judge to require the witness to answer the posed questions must be made more than once, do so. If the judge fails to rule in your favor, you can not give up the ghost and abandon your position. Keep at it, and at it, and at it. That's what Cross-examination is about. You're controlling the situation, not anyone else; especially not the witness.

10.04 Ask for a Sidebar

If the judge permits the witness to wander all about, giving any answer that he or she wishes, and overrules each motion that you make to control the witness, ask for a sidebar to address the judge out of the hearing of the jury. If the Judge grants the sidebar, say, out of the hearing of the jury:

> CROSS-EXAMINER: Your Honor, I most respectfully object to Your Honor's interference with my Cross-examination, your curtailment of my Cross-examination, by permitting this witness to refuse to answer my questions, or to answer with gratuitous, nonresponsive remarks, and overruling each and every motion I make to conduct a proper Cross-examination.

> THE COURT: I'm not curtailing your Cross-examination, Counselor.

> CROSS-EXAMINER: Your Honor, the very fact that this witness refuses to answer questions, questions which, if Your Honor wishes to have the reporter read back, lend themselves quite easily to simple, direct replies, is a curtailment of my Cross-examination. I cannot compel proper answers. I can only form proper questions, which I believe I am doing. I ask the court to compel the witness to answer my questions. You have denied my applications and I abide by Your Honor's decision. However, I must make a record to object, on behalf of my client, to the curtailment of the Cross-examination.

> THE COURT: Your motion, Counselor, is denied.

Of course, the court may deny even your Application to have a sidebar in order to make the above remarks for the Record. No problem, by asking for a sidebar, and having the court refuse you such, you have already made a record for any future use. If you feel that the Record does not emphasize sufficiently the court's refusal to require proper answers to proper questions, and the debilitating effect the court is having on the course of the trial, you could underscore the court's actions, as follows:

CROSS-EXAMINER: Your Honor, may I have a sidebar?

THE COURT: You may not. Continue.

CROSS-EXAMINER: Your Honor, I would like to make an offer of proof for the record.

THE COURT: You may not.

CROSS-EXAMINER: Is Your Honor refusing to permit me to make or preserve the record?

THE COURT: I'm telling you to proceed or I shall have the witness step down from the witness chair.

You've already made a great Record. You needn't go further. Nor was any of this done with anger or bitterness. You may have been reluctant. But that doesn't appear on your face or the Record. Remember that it is not necessary to have every aspect of the trial go your way. What is necessary is your persistence in protecting your client's interests, and the trial record, respectfully, but vigorously. The court may be piqued, on occasion, by your persistence, but, hopefully, shall respect you for it. What's more, the court's future rulings may be much closer to the proper line, closer to the balanced middle, once you let the court know, often and early, that you know what you are doing, that you are a fighter, and that you intend to vigorously protect the Record and your client.

11.

Never Ask a Question Unless You Already Know the Answer

11.01 What Does This Mean? How Is It Possible?

All cross-examiners, neophytes as well as seasoned veterans, have heard the bromide quoted above—*never ask a question unless you already know the answer.* Having heard such admonition, each of you have probably wondered, as I did when I first heard that phrase, what does that mean? If the statement literally means what it seems to mean, how can you possibly know in advance answers to questions you haven't even asked? How can you possibly know the testimony of the Adverse Witness unless you first ask questions and receive answers?

The answer to your questions and the solution of your quandary—as most everything connected with Cross-examination—are resolved by strict discipline. As hammered home in preceding chapters, strictly-disciplined interrogation is the key to effective, aggressive Cross-examination. If your question is properly put, and is one in which you supply all the information the jury hears, permitting the witness only the very limited function of affirming or denying your posed question, you have, automatically, reduced the *possible* answers to two: an affirmation of your question—yes; or a denial of your question—no.

Think about that! Obviously, if you ask sloppy, random questions, permitting the witness to answer in any rambling fashion he or she chooses, how can you possibly know what the witness will answer? You can't! When Cross-examination is a sloppy, random thing, buffeting you in any direction the witness chooses, like a ship at sea during a storm without a rudder, there cannot possibly be direction or control to your Cross-examination; no true and right course. The witness is controlling you, taking you anywhere he or she wishes. On the other hand, if you employ strict discipline to manage the

117

witness, to limit the questions, going small, patient, interrogating steps, rather than asking humongous general questions, if you are attempting to contain the witness, leaving the witness only the choice of affirming or denying the information you pose in your question, you are obviously substantially closer to your goal of knowing what the answer to your question will be—even before you ask it.

11.02 Not the End of the Story

While reducing the potential answers to either yes or no is certainly some progress toward the goal of knowing what the answers to your questions are before you ask them, it is not the end of the line by any means. In fact, it is just the beginning. The next step in being able to know in advance the witness's answers to your questions is to formulate questions that can only be answered in a fashion you already know, based upon information already supplied by the Direct examination, by the pre-trial or on-trial discovery, that has been uncovered in some prior statement, inconsistent or otherwise.

11.03 Neutralizing Harmful Effect

Your aim in Cross-examination is to make progress toward neutralizing the harmful effect or credibility of the Adverse Witness in the eyes of the trier of the fact. This can be done in several ways: by underscoring the witness's lack of awareness; by undermining the accuracy of the witness's account of the event; by casting doubt on the credibility or moral character of the witness; by bringing to the jury's attention the fact that the witness has an interest in seeing the adverse party successful. With some witnesses, all this can be accomplished; with others, perhaps only one of them. Your aim is to inject as many of the neutralizing elements as you are able, to erode any confidence or reliability the jury may see in the witness. To do so, however, you must NOT shoot from the hip with questions that *you hope* might bring out some factor you wish the jury to hear, if only the witness would give the desired answer. The witness may be able to shoot from the hip right back.

True, an occasional hip shot may hit its mark. But that is a matter of luck. What you are desirous of developing is a method, a skill that shall permit you to be a successful, effective marksman on all occasions, not a potluck hip shooter who occasionally may do an effective job.

Therefore, in analyzing your approach to the witness, in preparing your Cross-examination script and your line of attack, review the information you have on hand, and, utilizing that, carefully develop the lines of questions which you intend to use. Do not dive into a pond you do not know, the bottom of which you do not see. If you know the witness has a background which has some antisocial history, use it; if there is a criminal record, use it; if the Direct testimony is illogical and inaccurate, attack it; and if the witness has given prior statements which are inconsistent with the trial testimony, spread them before the jury. All of this must be funneled to the witness through controlled questions. Even if you have a great deal of information with which to cross-examine the witness, you are not permitted to just throw it wholesale at the witness. Be patient. You'll get there. Get there properly.

By formulating questions based on information you are sure of, you naturally already know the answers to the questions you will pose, and your task is merely to orchestrate that information in such fashion as to bring out its most damaging-to-the-witness effect. Thus, when utilizing prior inconsistent statements, the witness should be led into the trap of repeating the Direct testimony, thereby emphasizing, further sinking the hook of the inconsistent predicate that you are going to attack. For example, if, by his trial testimony, the witness identifies your client as being involved in the incident at issue, but previously gave a statement to the police, a few minutes after the actual incident, in which statement he indicated he *could not* identify your client, then purposely lead the witness into the area of identification. When you have the witness confirm that he has no doubt that your client is, in fact, the person he saw at the incident, take out your inconsistent statement, and laying the proper foundation destroy the witness's credibility based upon the prior inconsistency made moments after the event occurred. (See Chapters 13 through 17.)

Even though you may not know with total certitude whether the witness will or will not, on trial, make an identification of your client in the above example, you can know with precision that the witness shall give one of the two following answers: either, that the witness can identify your client; or, that he can not. You must be prepared for either answer. If the witness answers in a fashion helpful to your cause that he can not make the identification: fine. If he says he can make the identification, you are prepared to destroy the witness's answer with the prior inconsistent statement you have in hand. Thus, by formulating your questions, the only possible answers to which are either perfectly acceptable to you, or ones for which you are totally prepared to destroy the witness's credibility, you have arrived at the cross-examiner's Valhalla—awareness of the answer (or the two possible answers) before you ask the question.

11.04 Be Prepared with Fact

In all situations where you cross-examine you should have information already on hand before you formulate your questions. Have a police report, medical history from the hospital, doctor's report, prior statement, testimony given at an E.B.T. or Grand Jury appearance, testimony from a prior trial, or merely the exactly recorded Direct testimony. Based solely on this known information, you should mount your attack. Indeed, it is ludicrous to mount an attack with unknowns, without information, groping like a blind person in the dark, into areas that are totally foreign to you. You may be destroyed by the very question that you *hope* brings victory.

Since your goal is not to exercise your vocal cords, but to get to the center of the circle and since there are 360 paths to that center, you should not haphazardly strike off on any path, regardless of whether or not you know the way along that path. Try only paths that you know and for which you have some information, instructions, or prior knowledge.

11.05 You Can Only Win a Battle Once

It is never necessary to beat a dead horse or a dead witness, and it is never necessary to show the jury how marvelously clever you are. Trick shots are not necessary. A straightforward demolition in front of the jury is satisfactory, and once done, is enough. Do not tempt the fates by trying to kill a witness twice; you may not be so successful the second time, and you may, in the bargain, resuscitate the drowned Adversary. Once you've made your point, leave well enough alone, and sit quietly, with the inner satisfaction that the jury is looking at the witness with a jaundiced eye.

Even if the ammunition you have on hand for Cross-examination is not sufficient for the total kill—which, I have already told you, is not very often available—or shall not permit you to damage the witness as dramatically as you might like before the jury, it is still the known quantity; you must use that known ammunition and it alone. The big kill that you thirst for and imagine may lie in the unknown, may or may not; you don't know. Worse, your destruction, not the witness's, may be lurking beneath that unknown surface. Satisfy your urge to attack the unknown with the adage: *that which lies beyond what is, is not.*

11.06 Your Manner of Inquiry Is Equally Important

Incidentally, there are ways of utilizing material which, when used to formulate a question correctly, dramatically, effectively, can be far more beneficial than if piddled away with some meandering, whimpering inquiry. You'll get more mileage from a correctly asked question based on known information than you will from some redundant, formulated on the spot, hesitant, beating around the bush question with the same information. Thus, utilizing information at hand, ask only questions to which you already know the answers. Additionally, you must ask those questions in a fashion which is going to bring out the most damaging, most harmful answers from the witness. More about this in subsequent chapters.

12.

Exceptions to the Strict Discipline Rule

12.01 Merely an Appearance of Permissiveness

There are exceptions to every rule, even the strict discipline rule of the Cross-examiner. Actually, this apparent exception is merely that: an apparition. The cross-examiner never abandons his or her strict discipline. However, for special purposes, the appearance of a lack of discipline may be required in order to permit witnesses a longer rope with which to ultimately hang themselves.

12.02 The Repetitive, Vengeful Witness

There is a certain type witness, often a victim or a person close to a victim of an accident or crime, who is so intent upon wreaking vengeance upon your client that his or her testimony is oozing with the venom of constant repetitions of the harmful facts of the case, hoping to inundate your client with culpability. This type of witness will repeat her testimony at almost every question, regardless of whether the answer is responsive to the question or not. In other words, the witness will attempt to bury you with her testimony at each and every opportunity, going out of her way to be harmful, and to repeat the sordid details of her testimony and add gratuitous remarks to practically every answer.

    One method of coping with such a situation is, as in jujitsu, to utilize the energy and strength of the witness for your own purpose. That is, you might purposely lead the garrulous witness into waters where she has constant opportunities to repeat the story over and over again before the jury. While the initial recitation before the jury may be harmful, multiple repetitions of the same fact pattern—if in the same words, even better—often leads the jury to suspect the evil purpose and intent of the witness. In short, the jury begins to think that the witness, like Hamlet's mother, "doth protest too much." In such case, the credibility of the witness may begin to suffer with each repetition and with the obvious, extraordinary effort that that witness exerts to ensure your client's demise.

Although this exception to strict discipline may be efficacious on rare occasion, the strict rule and the better practice is always to curtail and contain the witness and not permit a witness to repeat harmful testimony before the jury. Where, however, the witness is obviously and purposely attempting to damage your position, where the witness is attempting overkill, and such attempted overkill is detrimental to the Adverse Witness's credibility and standing before the jury, you may carefully permit that witness to "protest too much."

12.03 Example—The Garrulous Witness

Q: Mr. Witness, in conducting your own business, you had been guilty of acts which were criminal in nature, were you not?

A: True. I was guilty of many things. I acknowledged that by already pleading guilty to having committed several crimes. That's why I'm here testifying. But I was not the only one who participated in criminal activities. Other people did too. Your client was involved with me.

Assume that this is not the first answer that this witness has given which contains similar gratuitous remarks implicating your client. He has early manifested an intent to lard on the same "I am guilty" story, dragging your client in as a participant in such illegality. Since the witness has already sowed the harmful seed in the jury's mind, it may be that your best defense against such purposeful and repetitious testimony is to let that excess venom become very obvious to the jury, unmasking the witness's singular purpose to harm your client at every turn and every question. Often, such a witness not only lards on the harmful testimony, but doles it out in almost the exact same language. True, causing such witness to repeat his testimony obviously shall repeat the harmful recitation for the jury. However, when the testimony is almost verbatim, each time, you may actually be undoing the harm to your client. If the jury believed the witness the first time around, that was enough to harm your client. The second or third repetition does not cause the jury to hear anything more harmful to your client than they've already heard. But the repetition, whether verbatim or not, has a tendency to make the jury begin to question the intent of the witness, and this begins to erode the credibility and the veracity of the witness. Let the jury ask themselves whether this is truthful testimony or a programmed rendition of carefully rehearsed material.

12.04 Example—The Verbatim Repetition Witness

If the witness is a verbatim repeater, you might lead the witness to testify again about the incident as follows:

> Q: Now you said, Mr. Witness, that you saw my client come around the corner in his car while you were standing in front of Miller's store, and that you saw what occurred thereafter?
>
> A: I sure did.
>
> Q: And what was that?
>
> A: I saw this car come around the corner. I was standing near the door of the store.
>
> Q: And, of course, you could see Mr. Injured at this time?
>
> A: Sure. He was standing by his car. He was just about to get in, when I heard this car come squealing around the corner—it was burning rubber, you know—like the kids say—and then the car comes fast along the street, and it kind of fishtailed and slipped and slid, and pinned Mr. Injured between his car and the other car.
>
> Q: Before you came to court today, you discussed the case with Mr. Adversary, the lawyer for Mr. Injured, or someone from his office, did you not?
>
> A: What do you mean discussed the case with him?
>
> Q: You've talked about what happened at the time of the accident with Mr. Adversary or someone from his office, haven't you?
>
> A: Yes.

Q: And, in discussing the case, did there come a time you practiced giving your testimony, as if you were at trial, being cross-examined, by Mr. Adversary, or someone in his office, to get you prepared to testify here in court today?

A: No.

Q: Is it your testimony that you never went over your testimony with Mr. Adversary?

A: We discussed it.

Q: And did you discuss questions that might be asked, answers that you might give?

A: A little.

Q: How many times is a little?

A: Two or three times.

Q: Three or four times, perhaps?

A: Perhaps.

Q: And, when you went over the questions that might be asked, the answers that you might give, you sometimes went over them a couple of times, so you would be sure you didn't make mistakes.

A: Not really.

Q: You were going over it so Mr. Adversary would know that you remembered what you were going to say, weren't you?

A: I don't know why he wanted me to go over it.

Q: But there's no question about the fact that you went over it maybe three or four times before you came in here today?

A: No, no question.

Q: Now, this noise that you've described the other car making when it came around the corner, can you be certain that's what you heard?

A: Sure. It came around the corner squealing—burning rubber, like the kids say, and then the car came fast along the street and it fishtailed, and slipped and slid, and pinned Mr. Injured between his car and the other car.

> Q: And, of course, you were able to tell whose car that other car was, weren't you?

> A: Sure, I had seen it often enough; it belonged to the Watson kid.

> Q: There's no question in your mind about that noise now? Perhaps it was the rattling of a broken part on the car? This wasn't a new car, this other car, was it?

> A: No sir. But there wasn't any rattling. It was squealing—burning rubber, as the kids say.

> Q: Perhaps this slipping and sliding noise, when the car came around the corner was from a different car?

> A: It wasn't a slipping, sliding sound, and it sure didn't come from a different car.

> Q: I'm sorry. You describe it then, for the jury.

> A: The car came around the corner squealing, burning rubber like the kids say.

Now if you heard that, if the ordinary juror hears that, you begin to discount it, despite the fact that you're hearing it repeated, or, for the very reason that you heard it repeated. The jury may very well tend to discount the testimony, or some of it, of a witness who is merely reciting by rote. Again, the repetition of the same story is not going to be any more harmful the fourth time it's repeated than it was the first time, and if doubts are caused in the minds of the jurors who think that, perhaps, this has all been rehearsed and planned to harm your client, it shall have exactly the opposite effect— even though the witness does not change a word of his testimony.

12.05 Example—The Negative or Bust Witness

Sometimes, and not as rarely as you might think, witnesses on the stand are so nervous or frightened that their emotional state causes them to react rather than think, to testify automatically, by reaction, not by rehearsal, as did the witness in the previous paragraphs. At such time, a strange phenomenon can take place: the witness, testifying against the position of the cross-examiner, unable to think clearly, will give answers that are opposite the answer that the *inflection* of the cross-examiner's voice appears to be expecting. For instance:

Q: You didn't actually see Mr. Defendant on the fire escape coming out of the burglarized apartment, though, did you?

A: Yes, I did.

Q: Did you get a chance to see his face?

A: Sure.

These questions are helping to bury you. You shouldn't cause them to be repeated unless they fit into the purposeful pattern that you are weaving for the jury. However, you may find that, at the same time, the nervous—perhaps frustrated by your persistence—witness shall begin merely to react negatively to any question that you, the enemy, ask. If that be the case, use the witness to your own advantage by asking questions which sound as if they seek answers exactly opposite from the answers you actually desire. For instance:

Q: When you first saw this man, he wasn't actually inside the apartment, was he?

A: Yes, he was.

Q: You didn't see him through the curtains, though, did you?

A: Sure I did.

Q: You're testifying that that's when you first saw him?

A: That's right.

Q: You've already testified that you saw this man for about two seconds. Now, when you were in the street, watching this someone inside the apartment, you weren't nervous, were you?

A: Yes, I was, a little.

Q: And when the person inside started to come toward the window, to come out, you stood right there in the open waiting for him, didn't you?

A: No.

Q: You didn't turn, to find a place to hide, did you?

A: Yes, I hid so I could look at him.

Q: You didn't have to look for a place to hide, did you?

A: Yes, I did.

Q: Where did you look?

A: Under the stoop, there's a place where they keep the garbage cans.

Q: You went to that place to hide?

A: Right.

Q: How far is it from the window you were looking into?

A: From here to where you're standing.

CROSS-EXAMINER: Would the court accept four feet as the distance between the witness and myself, for the record?

THE COURT: That seems about right.

Q: And this place where the garbage cans were—a man coming from the apartment could see you right away when he came out, right?

A: No, he couldn't.

Q: You don't mean that the place where you hid was hidden from the man when he came out?

A: Yes, it was.

Q: It wasn't behind the stoop going into the building, was it?

A: Yes, that's where I went.

Q: You didn't have to move to get to that spot, did you?

A: Yes, I did.

Q: You ran to get there, right?

A: I walked there.

Q: You walked sideways or backwards, right?

A: No, I didn't.

Q: How did you walk?

A: I turned quick, moved there, then I looked.

Q: This man that came out, did he come out and walk toward the stoop or away from it?

A: Away from it, toward First Avenue.

Q: That would be away from the stoop?

A: Right.

Q: So the man came out of the window, facing the stoop, and then moved down the block backwards, facing you?

A: He didn't walk backwards.

Q: He was walking normally, regular?

A: Sure.

Q: That wasn't away from you, was it?

A: Yes, away from me.

Q: His back was toward you.

A: Yes, his back was toward me.

Q: You couldn't see his face then, when he was walking away from you, could you?

A: Yes, I could.

Q: You didn't also see the man's face when he was inside the dark apartment, behind the curtains, did you?

A: A little.

Q: You couldn't see him though, when you turned to find your hiding place behind the stoop, could you?

A: I saw him, I saw him.

Q: And you also saw him when he came out of the window and turned toward First Avenue, didn't you?

A: That's right.

In your Cross-examination, you have set up such a set of improbabilities, taking advantage of the witness's almost automatic negative reaction to your questions, that even the probable becomes doubtful—that the witness might have seen the face of the burglar as he came out of the apartment. Thus, you have used the negative energy of the witness, intent upon destroying you and your client, to your own positive advantage. Remember, as was said earlier, the positive effect of Cross-examination is not registered by fireworks, lights flashing on and off, a bell ringing, or applause starting from the empty courtroom benches. The big kill is a rarity. It is also not where you totally humble the witness, causing him or her to crawl off the stand and slither along the floor, out of the courtroom. Cross-examination is effective, all that you could really want, if it causes the jurors to think to themselves *that witness isn't sure of what he saw* or if, for whatever reason, it causes the jurors to think that the witness is not reliable—not a liar—just not reliable or accurate or sure. Then you've won.

13.

Direct Examination

13.01 What Does Direct Examination Have to Do with It?

It might appear odd to find a chapter dealing with Direct Examination in a book aimed at unraveling the mysteries of Cross-Examination. However, since there is never Cross-Examination without there first having been Direct Examination of a witness—except, perhaps, at Depositions—and since the *Direct* frames the tone of the *Cross,* delineating the boundaries of your battleground, it is important that the subject and manner of Direct Examination be explored so that the Cross-examiner may then better understand the basic components of that which he intends to attack and, hopefully, decimate.

13.02 Redirect and Recross

Inasmuch as redirect and recross-examination are basically the same as their primary counterparts, except that their scope is circumscribed more narrowly—limited specifically to new areas or information uncovered by your Adversary's immediately prior examination of the witness—assume that the methods of Direct and Cross-Examination apply equally to redirect and re-Cross-examination, except for the limitation mentioned briefly above.

13.03 How to Prepare the Witness for Direct Examination

As there are exceptions to just about every rule, I cannot say that you should never call a witness to the stand for Direct testimony unless you have prepared that witness not only for your Direct, but also for the Cross-Examination that you can logically anticipate. The exceptions to the rule are rare, and, in the main, you should assiduously avoid putting an unprepared witness on the stand. Actually, it is more important to prepare your witness for the

Cross-Examination that will follow the Direct than it is to prepare the Direct testimony itself. For, a wily Cross-examiner, imbued with all the enthusiasm and confidence this book has buttressed, can weave a web around an unsuspecting Direct witness, making that witness appear foolish, mistaken, or unsure in front of the jury. Even unsureness is enough to unhorse your cause.

13.04 The Beginnings of Witness Preparation

At the outset of preparation, discuss the case with your prospective witness to find out what, in general, the witness can offer for the jury's consideration. This discussion may be quite informal and general. As you discuss the facts to which the witness will testify, probe the witness with questions to glean all the facts within the witness's knowledge. Keep in mind that most witnesses are not aware of the legal technicalities which must be proved with their testimony. As a result, their version of the incident may be quite lacking in the details that you know are necessary to your proofs and are required to make out a case. Therefore, probe in areas that are legally, technically significant, and most likely, you shall discover that the witness knows other facts which he or she was not aware were important. After getting your initiation into the facts of the case according to your witness, explain the proceedings which will occur in court, so that the witness is familiar with what will happen, that he or she shall take the stand, that the clerk or judge shall swear him or her to tell the truth, that he or she shall sit and be questioned, and the procedure will not, therefore, surprise and throw him or her off balance when taking the witness chair. This is most important.

13.05 Different Methods of Testifying

The first thing to explain to the witness concerning the proceedings which shall occur when the witness gives Direct testimony is that he or she must basically give a narrative of the incident and must not wait for you to probe into areas of your interest with leading questions. The witness ought to be well-advised that he or she must be prepared to give the entirety of his or her testimony, without very many questions emanating from the Direct examiner. Explain that otherwise, your Adversary will object and the judge will likely sustain the objection, as you are not permitted to prompt or lead the witness. With the necessity of a narrative in mind, go over the Direct testimony again, making sure that the witness is able to testify, giving all the salient and necessary information, without requiring you to prod and prompt more than a judge shall permit. You will be permitted, of course, to ask the witness questions and even interrupt the witness to ask for more details in certain areas. Even then, however, you shall not be permitted to use leading questions. Therefore, in the main, it is far better for your witness to be prepared to recite all the salient facts without prompting or leading.

An example of an acceptable presentation the facts that may be brought out on your witness's Direct testimony is as follows:

Q: Mr. Witness, on the 14th of June, 1980, where did you work?

A: Same place I work now, Miller's Nursery and Garden Shop.

Q: And on that date, do you remember seeing my client, Mr. Injured?

A: Yes. He came into the store to buy some flowers.

Q: And did you sell him the flowers?

A: Sure did.

Although this initial inquiry might technically be improperly leading, the court ordinarily permits such leading in preliminary areas which merely set the stage for the pertinent Direct testimony. To continue:

Q: And can you tell the court and jury *what else, if anything,* occurred thereafter? (The italicized language is the important wording.)

A: Mr. Injured left the store. I was talking with him and I walked to the front door; I wanted to sweep the front of the store. I walked him to the door. We talked a couple of minutes. Then we waved goodbye. He went to the curb to his car and was getting into the car. Another car came around the corner. I was still standing in the doorway, just looking toward the street. This other car, as I said, came around the corner . . .

Q: Let me interrupt to ask you this, what kind of car was it that came around the corner, if you recall, Mr. Witness?

A: It was a blue Chevrolet.

Q: Had you ever seen that car before?

A: Sure, plenty of times. It belonged to the Watson kid, Henry Watson's son. I saw him in that car plenty of times.

Q: Is there any question in your mind as to the owner of the car that came around that corner at that time?

A: Of course not. I recognized the car the minute it came around the corner.

In your Direct, as above, you should stop the Direct narrative occasionally to highlight the essentials for the jury. We shall continue:

Q: Very well, please continue.

A: So the car comes around the corner and it was making that noise when the tires are, you know, when they're peeling rubber, as the kids say.

Q: What do you mean that the tires were squealing and making noise?

A: The car was going so fast, the wheels couldn't catch, and were spinning, and that made a squealing noise.

Q: Go ahead, please continue.

A: So then the car kind of goes sliding and slipping, like it was out of control, and it sideswipes Mr. Injured's car, pinning him between the two cars.

Q: What, if anything, happened then?

A: The other car kept going about 50 yards and then stopped. The driver got out.

Q: Did you see who got out of that other car?

A: Sure. The Watson kid.

Q: Do you happen to know the name of the Watson kid?

A: Dennis. Dennis Watson.

In the above Direct examination, there are no leading questions. The only interruptions of the witness were to develop more details from his already-given testimony before going further. This Direct might appear to the judge and jury to be smooth, factual, and complete. However, before the direct examiner prepared the witness, half the details were missing: details like the noise the car made as it sped around the comer and proceeded along the street; details like the witness being able to recognize the car because he had seen it many times before. The first time through the story in your office, the witness did not describe the incident as it appears above. However, several repetitions of the story, with the attorney's asking for facts to fill out the necessary elements required by the law, emphasizing certain facts, the testimony comes out smoothly, filled with the facts necessary to permit the jury to understand the incident.

> NOTE: *The preparation above referred to, which is necessary in order to have the witness recall all the details of an incident, does not, in any way, infer that the witness's preparation includes fabrication of facts which are not true or correct. It is intended to mean that the witness, a layman, ignorant of the law and the details necessary in the trial of the case, may not recognize the significance of particular event, and may not, therefore, recite certain of the facts which the attorney might find essential. The job of the trial attorney is to go over the recitation of the witness carefully, asking questions in areas which will uncover actual details which the witness did not think were important.*

13.06 Preparing the Witness for Cross-Examination

Bringing out the Direct examination is probably the smoothest and easiest part of preparing your witness to give his or her testimony on behalf of your client. The more difficult part is to prepare the same witness to be Cross-examined by your Adversary. Essentially, the method of preparing the witness to be Cross-examined is to subject that witness to as difficult and even impermissible a Cross-examination you can muster, in order to give that witness experience in being asked difficult, rapidly fired questions, and being hammered by an unfriendly examiner. When I suggest that you cross-examine the witness using impermissible questions, I mean that the witness should be bombarded with questions about every aspect of his testimony, even questions in areas which you believe your Adversary should not be permitted to venture. You can never tell what a judge might permit, and your witness should be prepared for everything and not be stuck without an answer to a question because you miscalculated.

13.07 The Most Basic Defense to Cross-Examination: The Witness Must Answer ONLY the Question Asked

The first thing that the witness being prepared for Cross-examination must know is that he or she is to answer only the questions the Cross-examiner asks, and not volunteer information not sought by the examiner. A method of bringing this point home to your witness is to instruct them as follows:

> COUNSEL: Now, when you are being asked questions by me on Direct examination, give the full recitation we have been discussing. But, on Cross-examination, your answers are different. You answer only the questions asked and nothing else. Do not volunteer information that was not asked for.
>
> WITNESS: I understand.
>
> COUNSEL: Fine. Is it raining out today?
>
> WITNESS: No, sunny.
>
> COUNSEL: Nobody asked about the sun. If the Cross-examiner were to ask you if it is raining out, you do not answer, "No, it's a nice, sunny day!" You were asked only about rain. The correct answer to the question "Is it raining out?" is "No."

In other words, your witness must be prepared to answer questions, and should be advised to answer questions, with as few words as possible, preferably yes or no. Explain to the witness that Cross-examination is not social conversation. It is a specific verbal intercourse with a purpose. The cross-examiner's purpose is different from your purpose. You want your witness, who you have prepared for Direct, to make the Cross-examiner work and think of the questions on his own with no information or help supplied by your witness with ammunition provided by way of volunteered information.

13.08 The Witness Can Expand His or Her Answers In Certain Areas

There are some areas where your witness may be permitted somewhat more expansive answers under Cross-examination. Those areas, however, are the areas of the case which inundate your Adversary with information *he does not want.* For instance, you can advise the witness that he or she should answer only yes or no to everything asked, *except* if the Cross-examiner wants to know about the last moments before the incident. See the following example.

Q: Now, the afternoon of Saturday, June 14th, was a rather hot day, wasn't it?

A: No.

Q: You're saying that, on the 14th, the weather was not good?

A: No.

Q: Then it was a nice day, the weather was good that day, correct?

A: Yes.

Q: I see. You're saying that it was pleasant, sunny, but not hot, is that it?

A: That's right, Counselor.

NOTE: *Your witness is making the Adversary work for every shred of information. That's exactly what should be happening. You Cross-examiners, reading this chapter only as material for your interest in Cross-examination, should note how the witness is giving you the runaround. What do you do to offset such tactics? Think about it.*

The examination of the witness continues:

Q: And, on this nice, sunny, but not hot day, you were standing on the sidewalk in front of Miller's store?

A: No.

Q: Did you just testify you were in front of Miller's store?

A: No.

CROSS-EXAMINER: Your Honor, may we have the stenographer read back the witness's Direct testimony?

THE COURT: That's not necessary. Just frame your next question. That'll be easier.

Q: Did you testify a few minutes ago, that when you first saw Mr. In-
     jured, you were in the store?

A: Yes.

Q: And then you both walked to the sidewalk in front of the store?

A: Not exactly.

Q: Well, what did you say?

A: I said I was still at the door, watching him get in his car.

*NOTE: Your well-prepared witness has just caused the Cross-examiner
to break from his control, to drop his guard, and ask the witness for
help. ("What did you say?") The Cross-examiner is getting exasperated
by your witness; just what you hoped for with all the preparation.*

Q: And then you say you saw a car come around the corner.

A: It came screaming around the corner, tires squealing. . .

Q: Just answer the question.

*NOTE: Just as you prepared him, your witness has inundated the
Cross-examiner, larding on the harmful part of the testimony. You can
tell from the Cross-examiner's reaction that he is well aware of being
inundated with harmful material. You Cross-examiners think about
being faced with such a well-prepared witness and how you would
cope with him.*

Q: You were standing in front of the store when the defendant's car
     came around the corner.

A: Came squealing around the corner. He was really going.

Q: All right, you wanted to get that in again, now you did it. Are you
     satisfied?

A: I'm just telling the truth.

CROSS-EXAMINER: Your Honor, would you instruct the witness just to
answer questions asked and not volunteer information?

THE COURT: Very well, Mr. Cross-examiner, but you asked for that answer. Mr. Witness, please only answer questions asked and don't volunteer information.

THE WITNESS: Yes, Your Honor.

Q: And then you saw the car of the defendant come into contact with the car of the plaintiff?

A: Well, first I saw the defendant lose control of his car. It fishtailed and skidded. . .

CROSS-EXAMINER: Your Honor, I move that the answer be stricken as nonresponsive and the witness instructed to only answer questions asked.

THE COURT: No, I'll let that answer stand. Proceed to your next question.

NOTE: The Cross-examiner is getting a hard time in the above example. That happens. The reason for the hard time is the same reason that you subjected your own witness, when you were preparing him or her for Direct, to a scathing preCross-examination. If your witness is familiarized with the hard times that may come, if you instruct him or her how to counteract the hard times, he or she will be prepared for everything and find the actual battle a lot easier than the grueling training through which you put him or her.

13.09 Using the Reticent Witness

Just as monosyllabic answers can unstring the bow of the inexperienced Cross-examiner, they can also be a tremendous help for the crafty Cross-examiner. Single word answers can be pursued to advantage by the Cross-examiner who knows what he or she is doing. For example, you are about to embark on Cross-examination in a homicide case. The detective has testified on Direct examination about an oral confession (admission) that the defendant allegedly made, totally admitting the commission of the crime, describing the details of how he shot a policeman. See the Direct examination that follows.

Q: Now, detective, will you tell this court and jury, what, if anything, you said to the defendant at that point and what, if anything, he said to you?

A: Yes, sir. I said to the defendant, "Now, calm down. Sit down, sit down. Calm down. Relax. You want to tell me what happened today? You want to tell me the truth?" And he said, 'Yes.'"

Q: All right. You said, "You want to tell me the truth?" Please proceed.

A: And he said that he opened the window but he couldn't get into the apartment because the gate which was on the inside of the window was locked. Then he said he came back up the fire escape. And that he and his partner started to lift the TV set over the roof when he heard a noise on the fire escape. And he walked over to the edge of the roof, and he looked down the fire escape. And he saw a police officer coming up the fire escape. And he said to his partner, "La jara, la jara." I asked him what that meant. He said, "The cops, the cops." Then I said, "Then what happened?" He said he hid and crouched down behind the stairway wall, and he saw the cop go by him, and he had his gun in his hand, and he was pointing it at his partner. And he said that he was afraid, he saw the gun. At that point, the defendant put his hands over his face, and he said, "Mi Dios, Mi Dios! I did it! I did it!" And I said, "What did you do?" He said, "I shot the officer. I shot him in the back."

Such Direct testimony is formidable, to say the least. Think about it. The detective is not describing a physical scene. He's describing what he *heard*. It's pretty hard to dispute what a person—particularly a trained detective—said he *heard*, not what he physically observed; what he says he heard. How do you dispute that? Read on!

At the end of the Direct, the prosecutor hands you a notebook; it contains the detective's notes allegedly written immediately after the confession was made. Nothing else appears in the notebook except a repetition, almost verbatim, of what the detective has just testified to on direct. There is no other written material, notes, or reports concerning the confession. Think about how you, being the Cross-examiner about to stand on your feet, would handle the situation. To wit, a police detective of many years experience and reputation is testifying; the jury will tend to believe him. The only prior statement or written notes by the witness repeats, almost verbatim, his

Direct testimony; he is a truly professional witness who gives you no information whatsoever, except to answer your question, leaving you groping. How would you handle the examination?

Let's get into the Cross-examination:

> Q: Now, detective, you said that the defendant said he was lifting the goods over the roof, and he went to the edge to look over the fire escape, is that correct?
>
> A: He said he went to the edge of the roof and looked over the fire escape; yes, sir.
>
> Q: Now, do you know where the fire escape is on the building at 750 East 200th Street?
>
> A: Yes, sir.
>
> Q: It is at the rearmost portion of the building, isn't it?
>
> A: Yes, sir.
>
> Q: Did he say he told his partner—
>
> A: This is what he said, counsel: I told my partner, "La jara, la jara."
>
> Q: Did he say, "I yelled to him?"
>
> A: I just told you what he said, counselor.
>
> Q: He told him?
>
> A: Yes, sir.
>
> Q: And then, you say, the defendant took this position which you already demonstrated for us, and you assumed for us, is that correct? He took this position behind the wall?
>
> A: Yes. That is what he told me. He said he crouched down behind the wall. As a matter of course, counsel, the position I assumed was what he showed me later, you know, he demonstrated for me later—but at this time, he merely told me he crouched down.
>
> Q: Okay. Now, you say the defendant said he crouched down behind the wall of the stairway, is that correct?
>
> A: He had crouched down behind the stairway wall; yes, sir.

To this point, the detective is foiling every thrust of the Cross-examiner with his answers. At this point, the very purpose of this chapter is brought home fully. You must know how a witness has been prepared to testify, what you should anticipate, and be able, while still on your feet Cross-examining, to formulate a countermove. The countermove in the above situation is to take advantage of the terse answers, the pat story of the confession, and turn it to your advantage. The detective has testified about a fictional situation which has occurred in a police station. He has hammered his story down your throat. But the lifesaver is that the detective can't change his story—he's been too insistent in testifying to it. Nor can he add to it. He can't get away from it. He even has it written into the notebook which the prosecutor has handed to you. Notice how this now will become an advantage to you as you Cross-examine. Start out from the position that the detective's testimony did not provide all the details you might have sought had you been investigating.

Q: Now, detective, the defendant, when he told you about crouching behind the wall, did he say he crouched behind the wall of the bulkhead that covered the stairway?

A: No, sir. He said stairway wall.

Q: Would that mean inside the stairway?

MR. ADVERSARY: Your Honor, I object. He is asking the detective to interpret the language of this defendant and I object to it.

THE COURT: Objection sustained because of the form of the question.

Q: Did the defendant say he was outside?

A: You mean did he use those words, "I was outside?"

Q: In sum or substance?

A: No, he didn't, counsel.

Q: Did he say he was inside?

A: No, he didn't, counsel.

Q: Did you ask him where he was?

A: He told me where he was.

Q: Well, did he say he was outside or inside?

MR. ADVERSARY: Your Honor, I object to this. That has been answered.

THE COURT: Objection sustained.

Q: Now, you say that the defendant described how he grabbed this policeman, when the policeman went past him?

A: As he passed him, yes, sir.

Q: Well, did he say how far from where he was standing the policeman passed?

A: No.

Q: Did you ask him, "Well, did you have to take a step to grab the cop?"

A: No, counsel, I didn't.

Q: Did you ask him, "Did you have to run five steps and grab the cop?"

A: No.

Q: Did he say he just reached out and the cop was right there?

A: No, he didn't say that.

Q: Did you ask him, "Did you have to open the door of the roof to go out and grab the cop?"

A: No, sir.

Q: Did you ask him, "Were you hiding behind the door when you grabbed the cop?"

A: No, sir.

Q: Now, you say that the defendant told you that he jumped on the cop from behind?

A: Yes, sir.

Q: Now, did he tell you how far he had to jump?

A: No, sir, he didn't.

Q: Did the defendant tell you from what he jumped?

A: From what he jumped?

Q: From what? Did he tell you he was standing on the step when he jumped?

A: No, sir.

Q: Did you ask him where he was standing?

A: Did I ask him? No, sir.

Q: Did he tell you he was standing on the parapet wall when he jumped?

A: No, sir.

Q: Did he tell you he was standing on the bulkhead wall when he jumped?

A: He just said, "I jumped out."

Q: And you didn't then, and don't now know from where he jumped?

A: From behind the stairway wall.

Q: Which stairway wall did he say he was behind at the moment before he jumped?

A: He didn't say.

Q: And you didn't ask him to explain any of those details?

A: No, sir, I didn't.

Q: Detective, when you were asking this defendant these questions, it was with a mind toward someday perhaps having to appear in court to testify about what the defendant was telling you, wasn't it?

A: In part.

Q: And you wanted facts and particulars, didn't you, so you would have them accurately so you could, if necessary, testify accurately?

A: Yes, sir.

Q: All right, tell the jury which stairway wall that the defendant said he was behind, the inside or outside wall?

A: Your asking me if I know—

MR. ADVERSARY: I object to this.

THE COURT: If he knows, I will allow it. Overruled. Do you know, sir?

THE WITNESS: Not the one—will you repeat the question, sir? I am sorry.

MR. CROSS-EXAMINER: I will withdraw the question, Your Honor.

Q: When the defendant said he jumped onto the policeman, did he say the spot from which he jumped?

A: No, sir.

Q: Well, now, was it a jump where he was actually in the air or was it just a reaching out, a lunging?

A: I don't know, counsel.

Q: You didn't ask him that?

A: No, sir, I didn't.

Q: By the way, detective, you did say, did you not, that the defendant was calm and cooperative when you were questioning him?

A: I didn't question him. Just occasionally I said, "Go on" or "Continue."

Q: He was then, calm and cooperative?

A: Yes, sir.

Q: You didn't have to bully or pull this *story* out of him piecemeal, with hammer and tong?

A: No, sir.

Q: Did the defendant tell you whether or not he fell down with the policeman after he grabbed him?

A: No, sir.

Q: Did you ask him whether he fell down with the policeman after he grabbed him?

A: No, sir.

Q: Did you ask him if he and the policeman were still standing or were on the floor?

A: I didn't, no, sir.

Q: Did you ask him if he had a wrestling match for the gun?

A: No, I didn't ask him that.

Q: At any rate, the defendant said to you, you say, that he grabbed for the gun with his right hand. Is that correct?

A: Yes, sir.

Q: And then he got the gun, finally?

A: Yes, sir.

Q: Do you know whether he had to fight the policeman for it?

A: Do I know this, counselor? Do I know this of my own knowledge?

Q: Did the defendant tell you that he had to fight for the gun?

A: He said he struggled for the gun.

Q: Did you ask him that?

A: I didn't ask him that. No, sir.

Q: And you say he said he stepped back at that point, is that correct?

A: As the officer got up on his hands and knees.

Q: The defendant stepped back?

A: Yes, sir.

Q: Did he say how far he stepped back?

A: He just said he stepped back.

Q: Well, do you know where he was when he started to step back?

A: No, sir.

Q: Did you ask him that?

A: No, sir, I didn't.

Q: Did you ask him at what point he finally stopped—how far from the cop he was when he stopped?

A: I don't understand you, counselor.

Q: Well, you say he started to step back. I assume he stopped stepping back at one point.

A: He told me he stepped back.

Q: Well, did you ask him, "How many steps did you take, so you could supply that information to this jury?

A: No, sir, I didn't.

Q: Did you ask him, "How far away were you from the policeman when you shot?"

A: No, sir.

Q: Did you ask him, "At what point was the gun held?"

A: No.

Q: Did you ask him, "Were you holding it down low as you got up?"

A: No.

Q: Well, did you ask him if he held it up high?

A: No.

Q: You didn't know where the gun was held?

A: I don't know how he held the gun.

Q: And you didn't ask him for that information?

A: No, I didn't ask him that, no, sir.

Q: Did you ask him with what hand he fired the gun?

A: No, sir.

Q: At any rate, you say he said—the defendant said—that when he stepped back, he fired, is that correct?

A: Yes.

Q: Did he tell you that he shot all the bullets at the same time in a fusillade?

A: No, sir.

Q: And you didn't ask him how he shot the bullets?

A: I didn't ask him that, no, sir.

Q: Did he tell you, "I shot all the bullets from the same position?"

A: No, sir.

Q: Did you ask him if he shot all the bullets from the same position?

A: No, sir.

Q: He didn't tell you how he shot the gun?

A: You mean how—what position?

Q: What position it was in?

A: No, sir.

Q: The defendant never told you whether he was moving or standing still when he shot the gun?

A: No, sir.

Q: And you didn't ask him that either?

A: That is right.

This excerpt could go on far longer, but you get the idea. You can put the rest of the Cross-examination together yourself, reducing what appeared originally as rock-foundation police testimony to a far more vague, sketchy, incomplete recitation. Thus, you may very well use this technique to shake the credibility of a cocksure witness who attempts to stick as much harmful material as possible in front of the jury. Start picking apart those things beyond which the witness cannot tread. This is most often the case where there are reports, such as hospital reports, doctors reports, and police reports, and instances where the witness is bounded by the containments of records made months, even years, before. For further use of such documents, see Chapter 17, Use of Prior Inconsistent Statements to Third Persons, Not Reduced to Writing.

Inasmuch as this book is dedicated to the Cross-examiner, and is not a general trial book, further discussion of the methods of Direct testimony and the preparation of the witness therefor, shall be curtailed for that other book.

14.

Recalling the Direct Examination Exactly

14.01 You Can't Attack What You Can't Remember

At this point, it would be helpful for the prospective cross-examiner to know how to systematically record, completely and exactly, the Adverse Witness's Direct testimony in order, thereafter, to prepare a script for Cross-examination, and, in general, to prepare to attack the Adverse Witness and the Adversary's case.

14.02 Making Notes Is Essential

In order to cross-examine, you must be able to recall the Direct testimony exactly, verbatim. This does not mean you have to be a stenographer or have an eidetic memory to cross-examine; nor does it mean you have to hide a tape recorder on your person either. It does mean, however, that you must train yourself to capture the testifying witness's exact words, in writing, so that you will be able to refer back to that testimony for Cross-examination purposes, at any time, later in the trial, and again at Summation. Such training is not really as hard as it sounds on first reading. You do not have to record every word the witness utters. What you must do is capture every *answer* the witness utters and record it in your *notes*. The two italicized words in the preceding sentence are the essence of being able to recall the Direct examination exactly. You must record every answer fully. General impressions of the Direct, succinct abbreviations and random phrases *won't do*. Every answer must be noted in *writing*.

Even if you could remember each and every answer of the particular witness on the stand for the purpose of Cross-examination, you must be able to retain the answers of each witness to be able to cross-reference and cross-check the testimony of other, subsequent witnesses, and you must be able to put the whole case together for summation. You cannot, and should not even try to, remember the verbatim testimony of each witness in the trial from memory. Indeed, you should not waste your mental strength carrying around thousands of questions and answers, when it would be, and is, so much easier and more accurate to make notes at the very moment the witness is testifying. Use Albert Einstein's method: Never remember anything that you can look up. Einstein saved his mental gymnastics for thinking in new areas which really required his mental energies. So too, when you are at trial, save your mental energies for devising a formidable defense, not for recalling testimony that a previous witness gave two days or two weeks ago.

14.03 Even a Stenographic Record Is No Substitute

Even if you have available a daily transcript of the proceedings, you will find, if you follow the method of recording the Direct examination which appears in this chapter, that the transcript, barren of your notes, comments, and emphasis marks, requires perusal, takes up your time unnecessarily, and, while helpful for many purposes, is not actually a complete and total substitute for recording the Direct testimony yourself, in your own hand, in your own way, for your own later purposes.

14.04 The System

When an Adverse Witness takes the stand, prepare a page to record the testimony. Ordinarily, on a normal sheet of legal yellow pad I put a second margin one third of the page in from the right-hand edge. Thus, I have a piece of paper with two margins: one on the left side (printed), of about an inch, and the other, my own creation, on the right side, of about two inches. The left-hand, smaller margin is for marking and recording exhibits, evidence offered and introduced into the trial, and to record the time of day. It is also for reference notations to other materials, such as page references to Grand Jury minutes or Depositions, references to hospital or police reports, pages of the minutes of a transcript, or anything that will serve you, when on your feet cross-examining, in attacking, the Direct examination.

The right margin is for notes to yourself, comments, areas to question, to remind yourself to research certain points, to take a certain tack in your Cross-examination, to alert yourself to something significant when you are making up your Cross-examination script, or, if time does not permit preparation of such a script, to be used while you are on your feet cross-examining.

The center portion of the page you have prepared is to record the witness's answers. Notice, I specifically and purposefully did not say your Adversary's questions. However well articulated and delivered, your Adversary's question is not evidence and is not really significant. Only the answers of the witness are evidence, and that's all you have an interest in recording. Suppose, for instance, that your Adversary asks his witness, on Direct examination, whether she was standing on the corner of 86th Street and Park Avenue when the accident occurred. If you were writing down the question, you would have the following in your notes.

"Did you stand on 86th Street and Park Avenue at the time of the accident?"

The witness answers, "No."

Now what good is having your Adversary's question and the negative answer thereto in your notes? No good, that's what. Record only the witness's actual answers, not questions.

14.05 Recording the Testimony: Other Purposes

During a trial where daily copy of the proceedings are not available to either counsel or the court, your notes will be a wealth of specific, written information that will also serve you in excellent fashion, if necessary, to argue a point of law before the court or to cross-reference another witness's testimony. With such written notes, you will be able to take a position before the court, and demand that the stenographer read back from the actual trial minutes certain portions of the testimony, with the comforting assurance that when the notes are read back, exactly what you represented to the court shall appear there, and not some fairly similar, but also fairly dissimilar, inaccurate recollection of what you thought the witness had said.

14.06 How to Record the Testimony

In Chapter 13, there is an excerpt of Direct examination of a police detective in a homicide case. For present purposes, a portion of that testimony is reprinted here:

> Q: Now, Detective, will you tell this court and jury what, if anything, you said to the defendant at that point and what, if anything, he said to you?
>
> A: Yes, sir. I said to the defendant, "Now, calm down. Sit down, sit down. Calm down. Relax. You want to tell me what happened today? You want to tell me the truth?" And he said, "Yes."
>
> Q: All right, you said, "You want to tell me the truth?" Please proceed.
>
> A: And he said that he opened the window but he couldn't get into the apartment because the gate which was on the inside of the window was locked. Then he said he came back up the fire escape. And that he and his partner started to lift the TV set over the roof when he heard a noise on the fire escape. And he walked over to the edge of the roof, and he looked down the fire escape. And he saw a police officer coming up the fire escape. And he said to his partner, "La jara, la jara." I asked him what that meant. He said, "The cops, the cops." Then I said, "Then what happened?" He said he hid and crouched down behind the stairway wall, and he saw the cop go by him, and he had his gun in his hand, and he was pointing it at his partner. And he said that he was afraid; he saw the gun. At that point, the defendant put his hands over his face, and he said, "Mi Dios, Mi Dios! I did it! I did it!" And I said, "What did you do?" He said, "I shot the officer. I shot him in the back."

Had you been trial counsel to the defendant, there, at the very moment that the detective testified, you should have made notes of his testimony, so that you would be able to mount the attack that should follow on Cross-examination.

My notes would have read as follows:

Detective_____:

Sd to Δ, calm down, sit down;
sit dn.// calm dn // relax // want
to tell what happ // want to
tell me truth // "Yes" // sd he
opened window // couldn't get in //
gate, inside, locked // back up fire-esc.
Δ + F started lift TV over roof //
heard noise // walked to edge of roof //
saw P.D. coming up fire esc. // sd to
F, La Jara, La Jara // asked what
mean // "cops" // then what? // Δ hid
behind stair wall // saw cop go by //
had gun out // pointed at F // was
afraid // put hands over face // Mi Dios //
I did it // What did you do // Shot
P.D. in the back //

calm, cooperative?
telling all ?

where?
inside?
outside?

Notice that, while I have not recorded each and every word of the detective's Direct testimony, I have actually captured enough that I could, practically verbatim, read back to the court, my Adversary, or myself, days or weeks later, the entire testimony of that witness. Notice that there are no questions recorded; only testimony. As indicated previously, that's all you'll need. But you shall need every word of it, and you should not be so foolhardy as to presume that you can remember it without recording it in writing. Even if you could perform such a feat of cerebral legerdemain, you would be wasting valuable energy remembering something that an inanimate piece of paper makes no effort whatsoever to record and retain exactly.

This section concerning the recording of Direct testimony is so essential that, without it, you cannot be an effective, sustained cross-examiner. I will, therefore, include here another sample recordation of testimony. This excerpt is from a civil case where a doctor called by your Adversary is testifying about your client, the plaintiff, who has injured his back in an automobile accident. The doctor testifies that the plaintiff is not quite so ill or injured as he has claimed, that your client's back is not as seriously disturbed, and that, in general, much of the claimed injury is feigned.

YOUR ADVERSARY: Doctor, please tell the court and jury what the condition of health of the plaintiff was when you examined him on August 4, 1997.

DOCTOR: My examination at that time revealed a white male, 43 years of age, 68 inches tall, weighing 160 lbs. He appeared, at the time, to be in excellent health. He disrobed without discomfort, revealing a low, lumbosacral corset. Upon questioning, he said he had been wearing the same for a year. Parenthetically, there was very little evidence of use on the corset. The patient walked without a limp, and was able, when asked, to walk on his heels and toes. His trunk was in the midline, which means that he was erect, and his torso was not out of line; it was right where it was supposed to be. He was able to bend forward until his fingers were approximately two inches above his ankles. He was able to bend left and right, laterally, 20 degrees, and 15 degrees back. He actively restricted his forward bending. He was able to get onto the examination table easily. He resisted straight leg raising, raising to 70 degrees. The ankle jerks were slightly depressed. He claimed impaired sensation in the left lower extremity, except the thigh anteriorly, in front. This is not consistent with the alleged organic pathology. His left big toe did not extend. His reflexes were not definite. This might be an indication of some nerve root involvement. If it had been actual, the weakness of the left big toe would have been confirmatory. But, as I said, this resulted from the patient actively restricting his movements.

In recording this doctor's testimony, my notes might look something like the following:

12³⁵	Doctor Blank // exam revealed w/m/43/6'8"/160 lbs excellent health // disrobed // low, lumbosacral corset – wearing 1 yr. // very little evid of use // walked without limp // able to walk, toes and heels // trunk was in mid-line // bends until fingers 2" above ankles // 20° right left lateral, 15° back bending // actively restricts forward bending // onto exam table easily // resists straight leg raising 70° // ankle jerks slightly depressed // impaired sensation, left, lower, extremity, except thigh in front // not consistent with organic pathology // left big toe, not extended // reflexes not definite re: nerve root // if actual, weakness of left big toe would be confirmatory //	all assumption / no way to be sure / pain is subjective / if pain is real, opinion can confirm / not actual only because of arbitrary assumption

The real test of your ability to record testimony is to be able to refer back to the notes days or weeks after you record them and still be able, almost verbatim, to glean therefrom the testimony of the witness. I have, just for curiosity, dredged out notes taken at trials which ended years ago. Without so much as a hesitation, I have been able, again, to recite almost verbatim, the actual trial testimony from the notes. You shall be able to do the same thing. Later on, while you're reading the latter portions of this book, return to the sample recordations of Direct testimony which appear on these pages. Even in a week or a month, you will have no difficulty reading and recalling the exact testimony. That is a fantastic boost in your capacity to try a case, recall testimony, and put the case together.

> *NOTE: An occasional time reference can be seen at the side of the page of excerpted recordation. These references are for the purpose of knowing at approximately what time the witness testified to the specific information contained in your notes. In the event that there is some question during the trial which requires the stenographer to look through the stenographic notes for certain testimony, it shall be much easier and faster for the stenographer to find the questioned official testimony if you can indicate that the testimony was taken in the beginning or end of the morning session of a certain day, or right at the beginning or end of the afternoon session, etc.*

14.07 Also Note the Exhibits: The Left-Hand Margin

As you record the Direct testimony, as your Adversary offers exhibits into evidence, you should make notations in your left-hand margin of the exhibit number and a description of any exhibit, whether admitted into evidence or merely marked for identification. In this fashion, you shall have a complete record of the exhibits, be able to verify the clerk's records thereof at the end of the trial, and be able, at a glance, to know how many exhibits there should be, what they are, when they were introduced, by which witness, etc. Again, when preparing for summation, such notes shall prove an invaluable time-saver.

14.08 Another Use for the Left-Hand Margin

The left-hand margin is also for references to pages and documents which you have perused and have ascertained will be directly beneficial in your Cross-examination of the witness. For instance, while preparing Cross-examination, you have read over the notes of the Direct you have taken, and you have also determined that certain testimony does not square with your recollection of the same witness's statements as contained in other documents, E.B.Ts, reports, or prior testimony. Look at those other documents again; read them to make sure that your recollection was correct. Then note down the document and the page in your left-hand margin so that you can use the references specifically in preparing your Cross-examination script. These references may be to prior inconsistent statements made under oath or in writing by the witness, the use of which is explained in ensuing chapters. Later, when you have the document and page number marked on your Cross-examination script, you can, even in the midst of cross-examining the witness, see your notes and references, take up the document you have referenced, turn to the correct page, and with the continuous flow and rhythm so important to Cross-examination, hammer the witness with the punch of your questions, without being delayed or looking as if you are fumbling through documents in an unprepared fashion.

14.09 Preparation Permits Smoothness and Flow

All of the smooth, easy flow of a good Cross-examination does not come from the seat of the pants. It comes from careful preparation, note taking, cross-checking and cross-referencing, preparation of a Cross-examination script, and even a careful stacking of referenced, needed material, near where you will stand to cross-examine, so that you will have the time and the confidence to make it look as if you just stood up from the table and were able to easily trap a witness who was obviously trying to fool the jury. If you have to work too hard at tearing apart the witness, if you have to hurriedly search through pages of testimony while the witness, the court, and the jury idly watch you—which makes you more nervous, the witness more confident and calm—the jury may get an impression that the witness is a lot tougher than he really is, and that your apparent struggle to find material is in direct proportion to the truth and veracity of the witness's testimony. A little preparation will help you make the witness look like a pussycat.

14.10 Your Notes May Become Your Cross-Examination Script

All of the recording of testimony, the notes to yourself, and the exhibit and document references are intended for a two-fold purpose. The first is to record the testimony to put yourself in a position to be prepared to cross-examine the witness. The other purpose is to prepare a script to be used for that Cross-examination.

Ideally, you will have time to take your notes, and by careful reference, be able to actually put together an entire Cross-examination script, orchestrate it on paper, and develop nuances which occur to you in the calm of your library as you prepare to cross-examine the witness the next morning. (See Chapter 15.) However, be prepared for the judge to tell you to take five minutes and then begin Cross-examination, or even to stand right up and begin Cross-examination, right then and there, without the benefit of that calm library atmosphere. You should be prepared for such an event and should have made sufficient notes during your pre-trial or during-trial investigation, should know the documents at hand, and the other witness's testimony well enough, that in the twinkling of a star, you can do the necessary cross-checking and referencing, stand right up on your feet, and examine. Don't get nervous! With the instructions contained herein on preparing for Cross-examination, some advice on getting the time you need from a hard-nosed judge, and with experience, you will soon be able to prepare a basic, adequate, sometimes brilliant Cross-examination, in the very few minutes some judges allow before you begin to ask your questions.

Remember that the preparation is always the same. *Thorough*. It's just the time within which you make that preparation that varies from case to case.

15.

Preparing the Cross-Examination Script

15.01 An Actual Script

When the Direct testimony of each witness has been completed, theoretically, at least, you shall then have an opportunity to prepare for your Cross-examination of the witness. Ideally, you will be able to do so at your leisure, overnight, so that when you proceed to court the next morning, you will have a carefully orchestrated, cross-referenced Cross-examination script with which to work. The opportunity to prepare your Cross-examination script slowly, overnight, with plenty of time to consider and reconsider your approach to form, reform, and revise questions, even whole areas of questioning, is the ideal. Unfortunately, often you may not be afforded so luxurious an amount of time in which to prepare for the assault. Sometimes the witness, even if formidable in terms of substance of testimony or hurt inflicted, has only testified for a few minutes, perhaps a half hour.

The court, measuring the time necessary to prepare your Cross-examination by the amount of time the witness has testified, may permit you only a few minutes to formulate your attack. Other times, even if the Direct testimony of the witness took a substantial part of the morning session, there's still the entire afternoon session for you to cross-examine. Thus, regardless of how devoutly you wish for an overnight recess to prepare yourself, the court has an obligation to keep the trial moving briskly. In such case, you might have to make do with a luncheon recess in order to prepare for your Cross-examination. With a bit of practice, however, a luncheon recess shall become ample time for the preparation of at least enough Cross-examination to carry you through the afternoon session, so that, if necessary, you can prepare the remainder of your Cross-examination in the evening and continue in the morning.

15.02 The Better Prepared, the Less Time Required

If you have prepared for the trial thoroughly, as outlined in previous chapters, it should not be necessary to take very long to be ready to cross-examine any witness. Remember, you have already studied all the prior statements, testimony, and Depositions of the witness, and are mentally prepared to collate all that material with the Direct that you have just recorded in your notes. With time and experience, you will be able to put together an effective Cross-examination rapidly. Incidentally, as you are on your feet cross-examining, even if you have a full-blown Cross-examination script in hand, you should not be hidebound by that script. You should continually be revising and adjusting the Cross-examination to accommodate the twists and turns that inevitably arise as the witness twists and turns to elude the thrusts of your questions. That capacity and flexibility to improvise and formulate Cross-examination quickly, while on your feet, is the same capacity which permits you to formulate your attack well, quickly, and professionally, despite the shortness of preparation time.

15.03 Cross-Examination Is Not Improvisation

While you may occasionally be required to get up on your feet without the ideal, carefully created Cross-examination script, and while you may occasionally be required to improvise while on your feet in certain areas of your attack, Cross-examination should not be something that is done willy-nilly, attacking headlong with the first question that pops into your mind. The headlong attack is one that is obvious not only to you, but also to your Adversary and the witness. The area of inquiry that is so obvious to attack is also the area that obviously must be defended. Thus, this is also the area that the witness shall best be prepared to defend. A direct, immediate, headlong attack at the obvious target might be so well prepared for and rebuffed that you might find yourself sitting vanquished back at the counsel table without so much as a by-your-leave. Thus, when it is suggested that, with time and experience, you may be able to do a creditable job in standing up and attacking carefully, despite the fact that you haven't had a great deal of time for preparation, that does not mean that it's easy, that it doesn't take any preparation or practice, and that anyone with a law degree can do it the minute he or she stands on his or her feet. The fact is that most lawyers *cannot* do it. However, with practice, you will be able to do it.

With time, after preparing and conducting many Cross-examinations with full detail and full scripts, you may be able to quickly home in on the subtle approach, the right tack to use to begin to unravel the Adverse Witness's testimony. When you have developed that capacity, even if the judge gives you very little time to prepare, you can begin a proper Cross-examination; during recesses, luncheons, etc., you will be able to plan your continuing attack sufficiently enough to carry you to the next recess when you can breathe a little easier and plan for the ultimate moment of truth.

> NOTE: *Most of the basic pattern for your Cross-examination should already be in your head. All the digesting of the prior, pre-trial and on-trial information should be completed, waiting only for the Direct to be finished so that you may collate all the material. You may even have a basic idea where you want to begin your cross the moment the Direct ends. You might even have your first assault planned. But that doesn't mean you do not prepare—even if only for a few minutes—a careful, final battle plan.*

A crafty Cross-examiner, having analyzed the opponent's case, already knowing what ground the proffered witness would attempt to cover, and even without having heard the Direct, knowing in broad terms what the witness shall have to testify in order to support the Adversary's case, can plan basic countermoves in advance, waiting only to hear the Direct to know if his or her educated guess of what the Direct would be was correct. If it was, you are far ahead on the road of preparedness.

15.04 The Script Itself

Let's take a sample of Direct testimony, make the notes to record it, and then formulate a proper script from which to Cross-examine. As a test, while reading the following, make up your own notes on the Direct. The testimony is in a homicide case. The witness is a girlfriend of an alleged accomplice in the homicide. She testified that on the evening of the crime, three conspirators, including her now-cooperating boyfriend, came to her apartment to talk over the crime which was going to be committed. She testified on Direct as follows:

Q: Mrs. Witness, how long have you lived at 743 East 86th Street, Brooklyn?

A: Since June of 1992.

Q: And where do you live in this said building?

A: I have an apartment in the basement.

Q: And with whom do you live?

A: My son. He is 3 years old.

Q: Does anybody else live in the building?

A: On the first floor, Roger, my boyfriend's grandmother and aunt. And, on the second floor, his mother and father.

Q: How old are you, Mrs. Witness?

A: Twenty-three years old.

Q: And did you know Stanley A. Victim?

A: Yes, he was my uncle.

Q: Now on April 15, 1993, were you living at the same address?

A: Yes.

Q: Now can you tell what, if anything, happened on that evening?

A: Well, I had been in my apartment and I left and went up to the second floor, and I was there with Roger.

Q: Can you describe the apartment you were in?

A: Well, there is a main door which leads into a small foyer, and there is another door which leads into a kitchen where I was.

Q: And who else was up there at that time, besides yourself and Roger?

A: My son was asleep downstairs, but I think that Roger's mother was at home watching TV in her bedroom.

Q: And what else occurred, if anything?

A: About 8:30, or a little after, somebody came to the door downstairs. They came in and said Louie sent us here.

Q: Do you know who let them into the building?

A: No.

Q: Go ahead.

A: Anyway there were two men. I didn't know them. And they said Louie sent us here.

Q: Where were they when they said this?

A: In the foyer. On the second floor.

Q: And do you see anybody in this courtroom who resemble the individuals who you saw that evening?

A: The two men sitting there at that table.

DISTRICT ATTORNEY: Indicating the defendants, Your Honor?

THE COURT: Let the record show that the witness has indicated the two defendants.

Q: Is there any doubt in your mind that these are the men who came into the house that evening?

A: No.

Q: What happened after that, if anything?

A: I saw the two men walk into the kitchen and introduce themselves as Ken and Andy. I don't remember if each introduced himself or if one just said we're Ken and Andy. Anyways, they said that they had passed by the house a few times and it was dark there, and that they were going to go back in a while.

Q: Did you have an opportunity to observe these individuals on that occasion?

A: Sure, we were all sitting at the kitchen table.

Q: And who was doing the speaking, describe what had happened?

A: Ken did most of the talking. Andy was very quiet.

Q: Did the defendants look the same as they do now here in the courtroom?

A: Well, Ken was wearing glasses. Andy looks the same, but Ken had glasses.

Q: Now did they indicate whose house they had been to where the lights were out?

A: I don't remember if they said which house, but I was sure it was my uncle's.

Q: And when you say your uncle, you mean Stanley A. Victim?

A: Yes.

Q: Do you remember if anything else might have been said on that occasion?

A: No, I can't remember anything else.

Q: How far away from you were these people while all this conversation was going on?

A: Approximately five to six feet away.

Q: Was there any further conversation?

A: Well, there was other conversation, but I didn't hear it.

Q: Did Roger say anything in this conversation?

A: He didn't say very much, if anything.

Q: What happened then?

A: All of them left.

Q: Does that include Roger?

A: Yes. And when he was going down, I called to him and he turned around and said, "Don't worry."

Q: Did you know where they were going?

A: I had an idea where they were going.

Q: What did you do then?

A: I went down where my son was and I lay down.

Your notes, relative to the recordation of this Direct testimony, should look something like the note on page 167.

Based upon your careful study, you already know that the witness has made three prior oral statements, which have been recorded in writing. The first was to a police detective; the second to an assistant District Attorney on the same day as the one made to the detective; and the third to another Assistant District Attorney while the case was pending. Additionally, you know the witness testified under oath in front of the Grand Jury. Thus, you have three prior statements reduced to writing (see Chapter 19) and one prior statement made under oath (see Chapter 17) to collate and use in Cross-examination.

Joan Richards // 125 E 15th St //
6/25/79 same address // lived in basment 3½ yrs
with son 4 yrs old // 1st fl. Grand. + Aunt //
2nd fl., moth + fath. // 23 yrs old // deceas. uncle
day in ques. left bas. to 2nd fl // with Roger //
stairs lead to foyer and door // son was asleep
down st. // thinks Rogers moth at home, watch TV //
about 8³⁰ - little after // someone came to door //
doesn't know who let in // 2 men // didn't know //
said Louie sent them // said in 2nd fl. foyer //
(points out 2 Δs) // no doubt about it // walked
into kitchen // introd. as Andy and Ken //
doesn't remember if ea. introd himself // saw
both Δs clearly // said passed by house a
few times // dark there // go back in a while
Ken was quiet // only spoke to Andy //
Andy did most of talking // Andy wore glasses //
and mustache // doesn't remember if they said
which house // (Sure was uncle's) // doesn't
remember anything else they said // they
were 5 or 6 ft. away - maybe closer // was
other conversation betw 2 // didn't hear //

legitimate?
married?
Rogers son?

mustache ??

guessing

do anything

Call uncle?
PD?

never said
were
committing
crime

NOTE: *When there are multiple prior statements whether under oath or reduced to writing, a good practice is to analyze each of them in writing, side by side on a page, just as you would with Direct testimony. Thus, in connection with the four prior statements of this witness, I commit them to paper as follows. Being now familiar with the recording method, see if you can read what the actual statements were:*

		A		**B**
		DETECTIVE 3/23		ASS'T D.A. 3/23

A (Detective 3/23):
Louie said he'd set it up // send 2 guys // wanted to get into uncle's house // 2 men arrived // 6/25, little after 8 // stayed 20 min // 3 went to door // witness went down to own apt // 45 min. later, Roger came back alone // while in kitch, Andy said no one at home // no cars // go back before we go in to burg // all had been whisp //

B (Ass't D.A. 3/23):
Louie, few weeks before, at Marina, sitting on boat, talked of ripping off uncle / had to get others to help // Roger sin on conv. // Roger spoke to Louie after that // on 6/25 Roger spoke to Louie at Louie's house // on 6/25, 8 or a little after, 2 men came to house // no one else present // Louie sent us // Andy said it // drove around uncle's — no one there // Andy said it // all dark there // no one home // wait // then go back // they got up + left // Ken head down during conv // they spoke among themselves // didn't hear all // said pass by again // other guy didn't say anything // Roger agreed // Roger told witness about burg // they were there 15-20 mins // left 8:25, 8:30 // ½ hr - 45 min Roger returned // said not much happened // about 11, 11:30, fra. came, told about uncle dead // went to mother's.

C Asst D.A.	D Grand Jury
Saw Louie at marina // he	2 people came to home in evening
knew uncle // told about burg.	never saw before //
6/35 2 men came to house–Louie	came into house // someone else let in
sent us // Roger opened door	came upstairs // not much conv.
drove past uncle's // everything	talking in foyer // they said Louie sent us
dark // go back soon // Roger knew	passed uncle's a few times // ready to
uncle // called uncle Frank //	go out // that's all // ready to go
whispered among themselves // only	back // no one answered //
said hello to them // Roger said	whispered among themselves // that's all
nothing // 2 + Roger left // there	ever saw of them // introduced as
15 minutes // arrived 8:00–8:15 //	Andy + Ken only // found out Ken's
Roger returned // she had gone	name (last) after arrest //
downstairs // later Louie came	Andy had a thick mustache //
over + Roger left with Louie	
again //	

Now, fully armed, I prepare my Cross-examination script as follows:

	Richards	
	Richards not maiden name // what is	
	when married – divorced?	
	living with Roger – 3½ yrs	
	not married to Rog / son, 4 yrs	
	R not father // mother let stay in bast	
	Employed? not since child – 4 yrs	
	Roger supports / sole support? / welfare	
	advise welf., common law relation	
	looking for work?	
	who else lives at house	
	home on 6/25 – had been out –	
	with R. and his mother	
	see anyone in street	
	in parked car – double parked car	
	went up to 2nd fl.	
	later 2 men to door	
	Louie sent them	
	testimony – you do not know who said that	
B-7	actually, Andy said	
	Andy did most of talking	
C-39	whispering together	
	never saw before – never spoke before to Ken	
	only knew as Andy – Ken – no last names	

Andy had southern accent

men in court here—same men as 6/25

able to recognize from them

the way these men look — the same as the men 6/25

D 45 actually difficult because man had thick mustache

Louie sent them — knew Louie

met several weeks before — not with Andy or Ken

met at Marina — on boat

didn't see again before 6/28

expecting them

    if no — didn't know why there at first

    if yes — { had had prev conversations

        (with Louie about uncle rip-off

Deceased was uncle — blood uncle

mother's brother

families close — go to his home / he come to yours

    went to his house once — (12-13 yrs old)

show → recognize picture — except for body - uncle's house

photo of ever talk — ever in life — about ripping someone off

scene with Louie — just started talking about uncles

A-7 after convers — call uncle — mother - P.D.

B-3

    no one?

you testified — knew talking about uncle's home

weren't horrified — didn't scream for P.D.

    nothing?

The Cross-examination script displayed above appears at this point in the book merely as an example of the physical layout of a script, not necessarily for its completeness. There are many more things which are illustrated in ensuing chapters with which you must become familiar before you can put together detailed, complete, Cross-examination scripts. Therefore, merely view the script for its form, not as a completed script. Notice that the Cross-examination script is a unilateral document. It only contains your questions. Also notice that the attack begins slowly and subtly inquiring into the marital status (for those jurors who might be offended by a married woman with child subjected her child to her flagrant, meretricious relationship, we offer them something to think about). Then, it slowly develops the witness's relationship with the deceased, her blood uncle (for jurors offended by a young woman helping to plan, or at least knowing in advance, that her mother's brother was going to be the victim of a crime, we offer them something else to think about). Develop the Cross-examination subtly, leaving no gaping holes in the Direct testimony, but chinks, clouds, and nagging doubts.

15.05 What If There Are No Prior Inconsistent Statements?

It may very well be that, in a particular case, there are no prior inconsistent statements that you have been able to uncover. That does not mean that you can't Cross-examine the witness or that you don't prepare a script. It merely means that you have to pursue other methods to make the witness look bad and make the jury realize that the witness is not a reliable, credible person. For instance, inconsistencies may exist in the Direct testimony itself. Conflict between this witness's Direct and the testimony of other witnesses, other evidence already introduced, physical impossibilities, or all sorts of other things may exist and may be attacked. When you put your script together, when you orchestrate the dismembering of the witness, the full, dramatic, factual impact of all these discrepancies is revealed, fully-blown to the jury.

15.06 You Must Be Able to Vary the Script

While you may have spent considerable time on your preparation and line of attack, don't anticipate that it is a set speech or is carved in stone, or that you must follow it to the letter. You have set up the script as a guide which you follow carefully, unless some brilliant new idea or gaping new target appears on the scene. You may, based on an answer, go off on a tangent for a while, asking questions prompted by the witness's answers, then return to the script. You may abandon a particular tack you set up in the script which, because of the answers received, is no longer applicable or viable. Because you have prepared for the Cross-examination carefully and have thought out the attack, you should use the script as the basic outline of attack unless something significant arises to cause you to vary therefrom.

15.07 Preparation Is Always Necessary

As aforesaid, the preparation for Cross-examination is always the same; only the time in which you prepare varies. If the court permits you time to leisurely prepare yourself, you should do more detailed—not better—work with more cross-references, notes, etc. Because you have prepared so well in advance, done your thorough investigation, you should be able, *if necessary only,* after some experience, to put together a decent Cross-examination script or a substantial part thereof in a scant few minutes. Perhaps the judge gives you only ten minutes after the Direct to gather your thoughts, your notes, etc. This can not catch you totally off guard. You should use whatever time the judge allows to put together the first part of the examination. With your prior knowledge of all the information in the case, from your pre-trial and on-trial investigation, you can, in that time, put a good, basic start of the Cross-examination together.

If the witness is only a peripheral witness, with not much Direct testimony, you can probably put together the entire Cross-examination script in a few minutes. If the witness is one you intend to have on the stand for hours or days, you can assemble your script at different times. Work the first part of a long script in the few minutes the obstinate judge gives you after the Direct. That should carry you to lunch break or to the end of the day. If it carries you to the end of the day, then you're home free, and can prepare the rest of your script that night. If it carries you only to lunch break, during that lunch break, you prepare enough script to carry you to the end the day.

> NOTE: *If eating lunch is more important to you than preparing to cross-examine the witness, perhaps you should think of handling real-estate closings instead of trial advocacy.*

15.08 The Preliminary Breather Technique

Oftentimes, if you have a witness who has given Direct testimony near the end of the trial day, you can put together a preliminary, first-round Cross-examination script to carry you to the end of the day so that you can then prepare your heavy barrage overnight.

When you have an important witness you intend to have on the stand a long time, the preliminary script should already be completely in place. Use the preliminary examination to angle for the sidelines, for the lunch break, and overnight, so you can properly prepare a full-blown script which includes the Direct testimony. You can sometimes get such breathing room by undertaking to first examine the witness as to personal background, education, where he or she has lived throughout his or her life, where he or she has worked, etc., etc. You can usually gain about 25 to 45 minutes with this type of examination, at the end of which, depending on the time, you might indicate to the court:

> CROSS-EXAMINER: Your Honor, the next part of my examination is going to be quite lengthy. I wonder if this might be an appropriate time to take a break (or go to lunch or adjourn for the day) so that the jury can hear all the Cross-examination at one time rather than it being disjointed.

> THE COURT: Very well, ladies and gentlemen of the jury, we'll recess a little early today, and we'll begin a little earlier tomorrow morning to make up for it. Good night and do not discuss this case amongst yourselves or with anyone else.

Or perhaps the judge won't agree to take a break, in which case, you keep working to the recess, and then go to the law library in the courthouse, back to the office, or home to prepare the balance of your Cross-examination script. Be flexible; you're talented and experienced enough by now to handle the situation.

PART III

Prior Inconsistent Statements

16.

Prior Inconsistent Statements

16.01 A Truly Powerful Weapon

The following chapters, dealing with prior inconsistent statements, are most important to any person wanting to learn proper methods and techniques of Cross-examination. Prior inconsistencies, you shall find, are the single-most frequent and fertile ground upon which a Cross-examiner shall or can walk. There is nothing which can be utilized so effectively, or is so debilitating to a witness presented by your Adversary, than for the Cross-examiner to be armed with a statement the witness previously made, which statement contradicts the present trial testimony.

Therefore, pay the most strict attention to the material in this chapter. Study it carefully, because you're going to need it.

> NOTE: *Many a seasoned Adversary, and even a seasoned judge, has no idea how these prior inconsistent statements are properly used. Thus, you may find yourself, after objection by your Adversary, having to prove to the judge that your line of inquiry is proper. Contained herein is the ammunition for your assault.*

16.02 What Are Prior Inconsistent Statements?

A prior inconsistent statement is, basically, a statement made by a testifying witness on some prior occasion, which does not agree or coincide with the trial testimony the witness has given from the witness stand. While this must seem academic, it is amazing to see Cross-examiners attempt to use documents on Cross-examination, apparently as prior inconsistent statements, when neither the prior statement nor the Direct testimony is in the least inconsistent. In order for a statement, or a part thereof, to fall within the category of "inconsistent," there must be a specific area where the testimony at trial conflicts with the prior statement. It is *not* enough that the prior statement is in different language from the trial testimony, or that it is not given in the same order, or with the same detail, that not everything in the prior statement is testified to from the stand. In order for a prior statement to be usable as a prior inconsistent statement, it is *not* enough that the current testimony is not as complete as the prior statement. The contents of the prior statement must actually contradict or conflict with the witness's trial testimony, it must disagree, it must mean something completely different.

16.03 The Entire Statement Need Not Be Inconsistent

It is not necessary, however, in order to use such a prior inconsistent statement, that every single part of the prior statement disagree with every part of the trial testimony. There may be complete agreement between the prior statement and the trial testimony, *except,* for example, in the area of the time of the occurrence. The trial testimony may indicate the event occurred at 7:15 P.M. The prior statement may indicate, however, that the event occurred at 6:30 P.M. That is clearly an inconsistency which, if material, would permit the use of the statement on Cross-examination as a prior inconsistent statement.

> NOTE: *You should utilize the prior statement only for exploring the inconsistency. You do not have to utilize the entire statement. It is perfectly acceptable only to explore the area that is inconsistent.*

16.04 The Inconsistency Must Be Relevant and Material

The trial judge will restrict your inquiries during trial to areas which are proper, material, and relevant. Even though a statement qualifies as a prior inconsistent statement, it must also be relevant and material to the issue of the witness's credibility. There may be many inconsistencies in a statement which are totally insignificant, which in no fashion affect the witness's credibility. It is difficult to indicate specifically what would be relevant and material, for each case has its own peculiar facts, and what might be totally irrelevant in one trial would be the essence of another. Suffice it to say that belaboring a witness over minute inconsistencies, conflicts which are of no significance to the issue on trial, will have a reverse effect on the jury; that is, it will hammer home the fact that the witness must be reliable since you, the Cross-examiner, only find Tweedledum and Tweedledee about which to Cross-examine.

Make sure the inconsistency that you are going to explore has some real significance or purpose in your Cross-examination or forget it.

16.05 Caution: Inconsistencies Are Not Evidence In Chief

The Direct Testimony of a witness, the testimony that the witness gives before the jury, is called Evidence In Chief, that is, simply, part of the trial evidence. Testimony brought out about a prior inconsistent statement is *not* evidence in chief and *is not* evidence in the case at hand. This concept is most important and most often misunderstood.

The testimony given before the jury is the trial evidence. A prior statement, because it is, just that, a *prior* statement, not one offered to the jury as evidence, is brought out merely to attack the credibility of the Direct testimony, merely to cast new light and new coloration on the witness's present trial testimony or evidence. The only purpose of eliciting testimony about prior statements is to aid the jury's acceptance or rejection of the witness's truthfulness and reliability on Direct. Thus, again, the prior inconsistent statement, and what is brought out during an examination based on that prior statement is not evidence in chief—evidence in the case. It is merely utilized to affect credibility, and remains such.

In other words, your use of the prior inconsistent statements is restricted to crumbling the reliability of the witness's Direct testimony before the jury. If this is accomplished, there is no need to worry about the effect of that witness upon the jury. An argument at Summation can be mounted that the particular witness is not reliable based upon the inconsistency of that witness's testimony, based upon the different versions of the facts that the witness may have given. However, an argument at Summation cannot, subsequently, be founded upon the *evidence* contained in the prior inconsistent statement. Such prior statement is NOT evidence and does not exist in the case, except as it affects the jury's view and acceptance of the witness's Direct testimony.

16.06 A Devastating Weapon

Once the Cross-examiner understands the rules on the use of inconsistent statements, he or she has control of the single most devastating weapon with which to shatter the harmful effects of an Adverse Witness.

16.07 Kinds of Prior Inconsistent Statements

There are only four types of prior inconsistent statements which you may come across on trial (or in human communications of any kind):

1. made under oath;
2. in the handwriting of, or signed by, the witness;
3. made to a third person orally and reduced to writing by that third person; or,
4. made to a third person and not reduced to writing.

While all these are prior inconsistencies, they are each very different from the others, each governed by different rules, and each requires a different preliminary foundation before such inconsistency may be utilized on Cross-examination. Therefore, know all the rules concerning each prior inconsistency, since knowing how to use a prior inconsistency under oath won't, in the least, assist you in using a prior oral inconsistency made to a third party.

16.08 The Rules to Know

Certain universal rules have been fashioned which restrict or permit the Cross-examiner to dissect a witness on the stand by the use of any of the above prior inconsistent statements. These rules must be understood completely by the Cross-examiner in order that he or she be properly armed for the task ahead. Remember that Cross-examination should be smooth and controlled so that the trier of fact (court or jury) is permitted to get the full effect of the evidence you are uncovering by your questioning. Objections, colloquy with the court, and sidebar discussions to clarify the propriety of your use of prior statements only interrupt the flow of your examination. Therefore, it is imperative that you know the rules thoroughly and use the inconsistent statements properly. Only then do you stand a fair chance of having your Cross-examination flow as full and free as you prepared it.

16.09 Direct Confrontation of the Witness Only If the Inconsistent Statement Is Under Oath or in the Witness's Writing

A caution: In most jurisdictions, in order for a Cross-examiner to *directly* confront a witness with his or her own prior inconsistent statement, that is, directly Cross-examine the witness concerning his or her own prior inconsistent statement, that prior inconsistent statement must either have been:

1. made under oath;
2. must be completely handwritten by the witness whether signed or not; or
3. must at least be a statement subscribed or signed by the witness.

The reason for the strict requirement of oath or the handwriting is that these qualities give almost conclusive reliability to the fact that the witness actually made the prior statement. Additionally, all the other types of prior inconsistencies were made to third persons. Thus, it is the third person, not the witness himself or herself who is the "maker" of the statement. For the moment, remember, without the reliability of oath or handwriting, the issue at hand could devolve into the collateral issue of authenticity.

The rules concerning prior inconsistent statements are strictly enforced to preserve the integrity of the real issues on trial. Unless at least one of the three above specified requirements are present, the Cross-examiner cannot directly confront the witness with a prior inconsistent statement. There are other methods of using prior inconsistent statements which do not fall within the aforementioned categories; these shall be discussed in the following chapters.

17.

Prior Inconsistent Statements Made Under Oath

17.01 Statements Under Oath Defined

A prior inconsistent statement made under oath may be testimony from a prior trial; or testimony taken during a Deposition; at a preliminary hearing; or before a Grand Jury; or some other formal proceeding, at which the witness, under oath, made statements concerning the issues on trial. Obviously, to be inconsistent, these other statements must run, at least in part, afoul of the testimony given at the trial. Statements made under oath need not be in the handwriting of or signed by the witness in order to be used during Cross-examination. The reliability of the statement rises from the strength of the oath and the sanction of perjury attendant to the original giving of testimony.

17.02 Establishing the Prior Statement

During Cross-examination, in order to confront a witness with a prior inconsistency under oath, the cross-examiner must establish that:

1. the witness gave a previous statement under oath,
2. the time,
3. the place, and
4. the occasion of such previous testimony,

and then proceed with the Cross-examination to establish the inconsistency.

The following extract, taken directly from an actual criminal prosecution for attempted murder, tried in the Supreme Court, New York County, provides the proper method of utilizing a prior inconsistent statement made under oath.

Background

Your client, a man of approximately 45 years of age, with greying hair, is on trial for attempted murder. Two others not on trial and your client are accused of having beaten the complaining victim with a pool cue in a barroom. The victim has just testified that he had been in the bar many times and knew your client to be the regular bartender. He identified him as one of the men who struck him a terrible blow on the back of the head just as he was reaching for the door handle to leave the bar. The victim testified that he turned at the moment of impact, and clearly saw your client with a pool cue in his hand. The witness testifies that he then fell and awoke in the hospital.

The Previous Statement under Oath

At the conclusion of the witness's testimony, your Adversary hands you several pages of the witness's sworn Grand Jury testimony given three weeks after the incident. The District Attorney also gives you a copy of a police report made out by a police detective who visited the witness in the hospital the day after the attack. This latter document is not sworn nor subscribed by the witness, and is treated in Chapter 19, relating to prior inconsistent statements made to third parties, reduced to writing by the third party. The Grand Jury minutes you have just been given contain, inter alia, the following:

Q: Do you remember the 17th of August and being in the Tipple Inn in New York County?

A: Yes, that's the day they beat me.

Q: Will you tell the Grand Jury what happened to you on that occasion?

A: I was there having a few beers, you know. And then I got up to leave. I walked to the door. As I reached for the door, they were behind me.

Q: Who was behind you?

A: Three of them. A fat guy with blond hair, a skinny guy with black hair, and a guy with white hair.

Q: How were they standing?

A: Behind me.

Q: In what order were they standing, all together, single file?

A: The skinny guy and the blond guy were more or less side by side. The guy with the white hair was right there with them, maybe a little behind.

Q: And then what happened when you reached the door?

A: I reached for the door, you know. And then I caught this terrible shot on the head with something very hard. You know, it wasn't a fist or something. It was a hard object. I spun and saw them standing there. And this one guy had a pool cue in his hand.

Q: Which one had the pool cue in his hand?

A: The guy with the black hair.

Q: What happened after that?

A: After that, they started to beat me all over. I was on the ground. I woke up in the hospital.

Naturally, the Adverse Witness's trial testimony, attributing the actual weapon to your client *(your client is not "the guy with the black hair"),* is gravely inconsistent with his Grand Jury testimony.

17.03 Using the Inconsistency Under Oath

Now it is your function to take this Grand Jury testimony, which conflicts dramatically and significantly with the witness's trial testimony, and utilize it to hone the trial testimony, to get it right down to the shape of the truth—in this case, that your client was not the one who hit the victim with the pool cue. You might wonder, why bother? Perhaps it's just a slight mistake as to who wielded the pool cue; there's no question that the witness was beaten. True. But *by whom* is the quintessential question. The essence of the charge against your client is this witness's identification that *your client hit him with a pool cue.* If you can show the victim has made an erroneous identification, that the main witness is lying, mistaken, or confused, you are well on your way to neutralizing his entire testimony.

Before you begin to question the witness about his Grand Jury testimony, however, you should first reinforce his trial testimony about the man with the white hair wielding the pool cue. Sink it into the jurors' minds so that the witness cannot deviate from it.

In previous chapters, I have suggested that normally it is counterproductive to cause a witness to repeat his Direct testimony. Such repetition only assists your Adversary, reinforcing the direct case. However, there are exceptions, as in our current example, when you want to reinforce certain portions of the witness's Direct testimony to make sure it is clear and unequivocal, all for the purpose of making his unhorsing the more dramatic.

> NOTE: *The examination should be subtle, with the salient questions smoothly blended in a flow of other questions so as not to tip-off the direction or aim of your examination to the witness. (In the testimony following, the real meat questions relative to the prior inconsistent statement are marked with an asterisk.)*

17.04 The Cross-Examination

Q: Mr. Witness, you say there were three men behind you when you went to reach for the door; is that right?

A: Yes.

Q: One was fat and blond, correct?

A: Yes.

Q: And one was skinny with black hair?

A: Yes.

Q: The third person had the white hair, an older man?

A: That's right.

*Q: This is the man with the white hair here, isn't it? (you point to your own client).

A: Yes.

*Q: And according to your testimony, it was this man with the white hair who had the pool cue in his hand. Is that right?

A: He's the one.

Q: Before you started to leave the bar did anyone hit you, kick you, punch you; anything like that?

A: No. Only after I got to the door, then they hit me. He hit me (pointing to your client).

CROSS-EXAMINER: Your Honor, I ask that the answer be stricken as not responsive, and ask you to direct the witness to answer only the question asked and not make gratuitous remarks.

THE COURT: Yes, stricken. Mr. Witness, you must answer only the questions asked.

NOTE: *You might have ignored the gratuitous remarks as you are attempting to emphasize the witness's identification of your client. However, by objecting, you also underscore the testimony and the gratuitous remark.*

Q: Before you reached for the door, did you get punched, hit, kicked, or anything like that?

A: No.

Q: Before you reached for the door, did anyone curse you, say nasty things to you, insult you?

A: No.

Q: So that before you reached for the door, say as you were walking toward the door, there was nothing that had happened to you that was unusual, part of an assault or altercation of any sort; is that correct?

A: Yes.

Q: It was just an ordinary leaving of a bar, correct?

A: Yes.

Q: At that point, before you reached the door, there was no cause for you to be particularly suspicious of anyone in the bar, right?

A: Not until I got to the door.

Q: And then you reached for the doorknob, and only then, for the first time, felt this terrible blow, right?

A: Yes, he hit me with the pool cue. (The witness points to your client again.)

CROSS-EXAMINER: Your Honor, I ask that this answer be stricken and I again ask Your Honor to direct the witness to answer only the questions asked.

THE COURT: Mr. Witness, answer only questions. Don't make gratuitous remarks.

Q: Now, when you were at the door, ready to go out, and you reached
      for the doorknob, the men were behind you, right?

A: Right behind me.

*Q: And when you were at the door, ready to go out, reaching for the
      doorknob, which way were you facing?

A: I was reaching for the door, but I saw them.

*Q: The question is, when you were at the door, before ever being hit,
      without any suspicion, and you reached for the doorknob to go
      out, which way were you facing?

A: I was facing the door, but then I turned and saw him.

*Q: Before you were hit, then, you were facing the door, weren't you?

A: Yes, but I turned fast.

*Q: You didn't see anything behind you before you turned to look, did
      you?

A: I saw him, I saw him hit me.

Q: By the way, was it a hard blow on the head?

A: It was a terrible blow; very hard.

Q: Did it hurt?

A: You get hit on the head with a pool cue and see if it hurts.

Q: Did it knock you down?

A: Not right away. I went down though.

*Q: How many men had pool cues?

A: Only one—him. (Pointing to the defendant, your client.)

NOTE: *I'm sure you've noticed that the witness is trying to bury the
defendant. In the example, he is being permitted to do so because such
purposeful attack fits into the strategy.*

*Q: And this man is not the fat blond man, is he?

A: No.

*Q: And he's not the skinny man with the black hair, right?

A: Right.

Q: You're sure about that?

A: You look at him. He got blond hair?

(Now to utilize the prior statement under oath)

*Q: Do you remember testifying in front of the Grand Jury in this case, on October 2, 1996? (You now pick up the transcript and start thumbing through to the page you've previously marked. Let the witness and the jury see it coming.)

A: Yes.

*Q: You remember that, at that time, you were sworn to tell the truth, just as you were today?

A: I remember.

Q: And that was about two or three weeks after this assault took place, right?

A: Right.

*Q: By the way, was your memory of the event better three weeks after the incident took place, or today, eleven months later?

A: It was better then, I guess.

*Q: Do you remember being asked these questions at the Grand Jury and giving these answers? And please wait until I read both the questions and the answers to you and then advise the court and the jury if you remember being asked these questions and giving these answers. On page 16 (you advise the judge and prosecutor)
. . .

"QUESTION: And what happened when you reached the door?

"ANSWER: I reached for the door you know, and then I caught this awful shot on the head with something very hard. You know, it wasn't a fist or something. It was a hard object. I spun and saw them standing there. And this one guy had a pool cue in his hand.

"QUESTION: Which one had the pool cue in his hands?

"ANSWER: The one with the black hair.

*Q: Mr. Witness, do you remember those questions being asked in the Grand Jury and your telling the Grand Jury that the man with the black hair had the pool cue?

A: That's not the way it happened.

CROSS-EXAMINER: Your Honor, I object to the answer as unresponsive and again ask the court to direct the witness to answer.

THE COURT: Strike it. Answer the question. Read it back for him, Mr. Reporter.

Q: I'll rephrase it, Your Honor. Do you remember being asked those questions and giving those answers when you were under oath in front of the Grand Jury?

A: It's there, I said it, but it's not the way it happened.

CROSS-EXAMINER: Your Honor, will the District Attorney concede that I have read the portions of the Grand Jury testimony of this witness correctly, and exactly as they appear on the pages the District Attorney supplied?

DISTRICT ATTORNEY: Mr. Cross-examiner has read the minutes correctly, Your Honor.

Q: Was what you swore under oath in the Grand Jury true?

A: I don't remember saying that.

Q: Whether you remember or not, was what I read from the Grand Jury proceedings, two or three weeks after the assault, accurate?

A: That's not the way it happened.

You have now gained about as much as can be gained from the prior inconsistency. It's not necessary to beat the point to death. The jury sees the point, sees the inaccuracy and confusion of the witness; you've brought it squarely and firmly to their attention. Now, continue with other segments of your examination.

17.05 Civil or Criminal, the Use of the Oath Prior Inconsistency Is the Same

The use of prior inconsistency under oath is exactly the same, whether the trial issue is civil or criminal. In fact, both the subject of the trial and the source of the prior inconsistent statement is immaterial (Deposition, preliminary hearing, prior trial, etc.) as long as the inconsistent statement was under oath and was about the subject matter of the present testimony.

17.06 Sink Your Hook Deep in Front of the Jury

You would be well-serving your client to never forget that it is not enough merely to establish that the witness made a prior statement under oath concerning the subject matter at hand, or even that such prior statement is inconsistent with the present testimony. You must bring this point home effectively to the jury to have fulfilled your function.

In other words, it is not enough to merely drag the point into the courtroom, placing it dormant before the jury, without vitality, with only you, the judge, and your Adversary knowing its potential explosiveness. *Explode it!* The jurors are not lawyers. They may not realize the legal nuances of an undeveloped destruction. Make sure the jury sees it and knows what the significance is. Impale the witness (if you can) on the horns of inconsistency.

17.07 What Not to Do

The following excerpt of testimony will illustrate how a good piece of evidence can be frittered away when left unexploded in the witness's face. This is what you should *not* do with a glaring inconsistency given under oath on a prior occasion:

Q: You say the light was green in your favor when you were approaching the intersection of Main Street and 10th Avenue?

A: That's right.

Q: You're sure of that?

A: Yes.

Q: Do you remember testifying under oath at an Examination Before Trial on September 12, 1976?

A: Yes.

Q: Your Honor, I'd like these minutes marked for identification.

THE COURT: Very well, mark them.

Q: Read page 35 of these minutes to yourself, Mr. Witness, and when you are finished, I'll ask you other questions. (Hands the Deposition transcript to the witness.)

A: I've read it.

Q: Did you give those answers to those questions?

A: Yes, I guess I did.

Q: I offer the page in evidence, Your Honor.

THE COURT: No objection? Received in evidence.

At this point, the cross-examiner sits, prepared to read those minutes to the jury during Summation. You, the reader, have witnessed a total foul-up of good Cross-examination material. The jury doesn't know the significance of what occurred any more than you, the reader, do right this moment. By the time Summation comes along, they may have already forgotten that meaningless Cross-examination or, worse yet, formed an unfavorable opinion about your client's case. The able cross-examiner would have ripped into the witness, and brought any inconsistency to the jury's attention, precisely focusing the picture for jury scrutiny.

17.08 Focus Is Very Important

It is of the utmost importance that the jury's focus, thus, it's developing opinion, as it hears the unfolding evidence, be properly formed favorably to your cause at the first possible moment.

This is a new concept, one we haven't discussed before. Each piece of evidence has a tendency to influence the jury. You don't know exactly which one

is going to move one or the other of the jurors. Thus, when you have significant information, it is foolish indeed to be content to fold that information,
put it in your rucksack (backpack), and await Summation. To attempt to with-
hold good ammunition from the jury until Summation is to run the risk that
the jurors may make up their minds (although they're not supposed to) or
begin to form an opinion unfavorable to your client's case because you've been
holding significant information from them in order to have a spectacular Summation. Your Adversary, meanwhile, may feed them what he or she thinks is
salient and significant and may steal a march on having the jury think favorably toward his or her case. This may happen not because they have the better
case, but because you didn't help the jury form the proper perspective.

Get the pieces of the mosaic formed out in the open, in front of the jury.
Let them see and hear it happen. Summation should be a recapitulation of
what occurred during the trial, not a one-armed paperhanger's show.

17.09 The Proper Use

The far better approach for the cross-examiner in the last example would be
the following:

> Q: You say the light was green in your favor when you were approach-
> ing the intersection of Main Street and 10th Avenue?
>
> A: That's right.
>
> Q: You're sure about that?
>
> A: Yes.
>
> Q: Do you remember testifying under oath at a Deposition on Sep-
> tember 12, 1976?
>
> A: Yes.
>
> Q: Do you remember these questions being asked and giving these
> answers; please wait until I read both the questions and the an-
> swers, and then I'll ask you another question.

(You now read aloud the following.)

> Q: "Question: What street were you driving on?"
>
> A: "Answer: Main Street, approaching 10th Avenue."

Q: "Question: Was there a traffic light you could see at that point?"

A: "Answer: I couldn't see it. A tree blocked my view."

Q: "Question: When you couldn't see the traffic light, did you slow down?"

A: "Answer: No."

Q: "Question: Did you ever see the traffic light before you reached the intersection?"

A: "Answer: Yes, just before I reached it."

Q: "Question: What color was the light when you first saw it?"

A: "Answer: It just turned red."

Q: Do you remember, Mr. Witness, being asked those questions and giving those answers?

A: It must have been green before it turned red, right?

Q: Do you remember swearing under oath that you either didn't see the light or, when you did, before reaching the intersection, it turned red?

A: Yes.

Q: Was that the truth?

A: (Long pause—no answer.)

Q: I have no further questions.

Now the jury is focused. It can listen to the rest of the case more intelligently; the witness stands in a far different light now from what he did after the first example of his Cross-examination.

Don't let your Adversary build a fortification, don't let the witness erect a set of facts that you later have to tear down. If you destroy the enemy's bulwarks at every occasion, Summation should be an easy exercise of reminding the jury of all the failed attempts of your Adversary. You should not attempt to undo a bad impression at Summation. Rather, Summation should be a thorough recapitulation of all the devastating evidence that you brought to the jury's attention *during* the trial. Do not think the above illustration of what not to do is naive or insulting. In the midst of battle, while on your feet, you can easily *think* you did something effectively, but your cerebration was not put into words or action before the jury. It is still inside your head. Neither wishing nor thinking something makes it so. Discipline yourself to actually, and mechanically, like a pilot, use a checklist to be sure you did everything you should have.

17.10 Checklist for Prior Oath Inconsistency

1. Prior statement under oath
2. Inconsistent with present testimony
   a. mark the document for identification
3. Inquire as to recollection of prior testimony under oath
   a. as to date
   b. as to place or occasion
4. Read both question(s) and answer(s) to witness
5. Inquire whether the witness recalls such questions and giving such answers
6. Inquire whether facts of prior statement are correct . . .
7. . . . and present testimony in error
   a. if memory of events was better then than it is now
8. Inquire through court if Adversary concedes you read the transcript exactly as it appears

18.

Prior Handwritten or Signed Inconsistency—Not Under Oath

18.01 Handwriting or Signature Required

A prior inconsistent statement not made under oath can still be used for direct confrontation of the witness you cross-examine if, in fact, the prior statement was signed by the witness; or, if not signed, was at least made out in the witness's own handwriting.

Naturally, as with any prior inconsistent statement, the quintessential ingredient before undertaking Cross-examination based on such prior statement is that the statement *must actually be inconsistent with, or contradictory of,* the present trial testimony.

18.02 How to Use Such Statement

Once you've determined that an inconsistency between the trial testimony and a prior written or printed statement of the witness actually exists, you must then establish the authenticity of the prior document by having the witness identify his or her signature or handwriting. Thereafter, you must establish whether the witness recalls writing or signing such statement on the particular occasion it was made; i.e., immediately after the incident, or at the police station, or when an investigator interviewed the witness at home two months later. You must also establish that the reason that the information was written or signed was to record the fact of the event for the future; that when the statement was given, it was given truthfully; that (if only signed) the witness read the statement before signing it. You must then establish the prior statement, and, that the present testimony is inconsistent therewith. You must then attempt to show that the present testimony is not as accurate as the prior statement.

18.03 Establishing the Writing

Obviously, the *sine qua non,* in order to use a prior inconsistent statement in the handwriting of or signed by the witness, is to establish the fact that the document is, in fact, in the handwriting of or signed by the witness. Without that single ingredient being established, you have a document which cannot be used to cross-examine the witness directly. *You may be able to use another method to cross-examine with such statement, if it qualifies as a prior inconsistent statement made to a third person* (see Chapters 19 and 20, infra).

18.04 Laying the Foundation

The following are examples of preliminary examinations to establish the authenticity of a prior inconsistent statement, either (a) in the witness's handwriting, although it contains no signature, or (b) typed or handwritten by someone, and signed by the testifying witness.

(After having the exhibit marked for identification)

Q: I show you this document, Defendant's Exhibit B for Identification, and ask you if this is written in your handwriting.

A: (The witness begins to read the document.)

Q: It's not necessary for you to read the document at this time. The question is, is that document written in your handwriting?

A: Yes.

If the document is not made out in the handwriting of the witness, but rather in the handwriting of an investigator, a police officer, or someone else; or is typewritten, but contains what purports to be the witness's signature, then you inquire as follows:

Q: I show you this document, Defendant's Exhibit B for Identification, and ask you if that is your signature which appears at the bottom.

A: I didn't write this out.

Q: Do you know who did?

A: Not off the top of my head.

Q: In any event do you recognize the signature at the bottom as your own?

A: Yeah, that's my signature.

Now you are in a position to begin to utilize the prior inconsistent statement to discredit the witness.

18.05 Using the Written or Signed Inconsistency

On Direct testimony, the witness testified that he saw the defendant, on a ladder, cause certain canned goods to fall from a shelf in a grocery store onto the plaintiff's head. You now cross-examine:

Q: Who was present when you saw cans from the upper shelf fall on the plaintiff's head?

A: I heard the noise, turned, and saw the plaintiff just as he was hit with the cans and John Smith, the defendant, was on the ladder right next to him.

Q: You saw John Smith immediately as you turned after hearing the noise?

A: Absolutely.

CROSS-EXAMINER: Your Honor, I'd like to have this document marked for identification.

THE COURT: Very well, mark it.

Q: Mr. Witness, do you recognize this document, defendant's Exhibit B for Identification?

A: It's got my signature on the bottom.

Q: That is your signature?

A: Yes.

Q: You remember an investigator talking to you on April 15, 1997, at your home, about this case, and writing down what you said?

A: Yes.

Q: And when you signed this document, what is written on the pages before you, was already there?

A: Yes.

Q: And you read what the investigator wrote down before you signed your name on the bottom of the page?

A: Yes.

Q: In fact, there were some mistakes made by the investigator that were crossed out, and you put your initials next to the crossed out parts; isn't that correct?

A: Yes, those are my initials.

Q: Who wrote the initials which appear in the margins of this document?

A: I did.

Q: And when you read it, signed it, and initialed it, what you signed was an accurate account of what had occurred, wasn't it?

A: Yes.

Q: You weren't telling the investigator a phony story, were you?

A: No.

Q: And this statement was signed one week after the accident?

A: Yes.

Q: Was your memory of what occurred the day of the accident better one week after the accident or today, two years after the accident?

A: Better then, I'd say.

Q: May I have that document back, please. Do you recall that you told the investigator that, when you turned, you only saw the plaintiff on the floor and in your fright and concern you did not notice anyone else?

A: That's not correct. I did see the defendant.

Q: Would you read the second paragraph of this document? (You hand the document back to the witness.)

YOUR ADVERSARY: Your Honor, I object to Mr. Cross-examiner reading from a document not in evidence. Let Mr. Cross-examiner introduce the entire document in evidence.

CROSS-EXAMINER: Your Honor, this document deals with many other matters which are not relevant at this time. I do not offer the document in evidence. I merely wish to use it as a prior inconsistent statement. The witness has already identified the signature as his own.

THE COURT: Mr. Adversary, the document need not be introduced in evidence. You can introduce it on your own case if you see fit.

Q: Have you read the document?

A: Yes.

Q: And didn't you previously say to the investigator who visited you, that, in your fright and concern for the plaintiff, you did not pay attention to anyone else?

A: Yes.

Q: Did you not also say that you rushed over to help the plaintiff and that Mr. Smith, the defendant, came over and was also helping?

A: Yes.

Q: And isn't that the way it actually happened?

A: Not the way I recall it happening.

Q: Your memory of this was better, though, on April 15, 1997, was it not?

A: I guess it was.

18.06 Significantly Different from Use of a Statement Under Oath

Notice that, while still dealing with prior inconsistent statements, the use of a statement made under oath is quite different from one written or signed by the witness. In the oath statement, you ordinarily have questions and answers which must be read to the witness and he or she must then be asked if he recalls the questions being asked and giving the answers. In the written or signed statement by the witness, there are no questions or answers to be read, but rather an entire statement. In addition, you must either let the witness first read the handwritten or signed prior statement, then question the witness as to its contents; or, you must introduce the statement in evidence and read it—with the inconsistency it contains—to the jury. Ordinarily, as previously indicated, this document is NOT evidence in chief, but rather, intended only to affect the credibility of the witness. Thus, the court may refuse your offer of the document into evidence, and your use of it shall be limited to questioning the witness about the prior statement in order to test the accuracy and credibility of the witness.

As outlined in the above, excerpted, sample Cross-examination, however, the prior inconsistent statement need not be introduced in evidence in order to be utilized on Cross-examination. This holds true for both a prior statement under oath as well as a statement written or signed by the witness. And you may very well NOT want to introduce the document in evidence. Oftentimes, such a statement contains matters in addition to the prior inconsistency which you do not want the jury to see. There are times when you do wish the document, in toto, to be before the jury. If the document is strongly in your favor, or if the witness denies the inconsistency, it may become important for you to have the document introduced in evidence for later reference, or for tangible evidence of the inconsistency.

18.07 Introducing the Prior Inconsistent Document into Evidence

Having had the witness identify the handwriting or the signature as his or her own, you then establish the time, place, and occasion when such statement was made, and may offer the document into evidence. The court may allow the same into evidence. In the event that the court rules that the document is not allowed into evidence, you are not curtailed from using the document to question the witness.

18.08 The Reason the Document May Not Be Admitted into Evidence

Although the document is in the handwriting or is signed by the witness, thus qualifying it proper for introduction into evidence—as contrasted with a prior inconsistency recorded by a third person, but not signed by the witness—is that the document is not trial testimony, therefore, not evidence in chief. It is meant to affect the credibility, the accuracy, of the trial testimony. However, this particular type of statement actually straddles the line of admissible/inadmissible evidence, and the court may very well admit the same into evidence.

18.09 Use It Even If It Is Not in Evidence

Whether the document is or is not in evidence, it may be used to affect the credibility of the witness. This is done by questioning the witness about the document, laying a foundation for the prior inconsistent statement made by the witness concerning the facts of the case being heard by the jury. It is advisable not to coldly read a document to the jury, but rather to establish its foundation and the significance of the document with preliminary questions so that the inconsistency has some meaning.

For example, you have a witness on the stand who has testified that he saw your client on a fire escape leading away from the scene of a crime. You have in your hand a statement made to a police officer who was canvassing the area after the crime, in which the witness said he could not identify the man on the fire escape because he did not have a chance to see the man's face. You should inquire as follows:

> Q: Mr. Witness, you have said to the jury that Mr. Defendant is the man who you saw on the fire escape on the occasion in question?
>
> A: Yes.
>
> Q: Do you remember a police officer coming to your house to interview you on the very day of the crime, on the 15th of April, 1997?
>
> A: Yes, I remember.
>
> Q: And do you remember that, at that time, the police officer asked you certain questions about what you saw earlier that day?
>
> A: Yes.
>
> CROSS-EXAMINER: Your Honor, I would like this document marked for identification.
>
> THE COURT: Mark it defendant's Exhibit B for identification.

Q: I show you defendant's Exhibit B for identification and ask you if you recognize the signature on the bottom of it?

A: It's my signature.

Q: In fact, there are various mistakes made in the writing of the document, and there are initials next to the mistakes and the crossings out. Who wrote those initials?

A: I did.

Q: You read this document before you signed it and initialed it, did you not?

A: Yes.

Q: And, on the bottom, is that your signature?

A: Yes, it's mine.

Q: And that statement was true, at the time you signed it, wasn't it?

A: Yes.

Q: And didn't you say to the police officer at that time, and isn't it contained in that document, that you could not identify the man on the fire escape because you never had a chance to see the man's face?

A: Did I say that?

Q: That's the question. Perhaps the document, if you read it, will refresh your memory.

A: (He reads) That's what it says.

CROSS-EXAMINER: Your Honor, I offer the document in evidence.

THE COURT: Show it to Mr. Adversary. Any objection?

ADVERSARY: I do object, Your Honor, as being improper use of a prior statement.

THE COURT: No, I think it's proper. The witness has identified the signature as his own. Received.

CROSS-EXAMINER: Your Honor, at this time, I'd like to read part of this document to the jury.

ADVERSARY: Your Honor, if Mr. Cross-examiner is going to read from the exhibit, he should read all of it.

THE COURT: It's actually not necessary to read any of it to the jury. The document is in evidence. If there's a portion, however, that Mr. Cross-examiner doesn't read, and you want it read, I'll permit you to read it to the jury. Proceed.

CROSS-EXAMINER: I'm reading from Defendant's Exhibit B, now in evidence, which reads, in part, "I was in my apartment. I heard a noise on the fire escape. When I looked out the window, I saw a man going up to the next floor. I didn't get to see what he looked like, because he was already higher than my window."

Q: (To the witness) You did say to the police officer on the same day of the incident that you did not get to see what the man on the fire escape looked like because he was already higher than your window?

A: I guess I did.

Q: And that was true, was it not? You didn't see the man's face because he was already higher than your window when you looked out?

A: (The witness shrugs.)

CROSS-EXAMINER: I have no further questions, Your Honor.

18.10 Reminder Concerning Introduction into Evidence

(a) The document that you wish to use to cross-examine a witness as a prior inconsistent statement, whether that document be a prior statement under oath, a prior handwritten document, or one which has been merely subscribed by the witness, need not be introduced in evidence in order to use the same for Cross-examination.

(b) If you do wish to introduce the document in evidence, you need not read it to the jury at the time of introduction. However, in keeping with the concept of getting the evidence before the jury in order to form the minds of the jury, I strongly recommend that you do. If the document is significant enough to be introduced into evidence, it's significant enough for you to read to the jury and hammer home the point right then and there.

(c) When you do read from the document, you do NOT have to read the entire document. You can read as much of it as you desire. Your Adversary may object. The court may require you to read the entire document. But properly, you could read only the portions that relate to the inconsistency to the jury.

(d) Your Adversary can read the rest, any, all, or none of the rest of the document to the jury.

18.11 Only a Portion of the Document Can Be Introduced

As previously indicated, there are times when a document contains not only an inconsistency that you wish to have before the jury, but other extraneous, inflammatory, even damaging, material which should not be introduced into evidence. In this situation, you can request of the court that your introduction be limited to a particular portion of the prior statement. This is quite proper as the document is not evidence in chief. Even if introduced, it is only proof of the inconsistency and the tendency of that prior inconsistency to affect the credibility of the witness. Thus, the document may be introduced in limited version, redacted, for the limited purpose of affecting credibility.

Ordinarily, there is no difficulty eliminating extraneous material in the statement, as you can use blank paper to form a mask over the unwanted portion of the statement, having the clerk or someone on your staff copy the document so that only the pertinent part is showing, then admitting only the wanted document in evidence. You can, to save time, merely mask the portion necessary for the witness to see, then later, when the document is copied, substitute the excised version in place and stead of the original. The original may also be marked as a court's exhibit for preservation in the event of an appeal. You must be careful when handling a document that contains, in addition to the inconsistent statement, other damaging information. You may find yourself in the embarrassing position of attempting to offer only a portion of the document, and have your Adversary object, wanting the entire document in evidence. If the court insists that only the full document or nothing goes in, you may find yourself saying, in front of the jury, that you do not want the document in evidence. This may create, in the minds of the jury, that you are hiding something, that there is damaging material in the document, or in some other way diminish the significance of the document.

Thus, you have to weigh carefully if the entire document should be offered in evidence, or if you should only use it to affect credibility without the necessity of introducing any part of the document.

18.12 When the Witness Denies the Writing Is His or Hers

It is conceivable that the witness may deny that the signature on the document is his or her own, or deny that the handwriting in which the document is made out is his or her own. This can be a very serious problem as the identification of the writing is essential to an examination based upon a prior inconsistent statement allegedly written, or at least signed, in the handwriting of the witness.

Where, however, the document was made out by a third person, i.e., a police officer, an investigator, and only signed by the witness, when the witness denies that the signature is his own, you may treat the document as a prior inconsistent statement made to a third person and proceed to laying the foundation to bring in the third person to testify that the witness did indeed make such statement, exactly as it appears on the document. Where the document contains a typewritten or handwritten statement, allegedly made out by the witness, and the witness has denied signing the statement or the handwriting in which the statement is written, you have a very serious problem which must first be resolved by other proofs before you can further cross-examine the witness based on that statement.

18.13 Excerpt by an Expert

Sometimes just the sight of a prior statement that the witness has previously made and signed is enough to cause the witness to remember things that he or she is trying not to remember. The following is an excerpt of well-known Trial Advocate James M. LaRossa of New York cross-examining Dominic (Fat Dom) Borghese in a prosecution in Richmond County, New York. Mr. Borghese is a wily, uncooperative witness, trying at every step to foil Mr. LaRossa's questions. Mr. LaRossa gives you a fine example of staying with the witness, and working, working, working. See the following Cross-examination by Mr. LaRossa.

> Q: Have you ever met Detective Rauchet? Is that name familiar to you?
>
> A: Yeah.

Q: When did you meet him?

A: He came to pick me up at Allenwood.

Q: Brought you here to Staten Island?

A: Yes.

Q: By the way, when they brought you here to Staten Island and charged you, they put you in Atlantic Avenue?

A: Correct.

Q: And you didn't like Atlantic Avenue, did you?

A: No.

Q: Atlantic Avenue is a tough place?

A: Oh, yeah.

Q: Tough place to do time, right?

A: Yes.

Q: Not like Allenwood, right?

A: No.

Q: Did that help you make the decision that you should become a righteous man and cooperate?

MR. DRURY: Objection.

THE COURT: Overruled.

Q: Sir?

A: I don't believe so.

Q: Atlantic Avenue didn't help?

A: No.

Q: Did you tell Mr. Rauchet that your wire rooms made a profit of $310,000 a week?

A: No.

Q: I'm sorry, $310,000 for a ten-week period which would mean $31,000 a week?

A: Did I tell him that?

Q: Yes?

A: No.

Q: By the way, you loved to bet baseball, didn't you?

A: Yes.

Q: You would bet as much as how much? What was the biggest bet you have ever made?

A: $40,000, fifty.

Q: Didn't you make an $80,000 bet, on a game once?

A: I don't remember it, but it's possible.

Q: Do you remember $50,000?

A: I really don't remember exactly 50, but it might have went that high.

Q: Sir, did you ever tell a federal agent when you were being interviewed that you never made or lost any big monies from these bets?

A: Never made or lost? I don't understand that.

Q: In effect that they were small bets. Did you ever tell them your bets were small, tell a federal agent?

THE COURT: Do you want to specify who and where please?

Q: Do you remember being interviewed by a probation officer?

A: Once, yeah.

Q: When?

A: Cadman Plaza, I believe.

Q: Do you remember his name?

A: No, I don't.

Q: Do you remember when it was?

A: When I took the guilty pleas, when we made the deal.

Q: When was that?

A: Before 1994, 1993.

THE COURT: (to the jury) Let me explain something just briefly. Although the witness testified he was never on probation, sometimes a representative of the Probation department will prepare a report for a judge in aid of sentence, I guess that's what this might be, and Cadman Plaza would be a federal report to a federal judge prior to sentence.

Q: Do you remember, sir, being interviewed by that agent?

A: I was interviewed by a probation officer, yeah, with a lawyer there.

Q: Do you remember that you knew that that interview with the probation officer would result in a probation report?

A: Yes.

Q: And did you know that that report would go in front of a judge by the name of Sifton?

A: Yes.

Q: And did you know that Judge Sifton might very well use that to decide what your sentence would be? You knew that, didn't you?

A: The information I gave?

Q: Yes?

A: Yeah.

Q: Any question in your mind about it?

A: No.

Q: Did you tell that probation officer, sir, that you have never won or lost substantial sums of money gambling?

A: I might have, I don't remember saying it, but I might have.

Q: Is that true?

A: Never won or lost substantial? No, it's not true.

Q: That's a lie, right?

A: Yes.

Q: And if you told that to him, it would be a lie, right?

A: Yes.

Q: Let me show you what's been marked DB-127 please, and go to page 12. You have page 12?

A: I'm looking for it. (Perusing.) Yes.

Q: You have it?

A: Yes, I do.

Q: Do you see the paragraph number 48, entitled mental and emotional health?

A: Right.

Q: Do you remember that?

A: I read it.

Q: Did you tell that probation officer, sir, that you never won or lost substantial sums of money gambling, did you tell him that?

A: If I signed that paper, then I did.

Q: Sir, did you tell them that?

A: I don't recall.

Q: Well, sir, after this report was completed, was it given to you?

A: Maybe it was, I really don't remember.

Q: Maybe anything could have happened. Did you read that report?

A: Yeah, I just read this.

Q: No, did you read it before you were sentenced?

A: I don't remember, I don't think so.

Q: You don't think so. Do you remember Judge Sifton asking you whether you read that report?

A: Yeah, I might have said I did.

Q: You mean you lied to Judge Sifton?

A: I might have said I did and didn't read it. I'm sure it didn't mean
     nothing if I read it.

Q: Did you know, sir, that there is a federal crime, Title 18 Section
     1001, any time you lie to a federal agent or officer or employee it's
     a five-year felony, do you know that?

A: No, I didn't.

Q: You didn't know that?

A: No, I didn't.

Q: Did you think you were committing a crime when you lied to the
     probation officer?

MR. DRURY: Objection.

THE COURT: Overruled. Well, if you said that to the probation officer
that you never won or lost a lot of money, would that have been the
truth?

THE WITNESS: No, your Honor.

Q: Did you lie to that probation officer?

THE COURT: Do you remember saying that?

THE WITNESS: I don't remember saying it, but if I did it would be a lie.

Q: Do you remember telling the judge that you read that probation
     report?

A: No, I don't remember that.

Q: You don't remember that?

A: I didn't even talk to the judge, that's why I had a lawyer.

Q: You didn't answer any questions that the judge posed to you, sir?
     You don't remember that?

A: As far as the agreement, I don't remember, no.

Q: Do you remember when you pled guilty?

A: Yes, I do.

Q: Do you remember the judge asking you questions?

A: Yes.

Q: Do you remember the judge asking you whether you were taking any kind of medicine? Do you remember that?

A: Yes.

Q: Do you remember him asking you what you did in terms of the crime?

A: Yes.

Q: Do you remember answering those questions?

A: Yes.

Q: Do you remember going for sentence, sir?

A: Yes, I remember.

Q: Do you remember the judge asking you questions at the sentence?

A: Yes, I just said yes.

Q: That was the plea I asked you about before, this is the sentence?

A: Okay.

Q: Do you remember him asking you questions at the sentence?

A: If you refresh my memory.

Q: Do you remember whether he asked you if you were satisfied with the lawyer you were standing next to and the representation you had obtained, do you remember that?

A: Yes.

Q: Do you remember him asking you whether you had anything to say in terms of your sentence and what you were going to receive?

A: Yes.

Q: Do you remember that?

A: Yes.

Q: Do you remember him asking you whether or not you read that probation report and was there any errors in it?

A: I don't remember that, but if I answered him, I answered him, I don't remember.

Q: So if you said that you read it, it would have been a lie, right?

A: Right.

Q: Would you have lied to Judge Sifton if it was in your best interest that day?

A: Could be.

There is a more fulsome example of Mr. LaRossa's Cross-examination of this witness in the Supplement Section at the end of this book.

19.

Prior Inconsistent Oral Statement Made to a Third Person Reduced to Writing by the Third Person

19.01 Defined

Another form of inconsistent statement which can be utilized on Cross-examination is a prior inconsistency that was made orally to a third person, and that third person thereafter reduced said statement to writing. These statements may take the form of an oral description of an event made to a police officer at the scene of an accident, thereafter incorporated in the police officer's written official report; a statement made to a hospital attendant or nurse, thereafter incorporated into the hospital record; a statement made to an employer concerning the happening of an industrial accident, again being made part of a report by the employer; or any similar situation of a statement being made to any third person, who thereafter reduces said statement to writing.

19.02 Completely Different from Oath or Handwritten Inconsistency

While prior inconsistencies made orally to a third person are, indeed, prior inconsistencies, they are completely different from both a prior inconsistency made under oath or one made in the handwriting of the testifying witness.

As a result, the method of using an inconsistency that was made to a third party on Cross-examination is completely different from the methods to use the already discussed inconsistencies. The most significant difference is

215

that a statement previously made to a third person cannot be used directly to confront the testifying witness who has denied having made such prior statement. The reason you cannot use this type of statement to directly confront the witness is because this statement was recorded *by someone else, by a third party.*

In other words, this type of statement was put into writing or typewritten by someone else. It is, therefore, the statement of that other person—not the testifying witness. Think about that. The police officer, hospital attendant, or whoever made out the third party statement is not the witness. Where a third party created the report, it is only the third party who can be questioned about the making of the report. If, of course, the witness admits that he or she has made such prior inconsistent statement, you can pursue the conflict, the inconsistency, before the jury. You shall then be able to have full range to accomplish as much as you can accomplish with that portion of your Cross-examination. However, for the most part, witnesses on the stand are reluctant to admit that their present testimony is erroneous, or at least inconsistent with prior versions of the same event. This reluctance shall require you to use the inconsistency made to a third party in the manner described herein.

19.03 It Is Actually Hearsay

If the testifying witness denies having made a prior inconsistent statement to a third person, you may not directly confront or cross-examine the testifying witness with the fact that a third person attributes a prior, different and inconsistent statement to the witness. The reason for that is, without the stamp of authenticity of oath or the witness's own handwriting, a statement made to a third person, even where that third person had reduced the same to writing, runs full afoul of the hearsay rule.

Simply put, the writing of the third person, albeit that the writing indicates that the testifying witness made a prior inconsistent statement, is *not* the writing, the report, nor either technically or actually, the statement of the testying witness. The report is the report of the third person. How then can you confront the testifying witness directly with a report made by some other person? For example, a witness to an accident has told the police officer who responded that he, the witness, did not see the accident happen. The police officer writes such statement in his police report, properly and clearly attributing the statement to the witness. On the stand, the witness to the event testifies on Direct that he *did* actually see the accident occur. On Cross-examination, you may ask the witness whether or not, on prior occasions, the witness made inconsistent, contradictory statements concerning his view of the accident. But the witness denies having made such prior statement.

The Rules of Evidence, particularly the rule prohibiting the use of hearsay, as well as logic, do not permit you to confront the witness with the actual writing, questioning the testifying witness about a report made out by a third person. The testifying witness may simply respond with one or all of the following: I didn't say that; that's not my report; I don't know what that third person is talking about; I never made such a statement.

You may have a witness give in-court testimony that he or she was an actual eyewitness to the event and deny outright ever having made the purported prior inconsistent statement. The conflicting written report of the police officer is hearsay to the testifying witness, for it is the writing and the statement of a third person, not that of the testifying witness—even though the police officer's report attributes the prior statement to the testifying witness. Thus, you cannot directly cross-examine the witness concerning the content of the police officer's report; you *cannot* do anything more than that you've already done, that is, ask the witness if he or she made such a statement to the police officer. However, your quest does not end there. No, indeed. It merely begins there. For the asking of the question as to whether or not the witness made such a prior inconsistent statement to a third person, is merely the first step in laying the foundation for the use of this inconsistent statement.

A denial of having made the statement is the part of the foundation necessary to permit you *to call the third person to the witness stand* in order that the third person can give his or her account of the taking of the oral (inconsistent) statement from the testifying eyewitness.

Ordinarily, the third person is a disinterested person, independent of the litigation who is not likely to deviate from the statement that was previously made, particularly as it is in his or her handwriting or official report. Thus, this type of inconsistent statement, while different from the previously discussed inconsistencies, may be more cumbersome, but is no less an effective weapon for Cross-examination. Remember, however, unlike the statements covered in previous chapters, those which permit you to directly interrogate the witness about his or her own prior inconsistency, the inconsistency made to a third person requires a far different approach and method to use.

19.04 The Written Statement of the Third Person Must Be Introduced Through That Third Person

While you cannot use the oral statement made to a third person directly to cross-examine the testifying, denying witness, there is a method of utilizing such prior statement if the proper foundation is laid to call that third person to the stand to testify about the taking of the prior statement.

19.05 Laying the Foundation

An example of the method of using a prior inconsistent oral statement to a third person, which statement was reduced to writing by the third person, is in order.

Background

This is an excerpt from a homicide trial in New York County Supreme Court. The testifying witness had made many prior statements to police officers who the witness thought were, at the time, violating their duty by accepting bribes to cover up the witness's illegal activities. Actually, the police officers were making reports of every conversation had with the witness, and these reports were turned over to defense counsel for Cross-examination purposes after the witness's Direct testimony. Amongst the statements turned over was a report in which the witness had described to two police officers how he, the witness, had murdered someone (not the subject in the prosecution in the case on trial). The testifying witness, when asked by the cross-examiner, denies ever having made such a statement to any police officer.

The following report of the police officer serves two purposes. It becomes, not only a prior inconsistent statement of the testifying witness, but, at the same time, serves to further undercut the reliability of the witness by showing a propensity of the witness to vicious and criminal acts and an immoral character, which is a subject we shall explore in more depth infra.

The Police Report Says

"Clark met with us in the Two Steps Down Inn on the evening of April 15, 1972, at or about 8 P.M. It was a meeting to collect the money for the week. He invited us to have drinks with him, which we did. While speaking generally, the witness related to us how he had murdered a person known as John Smith, in Florida, in 1991. Clark told us that John Smith was involved in a scheme to bankrupt a chewing gum business with Clark, but that since the police were then investigating the business, Smith was very nervous and had said he would not lie to the police if they questioned him. Clark told us how he lured Smith to Florida on a fishing trip. That when out of sight of land (Key Largo) on the boat, he shot Smith in the chest with a .38 caliber revolver. He shot twice. When he went to grab Smith by the arm to lift him over the side, Smith grabbed Clark. At that point, Clark took a fishing knife he used to clean fish and stabbed Smith repeatedly in the chest until the knife broke in Smith's chest. He then picked up a gasoline can and beat Smith over the head with the can. Afterward, Jones who had also come from New York to Florida with Clark and Smith, and who had been steering the boat, took a .22 caliber rifle and shot Smith in the head. The two of them, then, with handcuffs, tied Smith to a heavy weight on the boat, and threw Smith overboard.

"Clark said that the water was so clear that he could see Smith on the bottom, after he was thrown overboard, with his eyes still open. That he had nightmares for months thinking about Smith in the water.

"I questioned Clark as much as I could, but could get no better location for Smith's dumping site than somewhere off Key Largo. We indicated that we thought he was making the entire story about Smith up, but he swore it was true.

"Further investigation from official police files reveal that one John Smith of the address given by Clark reportedly left for Washington in 1991 and has not been seen or heard from since."

Det. M. Johnson.
Countersigned: Lt. John Official

Standing, armed with this police report, ready to cross-examine, you can rely on one thing for certain. The Adverse Witness is not likely to admit to you or the jury, on the stand, that he is guilty of murder. If he does, of course, you're substantially on your way to discrediting him. However, if he runs true to form, you can question him about the statement and the murder in Florida, which he shall likely deny. Such denial shall create the inconsistency with the statement he made to the police.

In addition to the fact that you, as cross-examiner, can fairly well count on the testifying witness to deny his complicity in a homicide, you can fairly well rely on the fact that the disinterested police officer who made the foregoing official report in fulfillment of his official duties, who signed the same and had it countersigned by his superior, is very unlikely to testify that the report is inaccurate, untruthful, or in any fashion a deviation from actual events. This proposition is highly reasonable since a denial of the report by the officer would not only jeopardize the officer's credibility, but his job. Such a denial would indicate that the officer made out the official report with less than absolute rectitude.

Now, although you have substantial ammunition in your hand to show that the witness made a prior statement totally inconsistent with his trial posture of not being a murderer, and, therefore, to show that he is a highly immoral character as well as a liar—all to be buttressed by the rectitude and authority of the police department through the person of the detective who made the report—you must still lay a proper foundation or the judge will not permit you later to call the detective to the stand to testify about the prior statement.

19.06 Proper Foundation

In order to lay the necessary foundation to use this type of inconsistent statement, you are required to give the witness sufficient information to refresh his or her recollection, to recall his or her mind to the time, the place, and the person to whom the alleged statement was made, and you must also refresh the witness's recollection as to the content of the alleged statement. If you do not do all of the above in a specified fashion, you shall not have laid a proper foundation, and the court shall not permit you to call the third person to the stand to establish the prior statement. Thus, you must ask the witness the questions which fully give the witness the opportunity to be apprized of and to be reminded of the prior alleged statement he or she made, thereby giving the witness an opportunity to affirm or deny that he or she made such prior statement. If the witness agrees that he or she made the statement, then you have brought the inconsistency to the attention of the jury, and that is the end of that.

If, however, after you have duly provided sufficient foundation to remind the witness of the time, place, and content of the alleged prior inconsistency, the witness denies having made the statement, then you shall be permitted later to call the third person to the stand to testify about the prior statement.

NOTE: After laying the necessary predicate for the calling of a third person to whom a purported prior oral inconsistency was made, you do not immediately call the third party to the stand to give the lie to the Adverse Witness. Everything in a trial has a proper order. At the moment, obviously, because you are cross-examining an Adverse Witness proffered by your Adversary, you are on your Adversary's case. You have to wait until your case to call the third party witness to the stand as your witness. However, don't fret. Like the mosaicist you are becoming, if you work carefully and diligently, all the pieces of the trial mosaic shall be ready for your convincing Summation.

19.07 An Example of Laying the Foundation

Q: Do you know Detective Larry Johnson?

A: I do.

Q: Did you ever meet with Detective Johnson at the Two Steps Down Inn?

A: Many times.

Q: Do you recall meeting with him on the 15th of April, 1997?

A: I might have.

Q: Did you ever tell Detective Johnson, at the Two Steps Down Inn, on April 15, 1997, that you had participated in the murder of an individual named Smith?

A: No.

NOTE: Be prepared for the answer that "yes" I did tell Detective Johnson that I murdered Smith. In case you get that answer, you have to be prepared to flesh out your examination in order to spread the harm or unreliability inherent in the witness admitting murder. In the event that you get a negative response, however, you go on.

Q: Did you tell Detective Johnson, at that time and place, that is, the Two Steps Down Inn on April 15th, 1997, that you had a scheme with Smith to bankrupt a chewing gum firm?

A: No.

Q: Did you tell Detective Johnson, at that time and place, that Smith told you he was going to tell the police everything he knew when they questioned him?

A: No.

Q: Did you tell Detective Johnson, at that time and place, that you lured Smith to Florida on a fishing trip?

A: I never did, no.

NOTE: *You cannot be asking the witness these questions by reading directly from the statement of Detective Johnson, for that, in addition to being hearsay, would be reading from something not in evidence. Thus, you have to remember the things that Detective Johnson's statement contains and ask the questions without reading from the statement. Surely, you are permitted, from time to time, to check your notes, in which, of course, you have Johnson's statement. But you cannot read from it, word for word, in front of the jury.*

NOTE: *Each denial to each of your specific questions,* eo instante, *creates another specific area about which to inquire of Detective Johnson when you call him to the stand. This is the reason to go through the statements in detail.*

Q: Did you tell Detective Johnson, and assume that all these questions relate to the same time and place, that is the Two Steps Down Inn, on April 15, 1997, did you tell Detective Johnson that you shot Smith with a .38 caliber revolver in the chest?

A: Absolutely not.

Q: Did you tell Detective Johnson at that time and place that thereafter, in attempting to throw Smith overboard, Smith grabbed your hand?

A: No.

Q: Did you tell Detective Johnson that you panicked and grabbed a scaling knife and began stabbing Smith in the chest many times?

A: No.

Q: Did you tell Detective Johnson at that time and place that the knife broke in Smith's chest?

A: No.

Q: Did you tell Detective Johnson that you then began to hit Smith in the head with a gasoline can?

A: No.

Q: Did you then tell Detective Johnson at the Two Steps Down Inn on April 15, 1997, that you then handcuffed Smith to a barbell and threw him overboard?

A: No.

Q: Did you then tell Detective Johnson at that time and place that you had nightmares for months because you could see Smith looking up through the water with his eyes open?

A: No.

Now you have laid the necessary predicate, you have set the stage for calling the third person (Detective Johnson) to the stand, having nailed down the witness's position firmly for the jury.

As indicated in Chapter One, the trial is like assembling a mosaic. The ultimate aim of Cross-examination is to form pieces of that mosaic which shall all be brought into sharp focus for the jury at Summation. Remember that the entire picture need not be put together in one continuous movement. In the case of the witness who has just now denied both the murder and ever having spoken to Detective Johnson about it, you must permit the witness to step down from the stand, the fuse on the bomb of the prior oral inconsistency set but, at the moment, unexploded.

At this point, your Adversary continues with his or her evidence in chief. You must bide your time until it is your turn to introduce evidence. Meanwhile, if there are any steps that must be taken to ensure the appearance of the third person, Detective Johnson, at the trial, such as a subpoena, or an order from the court to order the Prosecutor to produce Detective Johnson when you require him, you should undertake them immediately. When the appropriate moment arrives, you put the third person (here, Detective Johnson) on the stand.

19.08 The Third Person Inquiry

Q: Detective Johnson, by whom are you employed?

A: The Police Department, City of New York.

Q: And your assignment?

A: Vice Squad.

Q: How long have you been a detective?

A: Eleven years.

Q: And in 1997, did you know a person by the name of Harold Clark?

A: Yes.

Q: In reference to an official investigation?

A: Yes.

Q: Can you tell the court and jury about that investigation?

A: We were investigating prostitution, and we had reason to believe that Mr. Clark was involved. We questioned him. On that occasion, he suggested that he could make it worth my while if I cooperated with him, soft pedaled my investigation of him. I indicated to him that I would think about it. I reported the same to my superiors, and they indicated that I should make it appear that I was going along with him so that I could get further information which might otherwise be unavailable.

Q: And did you go along and work with Clark?

A: I made it appear that way.

Q: Did you take money from him?

A: I did, several times. Thereafter, I vouchered the money, and made a report each time that I did.

Q: So that you were just pretending to be taking a bribe from Clark?

A: That's right, sir.

Q: And did you meet with Clark on April 15, 1997?

A: I believe I did, sir.

Q: I show you this, which I have had marked defendant's Exhibit H for identification. I ask you if you know what this is?

A: It's a copy of a DD 5, a report which I turned in concerning Clark.

Q: Is your signature on the bottom of this document?

A: It is.

Q: And was this document, your report, also countersigned by some-one?

A: It was. By Lieutenant John Official.

Q: And was this report turned in as an official report in compliance with your official duties as a detective on the police force?

A: It was.

NOTE: *You own this witness, because he is not going to try to sidestep his own official report. You can play him like a harp—assuming you know how to play a harp.*

Q: And when you made the same out, you were making it out carefully and as accurately as you could, knowing that it was an official report?

A: Yes, sir.

Q: Did Clark tell you that a person named Smith had said he was going to tell all he knew to the police, if and when questioned about the chewing gum scheme?

A: He did.

Q: Did Clark tell you that he lured Smith to Key Largo, Florida, for a fishing trip?

A: I believe he did.

Q: Is there any doubt about the fact that he said that?

A: I'm not too sure about each thing he said. We met and spoke many times.

Q: Look at your report, defendant's Exhibit H for identification, Detective, and see if, after reading it, your memory is refreshed on that point.

A: (After reading) He did say that.

Q: Did he also say, Clark, that is, that when out of sight of land, he shot Smith with a .38 caliber pistol?

A: He did.

Q: Did he say, Clark say, that when attempting to throw Smith overboard, that Smith grabbed his hand?

A: He did, sir.

Q: Did Clark tell you that he then started to stab Smith in the chest with a scaling knife?

A: A fishing knife; yes, sir.

Q: Did Clark also say that the knife broke in Smith's chest?

A: Yes, sir.

Q: Did he tell you that he then started hitting him on the head with a gasoline can?

A: Yes.

Q: Did Clark also tell you that another person named Jones, on the boat, also from New York, shot Smith with a .22 caliber rifle?

A: Yes, I believe he did.

Q: Is there a question about that in your mind, Detective?

A: No, not really.

Q: Is there any doubt in your mind that Clark said these things to you?

A: That he said them? No, sir.

Q: Did Clark also say that he and this other person threw Smith overboard and that he was attached to a weight by handcuffs?

A: Yes, sir.

Q: Did he say he had nightmares for months after that, thinking about Smith with his eyes open on the bottom of the sea?

A: Yes, sir.

Q: Did there come a time when you told Clark that you doubted his story.

A: Yes, sir.

Q: Did Clark swear to you that the things he told you were true?

A: I'm not sure about that.

Q: Would you read your report and see if that refreshes your memory?

A: (After reading) I told him I didn't believe him and he swore that it was true, yes, sir.

You have now completed all the steps in the use of that prior inconsistent statement, and the credibility and reliability of the witness is squarely before the jury for its determination.

19.09 Checklist

To use a prior inconsistent oral statement made by the testifying witness to a third person, you must first:

1. apprize the witness on the stand of:
   a. where,
   b. when, and
   c. to whom a statement had previously been made.
2. inquire specifically of the testifying witness if he or she had ever said (whatever was said) to such a person, at such a time and place, and so on, thus establishing the witness's trial testimony.
3. call the third person to the witness stand to testify to the actual, original inconsistent statement.

20.

Oral, Unsworn, Prior Inconsistent Statements Made to Third Persons, Not Reduced to Writing

20.01 Prior Oral Statements Made at Any Prior Time

The final variation of a prior inconsistent statement is one that may take the form of an oral statement made to a third person, say to the previously mentioned police officer at the scene of an accident, the hospital attendant or doctor, or to any third person on any prior occasion, *which has never been memorialized in writing or into any sort of report.*

20.02 Different Again

This type of prior inconsistent oral statement must also be treated by the cross-examiner in different fashion from prior inconsistent statements under oath, or in the witness's writing, and, even, prior inconsistencies made to third persons that were thereafter memorialized in some fashion. The reason, of course, is that these inconsistencies have neither the indicia of reliability attached to a statement made under oath at a formal proceeding, nor the authenticity of one that has been handwritten or signed by the person who made it, nor even the unchangeable prospect of a statement made to a third person which was then and there memorialized by the third person in some fashion. In short, this type of prior inconsistency is the most unstable and volatile of all the prior inconsistencies. For, in addition to not having been made by the witness, it was not memorialized, and is therefore subject to the infirmity of memory, reliability, and credibility of the third person who heard it.

20.03 These Inconsistencies Cannot Be Used for Direct Confrontation

As with the prior oral inconsistency that was reduced to writing by the third person, these unmemorialized, oral inconsistencies cannot be used by the cross-examiner to directly confront the witness as you might do with a prior inconsistency made under oath or made in the handwriting of the witness. This inconsistency must be used in a fashion similar to the prior inconsistency made to a third person which was recorded, i.e., when you become aware of such a prior oral inconsistency, you must lay the proper foundation by asking the witness whether or not, on a particular day, at a particular place, to a particular person, he or she said whatever it is that comprises the inconsistency. If the witness admits the prior inconsistency, of course, then you have effectively brought out before the jury the possible unreliability or lack of credibility of the witness. If, on the other hand, the witness denies making such prior oral statement, you then proceed to those steps which are required to lay the proper foundation to bring forward the third person to testify as to the prior oral statement.

The reason that you may not directly confront the witness with the third person's version of what was said on a prior occasion is, obviously, that the witness on the stand has testified such oral statement was never made. As to the testifying witness, the purported recitation of a prior statement of the witness by the third person is hearsay. As such, the witness cannot be cross-examined about what someone else says the witness said. The only one who can be cross-examined—and that is the bottom-line test of admissibility—about the oral prior statement is the third person who alleges that the statement was made.

20.04 Statements to Third Persons Are Volatile

A word of caution concerning the use of unrecorded third person statements is necessary. Cross-examination based on unmemorialized, prior, inconsistent oral statements is more difficult and unquestionably more dangerous than other types of prior inconsistencies because of the very fact that the inconsistency has not been memorialized and is not, therefore, as unchanging as is a statement sworn, signed, or otherwise recorded.

The oral-only inconsistency is subject to the frailties of all verbal communication, including forgetfulness, variation, haziness, and even denial by the third person that such a statement was ever made. Thus, such non-recorded statement is assailable by your Adversary in far more ways than one which has been memorialized in a transcript, written down, or recorded, and is, therefore, a far more unknown, changing, insecure device. The statement that you are now dealing with is as volatile and unstable as nitroglycerine. It could be perfectly benign, yet it is subject to blow up in your face. Be sure of your third person and of what he or she will testify *before* you rest too much of your case on his or her anticipated testimony and before you get yourself totally committed to this line of Cross-examination. Once sure, however, this type of statement can be as effective a method of discrediting a testifying witness as any of the others already discussed.

20.05 Laying the Foundation for Oral Inconsistency

The method of laying a foundation for Cross-examination based on an un-memorialized oral inconsistency is similar to the foundation needed for the inconsistencies to third persons which had, in fact, been memorialized (see Chapter 19). Even though similar, however, the foundation is somewhat different from the foundation required for an inconsistency made under oath or in the handwriting of the third person. When you are aware that the testifying witness may have made a prior oral statement to a third person that is directly contradictory of the testimony you have just heard from the witness's own mouth on Direct, in order to use such prior oral inconsistency, you must:

1. remind the witness of the time, place, and person to whom something inconsistent to the trial testimony was said;
2. remind the witness of what he or she purportedly said that was inconsistent;
3. ask the witness whether he or she made such inconsistent statement; and
4. be ready to produce the third person who heard such inconsistency to testify.

20.06 Example of Foundation

An example of the foundation that must be laid in order to use such unrecorded, prior, inconsistent, oral statement made to a third person is as follows:

Background: The situation at hand is an accident where an eyewitness, immediately after the event, told a storekeeper at, or near, the scene of the accident something different from the Direct trial testimony of the eyewitness.

Q: You've testified on Direct examination that you saw the vehicle of the defendant go through a stop sign and crash directly into the side of the plaintiff's vehicle, isn't that right?

A: That's right.

Q: Do you recall, just after the accident, that you spoke to Mr. Mint, the owner of the hardware store in front of which the accident occurred?

A: I'm not sure if he is the owner.

Q: Whether the man you spoke to is the owner or not, you do recall speaking, just after the accident, to the man who worked in the hardware store, don't you?

A: Yes. He came out to see what happened, and we were talking while we waited for the police and the ambulance to arrive.

Q: So there's no question in your mind that you do remember speaking to the man, whether he owned the hardware store or not, who was working in the hardware store at the time of the accident.

A: No question.

Q: You discussed the accident with him as you waited, didn't you?

A: I don't know if we discussed it. We spoke about it, mentioned it. I mean, it was right there in front of the two of us.

Q: At that time and at that place, right after the accident, while you were in front of the hardware store, did you say to the man from the hardware store that you had been looking in the window of the store at the tools, and heard a big crash behind you, and you turned to see the cars for the first time?

A: Did I say that?

Q: That's the question; do you remember ever saying, immediately after the accident, to the man from the hardware store, that you were looking in the store window at the moment that the crash occurred?

A: I never said that.

The above constitutes the necessary predicate or foundation for your use, later, on your own case, of the hardware store owner who you expect to testify that the current witness told him that he had been looking in the store window, and did not, in fact, see the accident occur. To the impatient, that does not seem like a total destruction of the witness. You're right; it is not. However, you have laid the necessary predicate for the third party to be called—on your case—to testify to the oral inconsistency. This is the perfect example of the mosaic quality of the Cross-examination, and the case in general. You have formed the piece of the case, right in front of the jury, by establishing that this witness denies ever having made a contradictory-to-the-Direct statement. Later, you shall call the third person to whom the statement was made. Each piece, although widely separated in time and place during the trial, will ultimately fit together. Form each piece precisely, knowing what the next pieces shall be and what the ultimate argument to the jury is going to be. Remember, not all Cross-examination is dramatic, accompanied by drum rolls and bands blaring. Be more content with strong, effective, workperson-like Cross-examination that is precise, effective, and, ultimately, destructive.

20.07 The Third-Party Examination

Having completed the above foundation for the use of an unrecorded prior inconsistent oral statement made to a third person, in this case, the owner or worker from the hardware store, you must now produce the third person for testimony on your own case. It is unlikely that your Adversary is going to call the third party to the stand. If he or she does, so much the better, for you can cross-examine the third party about the contradictory statement of the former witness. If the Adversary does not call that third-person witness to the stand, then on your case in chief, or on your rebuttal, call that third-person witness to the stand solely for the purpose of affecting the credibility of the testifying eyewitness. When you have that third-person witness on the stand, your examination should be as follows:

Q: Sir, do you own the hardware store located at 54 Main Street?

A: Yes.

Q: And were you at your place of business on the 31st of May, 1997?

A: I was.

Q: Did an accident occur on that day, in the street in front of your store?

A: It did. Two cars crashed in the street right in front of my store.

Q: Did you see the accident yourself?

A: No, I did not.

NOTE: *By establishing this lack of eyewitness experience on the part of the store owner, you eliminate a potential witness through whom, on Cross-examination, your Adversary might establish his or her case.*

Q: Did you go out of your store at any time after the accident?

A: Sure. Right after the accident. I heard the noise and went out to see what happened.

Q: By the way, do you know Mr. Eyewitness?

A: Yes. I know him from around town. I've seen him many times around town.

Q: Did you see him on the day of the accident?

A: When I went outside, he was standing right in front of my store.

Q: Did you have a conversation with him?

A: Not much. I asked him what happened.

Q: Did Mr. Eyewitness say anything?

A: He said he didn't know exactly either. He said he was looking at the shovels in my window, it was springtime, you know; and he heard a crash behind him. When he looked, the cars had already crashed.

Q: This is what Mr. Eyewitness said to you as you stood outside your store?

A: Yes.

Q: Is there any question in your mind that that's what Mr. Eyewitness said?

A: Of course not, why should there be?

True, you did not give the big kill to the original witness while he or she was on the stand, or at least not the big, dramatic kill of the movies, nor did you instantly shove the big lie down the witness's throat. Yet, for the purposes of your client's case, you have effectively, ultimately, neutralized the eyewitness. Remember at summation all the pieces must be there, in evidence, having been put in place during the trial in order to put them together at summation. Keep in mind where you're going and make sure you touch all the bases on the way.

20.08 Be Sure of the Third Person's Testimony

It is essential, in this type of examination, that you first investigate and ferret out the prior statements of the witness. When you have carefully done this, and have found that the witness has made a prior inconsistent statement to a third person, you then should interview that third person to get a feel for his or her capacity to remember the prior statement, capacity to testify, capacity for truthfulness, etc. In other words, you do not want to put a witness on the stand cold, one to whom you have never spoken, or whose testimony remains a mystery to you. You could be very rudely surprised.

In fact, the best practice is always to treat the third-party witness in the same fashion as a direct eyewitness or any witness. Take a written statement from the prospective third-party witness, even a negative statement, about his or her recollection of the events, so that the third-person witness cannot have his or her memory suddenly refreshed by an eager Adversary and be transformed into a direct eyewitness. If you have taken a written statement from the third person that does not take the place of a memorialization of the original prior inconsistency of the testifying witness, of course. The inconsistency is still oral, still existing only in the mind of the third person. But, at least, it gives you some strength in your Cross-examination, knowing that the third party will not suffer amnesia or change of testimony after you put him or her on the stand. In addition, you shall be in a position to refresh the third person's recollection and keep the third person in line and from straying from his or her original statement to you, by showing the third person the written statement that he or she signed for you. Thus, be sure of the testimony of the third person, and try to have it nailed down before you put him or her on the stand to bolster your case. You want the third party's testimony to be a boost, not a knock on your case.

20.09 Checklist

1. Investigate and discover the prior inconsistency.
2. Be sure to interview the third person. Take a written statement.
3. When the original witness is on the stand, you must establish whether he or she recalls making a statement at:
   a. the time;
   b. the place;
   c. on the date;
   d. and to the third person (named or identified).
4. Ask the original witness if, on that occasion, to the specified third person, the following specific statement was made. Then specify the statement.
5. Upon a denial that such statement was made, you shall be in a position to produce the third person to testify.

20.10 Additional Commentary about Prior Inconsistencies

The preceding chapters have shown how to use prior inconsistent statements, whether sworn, written, or unwritten. Hugh Anthony Levine, a Trial Advocate of San Francisco, who was formerly an Assistant District Attorney of New York County, then an Assistant District Attorney in San Francisco, conducted a Cross-examination of a Federal Agent of the Department of Agriculture relating to a case charging a conspiracy to traffic in meat products which did not comply with USDA regulations. Three defendants moved to dismiss the indictment or to compel the government to abide by a cooperation agreement whereby the main defendant would receive a noncustodial sentence, and two others would not be charged.

At the evidentiary hearing, the Agent testified that there had been no firm agreement, and that the main defendant had cooperated without any promises whatever made by the Agents. The most significant aspect of Mr. Levine's Cross-examination is the use of an image projection device during the nonjury pre-trial hearing, enabling entire documents to be displayed to the court, the witness, and the prosecutor.

The use of this modern technique has a dual effect. First, the witness is confronted by the prior statements (in the Cross-examination, Mr. Levine relies on several of the various prior inconsistent statements discussed in previous chapters) entirely, projected on a screen. Moreover, the court can see the document at the same time. Psychologically, it creates an atmosphere where the witness cannot evade or escape as the document is looming in front of the judge who can readily grasp evasions, denials, and lack of candor by the witness at the very moment it is happening. This innovation of Mr. Levine's is something you should keep in mind. Naturally, such method could not be used before a jury, as the jury would be viewing a document not in evidence. See the following Cross-examination conducted by Mr. Levine.

Cross-Examination by Mr. Levine:

Q: When was the last time you did review those notes?

A: Hmm. Two months ago.

Q: Was it after you testified on Direct examination?

A: No.

Q: Well, if you don't mind I'll just ask you to peruse these four pages of notes. These are, first of all, agent Quinn's notes of the events of the day, March 26, 1993, at the Hershey residence, right?

A: They appear to be, yes.

Q: Just peruse them, please, for the time that it takes. (Pause)

MR. LEVINE: Your Honor, is that visible to you at this angle, or do I need to change the angle?

THE COURT: That's visible, but it's not clear enough to read.

MR. LEVINE: I mean, if the handwriting can be read, is the setup okay for you?

THE COURT: Yes, the setup is fine.

Q: All right. Are you finished perusing the notes?

A: Yes.

Q: All right. Just hang onto them. All right?

A: All right.

Q: Do you see anywhere in those notes a reference that the government would try to keep Tom Hershey from being disclosed up front?

A: No.

Q: Do you see in those notes a reference that Tom Hershey's identity would not be volunteered?

A: No.

Q: Do you see in those notes a reference that the government would try to keep Tom Hershey in the background?

A: No.

Q: Can we agree, now that we have gone through this perusal process, that those three commitments appear nowhere in agent Quinn's notes of March 26, 1993, right?

A: That's correct.

Q: And now, I'll ask you to peruse his memorandum of interview of that same day, two pages, and I'll ask you the same thing, whether the memorandum of interview contains any reference to those commitments. (Pause)

A: The question is?

Q: Does agent Quinn's memorandum of interview of Tom Hershey on March 26, 1993, contain any reference to those three commitments by you to Mr. Hershey that we have discussed?

A: No.

Q: And so you will agree with me, won't you, agent Hasheider, that even the designated note taker, agent Quinn, made no written record of those commitments by you to Tom Hershey?

A: They are not in his notes, that's correct.

Q: And you'll agree with me, won't you, that the written record made at the time, March 26, 1993, is incomplete about commitments made to Tom Hershey?

MR. LYONS: Objection, Your Honor. Calls for a conclusion of the witness whether it is complete or incomplete. The facts speak for themselves.

THE COURT: Overruled.

A: I don't know what Mr. Quinn—he took the notes. I didn't take the notes.

Q: Now, the fact is that these commitments, these three commitments that we've recited here, first surfaced in any writing in agent Quinn's declaration, dated April 12 of 1995, regarding this motion, isn't that so?

A: I don't recall agent Quinn's declaration, so I can't answer that.

Q: All right. Well, don't you recall that that's the first writing of all of the writings that we have gone over, yours or anybody else's that I started off listing, in which these commitments to Tom Hershey are referred to?

A: Okay.

Q: You don't dispute that fact, do you?

A: No, I do not.

Q: Now, you prepared your declaration for this motion before agent Quinn prepared his, didn't you?

A: I believe so, yes.

Q: Your declaration is dated April 12 of 1995, and his is dated April 14 of 1995, correct?

A: I believe so.

Q: All right. Now, agent Hasheider, weren't there some other commitments that were made by you to Tom Hershey on March 26 of 1993 besides these three that we have mentioned so far?

A: No.

Q: Well, sir, did you not tell Tom Hershey that if he cooperated with you, you would call off the search warrant for Eddie Roper's place?

A: That's correct, yes.

Q: All right. And did you not tell him that if he cooperated with you, you would call off the search warrant that you had for Newt Frankfurter, Inc.?

A: That's correct.

Q: And in fact, you did come to call off those searches, correct?

A: That's correct.

Q: And you called them off because Tom Hershey cooperated, right?

A: That's correct.

Q: And you did it right there, that day, March 26 of 1993, correct?

A: That's correct.

Q: And you did it without any agreement between Assistant United States Attorney Lyons and any attorney for Tom Hershey, didn't you?

A: That's correct.

Q: Because there was no attorney for Tom Hershey at that point in time, correct?

A: Not to my knowledge.

Q: All right. Now, Mr. Lyons, referring to agent Quinn's memorandum of interview of March 26, 1993, he states, quote, "The agents explained that Hershey's cooperation with the investigation would be reported to the proper authorities and it would be taken into consideration in his pending drug case." And you're familiar with that being in his memorandum of interview, aren't you?

A: Yes.

Q: Now, that, too, was a commitment to Tom Hershey by you that was made on March 26 of 1993, wasn't it?

A: That statement was probably made by a B.N.E. agent.

Q: And the agents that are referred to are the state drug agents, correct?

A: Correct.

Q: This was something that you confirmed to him, right?

A: "Confirmed" meaning . . .

Q: That you agreed with it?

A: Yes.

Q: And again, you meant what you said about these things, about calling off the search for Eddie Roper's place and Newt Frankfurter, Inc. and about his cooperation being made known to the authorities in the drug case; you meant what you said about those things that day, didn't you?

A: Yes.

Q: And you intended to keep your word about those things, didn't you?

A: Certainly.

Q: All right. Now, there came a time you testified in front of the Grand Jury that returned the indictment in this case, that being February 28, 1994, right?

A: Yes.

Q: You remember that?

A: That I testified, yes.

Q: Was that the first time you ever testified in a federal Grand Jury?

A: No.

Q: Now, obviously, that event, the date of that testimony in 1994, was long before the defendants Hershey brought up this cooperation issue by their motion, right?

A: Yes.

Q: You recall, do you not, that a grand juror asked you after you had concluded your testimony, "Was anything promised to him," referring to Tom Hershey, "in terms of immunity or anything like that?" and then Mr. Lyons rephrased that question to, "Did you make him any promises?" And do you remember your answer being, "No, I did not make any promises." Do you have that in mind?

A: I don't recall the question.

(Pause, while Mr. Levine projects an image of the Grand Jury testimony.)

Q: Right here, "No, I did not make him any promises." Are you with me on that?

A: Yes.

Q: Now, agent Hasheider that testimony right there that just showed up on the screen, that wasn't the truth, the whole truth, and nothing but the truth, was it?

A: Promises in that scenario, I think, it probably had to do with the frame of my mind at the time the grand juror asked the question.

Q: You want to explain that answer a little more?

A: Surely. Promises with regard to his assistance with regard to the case is what you are asking me, correct?

Q: That's what the Grand Jury asked you, right?

A: Right.

Q: And you said, "No, there weren't any," right?

A: Right.

Q: But there were commitments that he wouldn't be disclosed up front and his identity wouldn't be volunteered to anyone, and they would try to keep him in the background; and that the search warrant for Roper would be called off, and the search warrant for Newt Frankfurter, Inc. would be called off, and his cooperation would be made known in connection with the drug case. All of those were commitments that had been made to him, right?

A: Some of those are commitments; some of those aren't. As far as we would try to keep his name out of the—disclosing his name, we would try to keep him in the background. Those are things that we would try to do. Now, as far as calling off the warrants, and that, they are not commitments to the Hersheys.

Q: Weren't they inducements to him to get him to cooperate?

A: Certainly, we wanted his cooperation and it would have jeopardized the case had we served the warrants, all three warrants, at the same time.

Q: All right. And it was something that he wanted you to do, call off those warrants, wasn't it?

A: No.

Q: Well, the fact of the matter is, the upshot of it, agent Hasheider, is you didn't tell the Grand Jury about any of these commitments that we have recited here in court when you were asked that question, right?

A: Correct.

Q: And you left the Grand Jury with the impression that there had been no promises to Tom Hershey, correct?

A: I suppose so.

Q: And it wasn't an entirely accurate impression that you left with them, was it?

A: I don't know. It seemed accurate to me.

Q: Now, you made those commitments that we have mentioned here as a federal agent in a federal criminal case, right?

A: Um-hum.

Q: And by what authority did you make them?

A: By what authority? I don't have any authority to make those commitments.

Q: Did you make them without authority?

A: I said, I don't consider those commitments, sir. We would try to do that as far as calling off the warrants, and that, those are my judgment calls, yes.

Q: But it was a commitment to try to keep his identity from being disclosed up front, right?

A: Correct.

Q: And it was a commitment to try not to volunteer his identity, correct?

A: Correct.

Q: And it was a commitment to try to keep him in the background, right?

A: Correct.

Q: And you made those to him, yourself, as your commitment to him, right?

A: No. They were attempts, attempts about getting his cooperation. I don't think they were commitments until actually we would have gotten a cooperation agreement.

Q: Well, sir, you've told us that you intended to keep your word about those things. Is that right?

A: I certainly would have.

Q: Now, did you ever do anything in the presence of Tom Hershey to suggest that you did not have the authority to make these commitments?

A: I told him he would have to do—anything that would occur with regard to a cooperation agreement would be between his attorney and Mr. Lyons.

Q: But to answer my question, these commitments—I've just recited them on several times, right?

A: Yes.

Q: Did you ever do anything in Tom Hershey's presence to suggest to him that you didn't have the authority to follow through on what you were committing to him?

A: I just said. I told him that anything that would have to be done would be through his attorney. That's what I suggested to him. So it's not that I had the authority, but he would have to acquire an attorney.

There is a more extended Cross-examination of the agent by Mr. Levine in the Supplement Section at the end of this book.

PART IV

Special Tools and Tactics

21.

Refreshing Recollection

21.01 Anything May Serve

When you are cross-examining a witness on the stand, and that witness testifies that he or she cannot recall a certain fact or event, his or her recollection may be refreshed by the use of any extrinsic object that may have a tendency to refresh that witness's recollection. You, the cross-examiner, may show the witness a menu from a restaurant which in no other fashion is relevant to the case; or a newspaper, or a piece of wood, a bumper from a car—in short, anything which shall jar the memory of the witness.

The essential predicates which must be present in order to refresh the witness's recollection by the use of such extrinsic objects are:

1. the memory of the witness must be first exhausted before you can resort to refreshing; and
2. the object used must tend to refresh or remind the witness of what he or she originally knew.

21.02 Refreshing Is Not Leading or a Substitute for the Witness's Knowledge

The use of extrinsic objects in order to refresh the recollection of the witness is just that: a refreshment of a memory or a knowledge that was originally there. In other words, the witness had to have known the information originally, and now has to state that he or she has no recollection of the fact or the event in order for you to be permitted to refresh that memory. The use of this object is not intended to permit the witness to read a document or see an exhibit, which shall supply to the witness information which he or she didn't possess on a previous occasion, or to make obvious the fact about which you want the witness to testify. Such an attempt shall immediately call for an objection by your Adversary and an adverse ruling from the court.

Refreshing recollection is just that—to refresh or jump start the witness's stalled memory. Thus, having seen the extrinsic object, the witness is given a hint, and is able, thereby, to recollect facts. The item, thus, is the springboard from which the witness can recall facts that he or she already knew.

21.03 Civil or Criminal, Plaintiff or Defendant, Direct or Cross

Refreshing recollection is a Trial Advocate's tool whether the Advocate is involved in a civil or criminal case, whether the Advocate represents the plaintiff or defendant, or whether the Advocate is presenting Direct testimony or is cross-examining. In short, it is a weapon that may be used any time a witness on the stand cannot recall something during his or her testimony. It is, therefore, not just for the cross-examiner. An Advocate eliciting Direct testimony from a witness, when he or she finds the witness stalled, may proffer a document or item to get the witness going again. Whether used on Direct or Cross-examination, the document or item may not be utilized in a leading fashion. As seen hereafter, the Advocate must be careful in laying the foundation for the item, and is not permitted to lead or suggest anything to the witness. The witness may be asked the simple question, after proper foundation is laid, whether the item refreshes his or her recollection of the subject matter.

21.04 Laying the Foundation

As usual, there is a foundation that first must be used before the refreshing recollection device may be used by the examining Advocate. The foundation for refreshing recollection is rather simple compared to some of the other formulae that have preceded this chapter. All that is necessary—but nonetheless essential—is that the witness indicate that he or she cannot remember—that he or she no longer remembers or has no present recollection of the fact sought by the questioner. That point of memory failure or stall *must* be reached before the questioner proffers the extrinsic object intended to refresh. And, the witness must testify that he or she doesn't *remember.* Refreshing recollection is not a way of supplying evidence to the witness. It is intended to refresh, not supply, information into the recollection. If the witness was to testify that he or she wasn't aware of something, that she never knew a particular fact, it would be ludicrous, in the extreme, to then proffer a document or object and ask the witness if that object refreshes her recollection. For example, in a civil case where the condition of the roadway and the weather are significant in order to show that the defendant was not acting prudently under the conditions then and there existing, you might ask an independent witness the following:

Q: And what were the weather conditions on the early morning of April 15, 1997?

A: I know it was nice later in the day. I'm not really sure about the early morning.

Q: You were awake in the early morning, were you not?

A: Oh, I was awake all right. I just don't, to tell you the truth, remember the weather early in the morning.

Q: I show you this which has been marked plaintiff's Exhibit One for identification (a newspaper from the day in question; on the front page is an article about a flash storm with lightning and thunder) and ask you whether this, in any fashion, refreshes your recollection of the weather early on that day?

A: (Scans the front page) Yes, it does.

Q: And do you now recall what the weather conditions were on the early morning of April 15, 1997?

A: There was a sudden kind of flash storm, with lightning and thunder. And a pretty heavy wind, now that I recollect. A couple of people drowned.

You might just as easily have handed the witness a copy of the weather bureau report of April 15th, a flood insurance policy, or a piece of siding from a barn—anything that might have jarred and thereby refreshed the witness's past recollection of the event. In other words, the purpose of the extrinsic object is to jar the witness's recall. It is totally unimportant what object it is that helps the witness to recollect. Remember that the extrinsic object is not intended to supply to the witness any information whatsoever; it is merely to trigger his or her past recollection.

21.05 Don't Be Premature

If the witness is not in such testimonial posture that her present memory and recollection of the event are exhausted, you may not resort to an attempt to refresh the witness's memory with extrinsic objects. For instance:

Q: What color was the car that you saw that day?

A: It was either blue or dark grey; dark blue or dark grey.

Q: I show you this, marked plaintiff's Exhibit Two for identification, and ask you whether this refreshes your recollection as to the actual color of the car you saw?

YOUR ADVERSARY: Objection, Your Honor, the witness hasn't indicated anything that suggests that her memory needs refreshment. She has testified the car was either blue or dark grey.

THE COURT: Quite correct. You haven't laid the proper foundation as yet, Ms. Advocate.

Q: Ms. Witness, did you get a good look at the car?

A: Actually, not very well, just a glimpse. I don't really know what color it was.

Q: I now show you this photograph, and ask you whether this refreshes your recollection as to the color of the car you saw that day?

YOUR ADVERSARY: Objection, Your Honor, the witness has testified she doesn't know because she didn't get a good look at the car. There is no refreshing necessary here. This is leading.

THE COURT: Quite correct, you still haven't laid the proper foundation, Ms. Cross-examiner.

This flurry of questions all resulting in your being set down by the judge is not helping you in front of the jury. Don't strain the situation where it is not called for. Don't attempt to use a piece of evidence improperly, or to conduct an improper examination of the witness. It could backfire by turning the judge or the jury against you. In this situation, however, if you had brought the witness to the following point, you would then have been permitted to refresh her recollection as to the color of the car:

Q: When you say the car was either blue or dark grey, you're saying for sure that it wasn't yellow, red, or brown?

A: No, it was either dark grey or blue, dark blue.

Q: And in order to give that answer, you have a picture in your mind, a recollection of what that car looked like, however vague the picture you recall.

A: Oh, I have a picture in my mind, all right. It was either dark grey or dark blue.

Q: Can you try to concentrate, and bring that memory into sharper focus and see if you can recollect whether it was the blue or dark grey you have testified about?

A: (The witness concentrates silently, then shakes her head.) No, I can't tell you exactly, to tell the truth.

Q: I show you this photograph and ask you whether or not this refreshes your recollection as to whether the car you saw was blue or dark grey.

A: (She studies the photograph.) No, it doesn't.

NOTE: *Once the witness tells you whether or not the photograph refreshes her recollection, she is then back in the present memory, and her testimony is from present recollection. In other words, the refreshment is intended only to bring her present memory up to date, to refresh it. The testimony that you elicit must be from the present memory.*

Thus, in this situation, where the witness testifies that the photograph does not refresh her recollection, you are not permitted to pursue the inquiry or argue with the witness that she *must* or *should* recall the color of the car. If, however, the object does refresh the recollection, then you may pursue your examination of the subject. For example:

Q: I show you this photograph and ask you whether or not it refreshes your recollection as to the color of the car you saw that day?

A: (She studies the photograph.) It does.

Q: And now that you've had the opportunity to refresh your recollection, what color was the car you saw?

A: Dark grey Oldsmobile.

21.06 You Are Bound by the Witness's Answer Whether the Object Refreshes Recollection

Once you show the object to the witness, the witness decides subjectively and unilaterally whether or not the object refreshes her recollection. This is, of course, as it must be, for there is no expert or mechanism in the world that can be put before the jury to convince the jury that when the witness said that her memory was not refreshed, it actually was, and that the witness was fabricating her testimony. *Only the witness knows if her memory has been refreshed.* And if she says it was *NOT,* then you are bound by such answer, and must proceed onto some other method of examination.

> CAUTION: *Misusing a piece of evidence which contains a prior inconsistent statement to refresh the witness's recollection of what she actually said may, in effect, also kill that piece of evidence for other use. Thus, be sure you are not using valuable Cross-examination material wastefully.*

21.07 The Extrinsic Object Is Not Evidence

Although you have used a certain extrinsic object to refresh the recollection of the witness, that object is not evidence and may not ordinarily be introduced into evidence based on the foundation used to permit refreshing the witness's recollection. The only purpose of the extrinsic object is to jar the present memory of the witness and, as previously indicated, the object can be anything whatever in the world, even unrelated to the case, so long as it tends to refresh the present recollection of the witness. Such an object is certainly not evidence which ordinarily can be introduced into evidence. The cross-examiner may, if her Adversary used some extrinsic object to refresh the witness's Direct testimony, use that same extrinsic object on Cross-examination, even attempt to introduce the extrinsic object into evidence, in order for the jury to gauge the reasonableness of that object's ability to refresh the witness's recollection. Since refreshment of memory is so subjective, attacking the witness or the extrinsic object and its capacity to refresh seems more than an exercise in futility. It shall tend to make your Cross-examination insignificant since you are reduced to arguing with the witness whether or not her memory has been refreshed. Moreover, there is no way you can win that argument.

21.08 Do Not Waste a Prior Inconsistent Statement to Refresh Recollection

Oftentimes a cross-examiner has in hand a document which indicates that the witness's prior version of the facts in the case were other than the present, on-trial testimony. Being so armed, the cross-examiner often totally misuses the document by using it to refresh the witness's recollection rather than attack the credibility of the witness with a prior inconsistency. For example, the cross-examiner has in her hand a prior inconsistent statement, signed by the witness, in which the witness indicated that the car she saw on the day of the accident was actually a rust-colored car. Let us use a prior set of questions and answers and revise them slightly, as follows:

Q: What color was the car that you saw that day?

A: It was either blue or dark grey. Dark blue or dark grey.

Q: When you say the car was either blue or dark grey, you're saying for sure that it wasn't yellow, or red, or brown?

A: No, it was either dark grey or dark blue.

Q: And in order to give that answer, you have a picture in your mind, a recollection of what that car looked like, however vague the picture you recall?

A: Oh, I have a picture in my mind, all right. It was either dark grey or dark blue.

Q: Can you try and concentrate and bring that memory into sharper focus, and see if you can recollect whether it was the blue or grey you have testified about.

A: (The witness concentrates, then shakes her head.) No, I can't tell you, to tell the truth.

Q: I show you this document and ask you whether or not it refreshes
     your recollection of what you actually saw that day.

THE COURT: Read that to yourself, Ms. Witness, and then just indicate
whether or not it refreshes your recollection.

A: (After reading.) It does not.

Q: You say that document does not refresh your recollection as to the
     color of the car you saw that day.

A: No, it doesn't.

You have now practically ruined a perfectly fine Cross-examination
weapon by showing it to the witness with the hope that she will be kind
enough recollect what she has no obligation to recollect, that is, that the car
was, in fact, rust-colored. Remember that whatever the witness says as to
whether or not her memory is refreshed cannot be changed by argument or
other contradiction. It would have been far better to use that document as a
prior inconsistent statement and then cross-examine accordingly. (See Chapter 18, supra.)

> NOTE: *Even though the Cross-examiner is permitted to utilize—now
> as a prior inconsistent statement—that very same document with which
> she attempted to refresh the witness's recollection, it has lost a great
> deal of its impact in front of the jury.*

Psychologically, it does not have the same dramatic punch as if it were
used originally as follows:

Q: In order to give the answer you've just given, you have a picture in
     your mind, a recollection of what that car looked like, however
     vague the picture that you recall.

A: Oh, I have a picture in my mind all right. It was either dark grey or
     dark blue.

Q: Do you recall that after the accident happened, the police arrived?

A: Yes, about ten minutes later.

Q: And were you still at the scene?

A: Sure.

Q: Did the police ask you any questions?

A: I believe they did.

Q: Your Honor, I'd like to have this document marked for identification.

THE COURT: Mark it.

NOTE: You can and should mark items that you wish to utilize and, perhaps, introduce into evidence as you go along. However, it is recommended that you premark exhibits, so that the marking of exhibits— since it is accomplished by the court reporter—does not impede the smooth flow of your examination. Let's go back one step right now.

Q: I show you what has been previously marked as defendant's Exhibit C for identification. Will you look at this document, Ms. Witness, and tell the jury whether or not that's your signature which appears at the bottom thereof.

A: (The witness begins to read the contents of the document.)

Q: It is not necessary Ms. Witness to read the document at this time. Just tell the court and jury if that's your signature on the bottom.

A: It is.

Q: (Taking the document back from the witness.) And you signed this document for the police, didn't you?

A: I didn't read it. If you let me read it, I'll tell you the answer.

Q: There's no question that that's your signature on the bottom, is there?

A: No, no question.

Q: I offer this document into evidence, Your Honor.

THE COURT: Show it to your Adversary.

YOUR ADVERSARY: May I have some questions on the voir dire, Your Honor.

THE COURT: Certainly.

YOUR ADVERSARY: Ms. Witness, did you read this document before you signed it?

A: No.

YOUR ADVERSARY: I object, Your Honor.

THE COURT: The witness has identified her own signature on it. I'll receive it.

Q: And when you spoke to the policeman that day (now reading from Exhibit 3 in evidence) you told the police that the car you saw was rust-colored?

YOUR ADVERSARY: Your Honor, the document speaks for itself, counsel can read it to the jury if he wishes.

THE COURT: She can, or she can read any portion of it, or refer to it in any way. If you want to read the rest of it to the jury, or whatever counsel leaves out, you certainly may do that. Can you answer the question?

A: What was the question again?

Q: May the reporter read the question to the witness, Your Honor?

THE COURT: Yes, read it.

Q: Having heard the stenographer read the question, can you tell the jury whether you told the police that the car was rust-colored?

A: If it says it there, that's what I must have said.

Q: And when you answered questions posed to you by the police, you were telling what you had just seen, weren't you?

A: I don't know what I told them. I don't remember much about the accident now.

Q: You must have remembered more about it then, ten minutes after the accident?

A: I guess so.

Q: And when you told the police that it was a rust car that caused the accident, that must have been the truth?

A: I guess so.

Thus, you have better used a document which might have been used to refresh the witness's recollection. Obviously, however, driving a spike into the witness's testimony by using the document to affect credibility as a prior inconsistent statement is far more effective than using the same document merely as a memory stimulant which permits the witness to give an answer with which you are going to be bound, i.e., "no, it doesn't refresh my memory." Of course, using the document as a prior inconsistent statement does not entirely eliminate the use of refreshing recollection in other areas covered by the statement where the witness's memory has actually stalled.

21.09 Past Recollection Recorded

There is another alternative use of an extrinsic document other than the refreshing of recollection or, on the opposite end of the spectrum, direct attack by use as a prior inconsistent statement. That alternative is *Past Recollection Recorded*. The extrinsic object necessary for use as past recollection recorded falls somewhere in the middle ground between the *anything* that can be used to refresh recollection and the specific prior inconsistent statement made directly by the testifying witness.

Although the direct frontal attack with a prior inconsistent statement is a far more effective device, what shall you do if the witness testifies she has NO memory of an event? You proffer the document to refresh recollection. The witness says "No," the document does not refresh recollection. Now what? What do you do when the extrinsic document does *not* refresh a recollection that has gone totally blank and, the witness *does not* testify from the stand in a manner which contradicts the statement you have in hand? Think quick. Your Adversary, in the cat-bird seat, is about to rise and object to your use of a prior *inconsistent* statement as being inappropriate for there is *no inconsistency*. The witness has said she doesn't remember and has not testified to any fact inconsistent with any prior statement. See the following example.

Q: Was the car which you saw dark blue or dark grey?

A: To tell you the truth, I can't remember.

Q: (You take out a document.) You recall speaking to the police who responded to the scene that night?

A: Yes.

Q: And did you describe for them the accident which occurred, what you observed?

YOUR ADVERSARY: (He, through discovery, knows what the statement says.) Your Honor, I'm going to object right here to any attempted use of any alleged statement.

THE COURT: Mr. Cross-examiner, what is the basis of your use of the statement which you are referring to?

CROSS-EXAMINER: A prior statement of this witness, which is certainly contradictory of the present testimony. The witness specifically described the car to the police, and now says he doesn't remember. That certainly is inconsistent.

YOUR ADVERSARY: Not within the rules of evidence, and I object to counsel's colloquy.

THE COURT: Good try, Mr. Cross-examiner, but you know that inconsistent actually means contradictory. There's no contradiction here. Sustained.

You have just been neutralized in your use of a document that's right in your hands, that the witness has made at some prior time, but which is *not* inconsistent (contradictory) to the present testimony. Are you going to just stand there with that document in hand? No, way! What to do? Simple. If it's not a prior inconsistent statement, usable as such, because the witness doesn't recall its contents, then it may be a past recollection recorded and you can use it as such.

21.10 Requisites

In order for you to utilize a document as past recollection recorded, these are the following requisites:

1. the witness's memory of the contents of the document, as well as the event, are exhausted;
2. the document was made at, or about, the time of the event or transaction;
3. the accuracy of the document, *when made,* is verified by the testifying witness.

21.11 Explanation

a) The absence of memory, in this situation, is virtually the same as that necessary before you can use extrinsic objects to refresh or jar the memory, that is, the witness has no recollection of the event. Use of the document (past recollection recorded, obviously, is limited to documents) as Past Recollection Recorded is *not* precluded by having tried to use the document to refresh recollection.

b) The extrinsic document happens to be a recordation of the event made by the testifying witness *at or about* the time of the event in issue (the old, more rigid rule was contemporaneous), when the facts were fresh and vivid in the witness's mind at the time of the recordation.

c) The testifying witness verifies the accuracy of the recordation when made, so that, although she doesn't recall the event or the contents of the recordation she made at the time the recordation was made, she does acknowledge that she did, in fact intend to record correctly what she observed.

If you establish all these criteria, you may then undertake to utilize the document as past recollection recorded. This does not mean that the jury has a chance to actually hold and read the document. It may. It is up to the judge. For sure, however, you, the Cross-examiner, may establish the necessary predicates above indicated, then introduce the statement in evidence. You may then have the witness read her statement to the jury, or you may be permitted to read the document to the jury. Such document becomes evidence in chief, and, is as if the testifying witness had actually pronounced the words contained therein, it becomes part of her testimony. Moreover, the judge may permit the document to be shown to the jury or even brought into the jury room.

Naturally, you keen observers have already said to yourself that the witness isn't just going to sit by and make life easy for you by saying, "Sure, even though I told you I don't recall the event, that document accurately reflects exactly what you want the jury to hear from my mouth." Probably true, but equally probable is the fact that the witness, when shown such a document, will either have her memory refreshed or she's going to realize that you have the document and that somehow you're going to bring it before the jury. In other words, the witness is ahoist on her own petard, she can't escape you. In fact, the witness probably knows that she is going to appear very foolish indeed, in the eyes of the jury, when her own report of the events does not refresh her memory.

But assume that happens and the witness decides to play hardball and doesn't at all remember the event, not even after you show her a document in which she had previously memorialized the entire event. You may make a move either to utilize the document as a prior inconsistent statement (if it contains information that conflicts with the witness's present testimony) or (if there is no conflict) as past recollection recorded. This tool can be used one way or the other. It is you, however, and your control of the situation that determines how you utilize the document. For example, you attempt to utilize the document as a prior inconsistent statement, *although there is very little conflict where the witness says that she doesn't remember the incident.* Your Adversary objects and the judge says:

> THE COURT: Yes, Mr. Cross-examiner, good try, but inconsistent actually means contradictory. There's no such contradiction here. Sustained.
>
> CROSS-EXAMINER: Very well, Your Honor.

Q: Do you recognize this document, Ms. Witness?

A: It looks like a report that I might have made out at the time of the incident.

Q: Were you required to make this statement for your work or in connection with your duties?

A: No.

Q: But, in any event, you made it out.

A: I might have, yes.

Q: And when did you make it out?

A: I guess right after the incident. I just jotted that down in a notebook I happened to be carrying.

Q: And did it reflect what you saw?

A: I can't say.

Q: Well, when you recorded this, you weren't writing a fiction piece, were you?

A: I don't understand your question.

Q: What you were writing had something to do with what you saw, didn't it? You weren't making up the things out of your imagination and writing them down here?

A: Oh, no.

Q: So that, basically, although you don't recall it now, this document contains your observations of the actual event at the very time of the event?

A: I guess you could put it that way.

CROSS-EXAMINER: Your Honor, as past recollection recorded, I offer the contents of this document, and the document itself, into evidence.

THE COURT: We'll mark it as a court exhibit, and you may read it to the jury. I'll reserve decision on whether or not the jury should see the actual document.

You did it. Perseverance and a complete knowledge of the various uses of documents, having a full complement of arrows in your quiver, carried the day for you again.

22.

Exploring Prior Illegal or Immoral Acts

22.01 Purpose

In addition to other material available to the cross-examiner, any illegal, immoral, or antisocial acts of the Adverse Witness can be utilized to attack that witness's credibility. These acts need not only be criminal or immoral, but can be any act which shows the Adverse Witness to be capable of deceit, distortion, unreliability, or a person who values and places his or her own interests above that of others or society in general, regardless of the consequences or harm that such act might cause others. Basically, the use of these antisocial acts on Cross-examination is to permit the jury to obtain a full view of the witness, to be better able to evaluate the witness and his or her testimony in light of his or her true character. Needless to say, despite antisocial acts, whether criminal or otherwise, a jury is still free to believe that the witness, despite his or her background or habits, is worthy of belief, at least in this one instance.

In the ordinary situation, having information that the witness has done some antisocial act in the past is not the beginning and end of your Cross-examination. It is not the material of which the hoped for "big kill" is made. It can help, of course. It can be damaging. But it can also be something that the jury can determine is insignificant or unimportant in the context of the testimony. For example, many times co-defendants in criminal cases cooperate with the prosecution and testify against their fellow accused, with the hope of gaining favor on their own behalf from the court which shall pass judgment on them. You have a perfect example of just such a witness in the person of "Sammy the Bull" Gravano, whose Cross-examination by Jay Goldberg has been excerpted for you in this book in several places. Mr. Gravano admitted 19 homicides and a deal with the prosecutor which would render him eligible for a possible sentence of probation. Mr. Gravano's testimony, despite what you might consider horrific and self-serving, was accepted by that jury to convict the persons against whom Gravano testified.

Thus, witnesses may have been guilty of murders and swindling, going back years and years; they may also have had self-serving purposes in testifying in a fashion acceptable to the prosecutor, yet, for the purpose of convicting the defendant against whom the witnesses testify, the jury often finds them sufficiently credible. How can that be? How can the jury accept the word of a murderer, a con man, a thief, a cheat—a person who lies to serve his own interests? I don't know. In their ordinary business dealings, I assume, if you or any member of any jury were presented with such a person, everyone would run as if they were being drawn into the jaws of death. In innumerable criminal cases, you'll find the jury accepting just such testimony and convicting other people based thereon. In the ordinary civil case, the cross-examiner does not run into anything quite so dramatic as Mr. Gravano, but you do run into witnesses who have unsavory aspects to their background. You can utilize such material, whether in a criminal or civil case, but remember that such material should be considered only another piece of the mosaic, and it should be used as such, something which adds to the weight of your Cross-examination, but which can hardly carry the entire weight of your Cross-examination.

22.02 Illegal Acts

When you become aware of the prior criminal history of an Adverse Witness, whether supplied by your Adversary or discovered by your own investigation, you are not bound to cross-examine merely about the convictions that the witness has suffered. You are equally permitted to delve into the underlying facts of any illegal or immoral act of the past, regardless of criminal conviction or even acquittal. However, there are different methods of using the different materials.

22.03 Convictions

If the witness has been convicted of a crime previously, you are able to ask the witness about that conviction and the underlying circumstances thereof as shown in the following example.

Q: Mr. Witness, on July 6, 1965, were you convicted of the crime of felonious assault in New York County?

A: Yes, I was.

Q: You were guilty of attacking someone physically?

A: I guess you could say that.

Q: You guess you were convicted of assaulting another human being? Was it not a woman, named Ada Doe, a sixty-three-year-old woman?

A: It was, it was.

Q: And were you also, on September 12, 1967, convicted of the crime of impersonating a police officer?

A: Yes, I was.

Q: You posed as someone you were not?

A: Right, right.

Q: In order to do this, you had to lie, to say things that were not true, to convince others of what you were saying to get some benefit for yourself, correct?

A: I didn't get much benefit out of it.

Q: But you had hoped you would, correct?

A: Right, right.

Q: And were you also, in July, 1978, convicted of the crime of murder?

A: Yes. And I did my time.

Q: How much time? When were you released from prison?

A: 1998. July, 1998.

Q: Just six months ago?

A: Right.

Q: And in that crime of murder that you said you were convicted of, was a woman, an eighty-year-old woman, murdered?

A: Yes, but I didn't do it.

Q: You were convicted of it, in a court of law, were you not?

A: Yes, I was. I already admitted that.

Q: Was this woman beaten to death with some blunt instrument?

A: Yes, but I didn't do it.

You have used the material as much as the law allows. Would the jury, doing some personal business, or having some personal dealings with this witness, accept anything that he says, knowing now what they know about him? It is highly doubtful. Will they accept such testimony to injure your client? Perhaps. But you have sown serious seeds for thought and doubt.

22.04 Non-Convictions

In addition to criminal acts of which the witness has been convicted, you are also permitted, under certain conditions, to ask about the underlying facts of criminal acts which were dismissed or about acts of which the witness was actually acquitted. The mere act of dismissal or acquittal—perhaps for failure of available proofs—does not mean that the event never occurred or that the witness did not commit the act. Be careful. You cannot ask about arrests. You must know exactly how to pose these questions or you will be cut short rather rudely by the court. Be prepared to justify your inquiry, since, even if you ask the questions carefully, most adversaries shall advise the judge that you are not permitted to ask such questions and many judges shall sustain the objection. Be prepared with citations and case law in your jurisdiction that support the position that you may ask just such questions.

You are not permitted to ask the witness if he or she had been arrested for a particular act. This is because, in our system of justice, the mere fact that a person has been arrested for (accused of) a crime is not sufficient for such fact to be used against him. Just as acquittal does not rule out the possibility that such act was, in fact, committed, so too, mere arrest does not mean that the act actually occurred. The witness may have been totally without guilt of such charges, arrested by error, and, when the authorities realized such lack of culpability, released the arrestee from custody. You are permitted, nonetheless, to ask questions as to whether or not the witness actually committed the immoral acts underlying the criminal charge. *Once again* you are bound by the witness's answer. In the event that you receive a negative answer, you are bound thereby. For instance, you find that the witness was arrested in 1995 for felonious assault and for grand larceny in 1997. As a result of the witness having had a superb cross-examining lawyer, there were no convictions. You are permitted to ask the following:

> Q: Mr. Witness, on June 6, 1995, did you assault a woman with a bottle in New York County?
>
> A: I was accused of it, but I was acquitted.

> CROSS-EXAMINER: I object, Your Honor, to the witness giving gratuitous remarks in front of the jury. I ask that Your Honor instruct the witness to answer the question asked. I also ask that the answer be stricken.
>
> THE COURT: Yes, strike the answer. The jury will disregard the answer. Just answer the questions asked, Mr. Witness.

After the witness has foiled your thrust so well with a gratuitous remark, perhaps it is unlikely that questions about the underlying facts can be of much significance in front of the jury, but they may be. You continue:

> Q: Did you, in fact, assault a woman, with a bottle on June 6, 1995?
>
> A: I already told you.
>
> Q: You've told what happened in court. I'm asking you if, you, in fact, actually hit a woman with a bottle on June 6, 1995?
>
> A: No.

Although you are getting negative answers, the witness may also be transmitting hostile, negative vibrations to the jury, which shall cause them to distrust or disbelieve him. Thus, you may be accomplishing something positive with your questions, despite the fact that the plain words of the trial transcript do not reveal, on their face, the damage that may be occurring.

> ADVERSARY: Your Honor, I object. Counsel has no good faith basis for asking that question.
>
> THE COURT: Come up, counselors. (You approach the bench.) Counselor (the judge asks you), what is the basis of this inquiry?
>
> CROSS-EXAMINER: Your Honor, I have the witnesses arrest record right here. I am entitled to explore the underlying facts.
>
> THE COURT: Very well. Step back. Proceed, Counselor.

Q: Did you, Mr. Witness, on February 11, 1997, steal several cars in
     the 48th Precinct in the Bronx, New York?

A: No, I didn't.

Are such questions worth it? Well, ordinarily, they certainly can't hurt,
and when laced with enough factual content, and the continued examination
is permitted by the court, the jury can realize there is some basis for your
questions, and such basis may give a jury pause.

22.05 Objections

Oftentimes, as above, your Adversary may impose an objection to your use
of non-conviction material to impeach the witness on the ground that the
witness was acquitted of the charges and that acquittal precludes any inquiry. Since you shall find that the law does permit you to inquire as to the
underlying facts of any illegal, immoral, or illicit act in the Adverse Witness's
past, regardless of whether or not a conviction resulted, you should research
the issue. Keep a list of the citations in your trial book, so you will be ready
to answer the objections when they crop up.

22.06 What's the Point?

As you are bound by the answer, and the witness is unlikely to give an affirmative answer, you wonder why bother? First, the sanction of a charge of
perjury in another and later proceeding is present. So you may get an honest
answer. Second, surely the jury that you selected shall catch the drift that
you are not asking the witness questions out of the blue when you inquire
about an event that occurred in a certain month, certain year, or even certain
day, in a certain place, against a certain victim. Not being able to determine
if the witness shall admit a particular bad act, nor being able to assess how
such negative responses to specific questions are going to affect the jury, you
might as well give it a shot and use the information—you miss 100 percent
of the birds at which you never fire your shotgun.

22.07 It Could Backfire

Backfiring can happen in the same way an ancient conviction may backfire,
that is, when the witness may have done an antisocial act forty years before,

and since then has led an exemplary life, has done great deeds for the community at large, is generous, honest, upstanding, etc. Asking such a witness questions about an event, even if true, may very well antagonize the jury against you and your cause. Inasmuch as the damage that you could effect by questions about an insignificant act in the long past may not compare to the backlash damage that you could do your own cause, it is extremely difficult to give a hard and fast rule as to the use or lack of use of such information about prior bad acts. Each situation and each witness stands alone and must be evaluated by you under all the attendant circumstances. If you decide that the damage that may be done to the witness is going to be greater than the backlash that may occur to yourself and your client, then, by all means, you should use the material. Just remember, you cannot ask about arrests. You can, however, ask about the underlying facts, regardless of whether or not an arrest resulted in an acquittal or dismissal.

22.08 Good Faith Essential

In order to pursue a line of inquiry as to immoral or illicit events, even those underlying arrests which did not blossom into prosecutions or convictions, you must have a good faith basis for the inquiry. While you do not have to—shall not be permitted to—prove the underlying events (those charges against the witness are collateral to the issues in the instant case) that does not mean you may inquire in bad faith, ask questions not based on fact, questions which are total figments of your imagination. Such behavior is sanctionable, perhaps contumacious, and should never be indulged in by a trial attorney of integrity.

22.09 Immoral and Illicit Acts

Even though not criminal, any acts which are antisocial, immoral, illicit, or loathsome, and basically have a tendency to give the jury a better insight into the witness's character are grist for the cross-examiner's mill. Again, you are bound by the witness's answer. The reason you are so bound is because the issues of the trial at hand are the issues to be adjudicated. Whether or not a witness did or did not, in fact, commit an immoral or illicit act at another time cannot be substituted or added to the issues to be decided. Thus, in an accident case, if you ask a nonparty witness whether or not he beat his wife, and he says he did not, you cannot bring in the wife who shall testify that he did beat her. For then the issue of the trial at bar becomes clouded with the question of the mini-issue: whether the witness actually beat his wife. Such is impermissible.

The above does not preclude your use of illicit acts for Cross-examination in an attempt to impeach the witness's credibility with the use thereof. You merely must accept the answers given to your questions. However, even negative answers may have an effect on the jury, since the jury may perceive that although the witness is saying *no*, the witness's discomfort at the questions and the witness's demeanor may cause the jury to disbelieve the answer. The jury may be so appalled by the shady background as to disbelieve the entirety of the witness's testimony. For example:

Q: Mr. Witness, do you have a drinking problem?

A: I have no problem with drinking, no.

Q: What I'm asking, Mr. Witness, is have you regularly been under the influence of alcohol to such an extent that your senses were unable to function properly?

A: Maybe a couple of times in my life, when I was a kid.

Q: Would it be more like several times a week, right now?

A: No.

Q: Have you such a problem with alcohol that you have to seek medical aid within recent time?

A: No.

Q: Have you, in fact, been hospitalized on several occasions as a result of such drinking?

A: No.

YOUR ADVERSARY: Your Honor, I object, and request that counsel and myself be permitted to approach at the sidebar.

THE COURT: Very well.

YOUR ADVERSARY (At the sidebar): Your Honor, these questions are improper and asked in bad faith. Counsel should know better than to ask such questions. I ask for some offer of proof as to good faith, or ask, in the alternative, that the court instruct the jury to disregard this line of questioning completely.

THE COURT: Ms. Cross-examiner?

CROSS-EXAMINER: Your Honor, I have proof that the witness has been hospitalized several times for chronic alcoholism. I intend to introduce such evidence.

YOUR ADVERSARY: That is totally collateral, even if true, Your Honor.

CROSS-EXAMINER: The witness is now perjuring himself in front of the jury, Your Honor, and I am permitted to show that. I am not now talking about his alcoholism. I'm talking about his untruthfulness right now, in front of the jury. I have certified proof of his hospitalization.

THE COURT: This is the main witness in the case. I'll permit it.

Thus, although you are stuck with the witness's answers in reference to illicit or immoral acts, the fact that you have proof and a good faith basis to support your position may stand you in sufficient good stead with the court to permit your inquiry.

22.10 Credibility Is Always In Issue

The above statement, that credibility is always in issue may help to resolve any contradictions which might seem to appear in foregoing paragraphs as to whether or not collateral issues, such as did or did not the witness engage in illegal, immoral, or illicit acts, may permissibly become part of the trial. A witness's credibility is never collateral. A witness's credibility is always in issue. Thus, if the witness testifies he did not commit an act, you are bound by the answer. However, if the witness testifies that he was not hospitalized and you have certified proof that he was, in fact, hospitalized for his alcoholism, you have to convince the judge that you should be permitted to bring that out in front of the jury.

> NOTE: *If the court thwarts your introduction into evidence of the hospitalization records indicated, you may nonetheless have them marked for identification and show them to the witness to see if they refresh the witness's recollection. Psychologically, both for the witness and the jury,*

such a showing may be quite effective and the witness's discomfort and demeanor may serve to prove what the witness has denied.

22.11 Checklist

1. You may inquire into illegal acts either when:
   a. the witness has been convicted of a crime, or
   b. the witness has actually committed an illegal act, regardless of arrest, conviction, or acquittal.
2. You may ask about the underlying facts of a criminal act, regardless of any arrest or the favorable result of prosecution procedures.
3. You may not allude to arrest, but rather just to the commission of the illegal or immoral act.
4. You may inquire about immoral or illicit acts at any time, but you are ordinarily bound by the witness's answer.
5. You are able to show the witness is unreliable by showing misstatements of fact not as to immorality, and so on, but as to events about which the witness has testified erroneously, falsely, or unreliably.

23.

Cross-Examining the Expert

23.01 The Expert Thinks Human Thoughts

The basic approach to cross-examining expert witnesses is to realize that an "expert" is no different from any other witness, *except* that he or she is talking about a specific, often technical subject, and they may use words which are particularly connected to that specialty. Notice I emphasize the words, not the thinking processes of the expert, may differ from those words that the average person uses daily.

The concepts of which the expert speaks may be specialized, but they must be logical, make progressive sense, be built upon appropriate foundations, and be expressible. Lawyers use a language of art that is not ordinary for laymen. Yet we know that behind the terms of art (hopefully) are common sense, basic concepts of logic, and physical and intellectual reality, forming a proper foundation for conclusions. The same is true for doctors, engineers, or atomic scientists. The human mind, even expert human minds, works the same way for all humans. While the expert may just use language or terms you might not ordinarily understand, if you learn to understand their specialized language and terms of art, you shall suddenly understand what they are saying. Thus, you shall have equalized yourself with them, leveled the playing field, and you can then proceed to cross-examine them.

23.02 Learning the Language

To best cross-examine the expert, familiarize yourself with the area of his expertise or at least the area about which you know he must testify relative to the issues or trial. You shall, as you research, *ipso facto*, familiarize yourself with the words or phrases which the expert may use. More than likely, the expert thinks that the language lawyers speak, the legal terms of art they use amongst themselves, are strange and undecipherable. Once you are familiar with the subject matter and terminology about which the expert shall testify, you shall be surprised that the expert is no longer talking a foreign language; the expert now talks a language you understand, and the validity of his testimony, or lack of it, and the logic of his thinking, or the lack of it, become immediately apparent to you.

23.03 Translate for the Jury

Oftentimes, the expert attempts to expand the significance and "specialness" of his field of expertise by using a language mere mortals do not ordinarily use (as aforesaid, lawyers and judges do the same). This hiding behind a smoke screen of arcane words, saying something rather ordinary in specialized nonordinary terms, is nothing more than window dressing. For example, a doctor might, for the jury, describe a sprained ankle as a subluxation of the peroneal tendon. That condition can and must be translated into lay terms—a sprained ankle—and it is your job, as cross-examiner, to do so.

The expert is presented to introduce and explain to the jury a specialized subject. The expert is not called to the stand to clarify for the jury what it means to walk up to a door and knock on it, nor to describe the sensation of buying a ticket to the cinema. These are common human experiences that require no special explanation. The expert's sole function is to help the jury understand a subject they may not have in common experience. The expert's opinion—as the judge will charge the jury—is not a substitute for the jury's thinking and deliberation. The expert is to help the jury understand the specialized subject matter so the jury may thereafter make a factual determination concerning that subject. The jury can't make such determination unless the expert's terms of art, the specialized words used in that specialty are broken down for them, reduced to layman's language so that the jury can digest and weigh the facts of the case, including the circumstances about which the expert has testified, in their true perspective.

For an example of such *reductio ad* laymen's language, thus reducing the impact of what is often nonsense in dressed-up terms, see the Cross-examination of a medical expert which appears immediately below. The doctor is testifying in a homicide case concerning a witness who has testified previously in the case. The defense is anticipated to claim, based upon

Discovery material turned over by the prosecution, that the witness is an alcoholic and hallucinated a confession by the defendant. The doctor has been presented to give an opinion that the witness may have been an alcoholic but was not hallucinating at the moment he heard the confession. The doctor-experts opinion is based on the assumed premise that the witness was describing what he had actually seen in a lucid moment, and was not having an alcoholic hallucination. Your task on Cross-examination is to have the doctor admit that if, in fact, the witness was hallucinating, the entire testimony is meaningless.

You shall often find that the expert disguises the testimony with which he or she supports his or her opinion in favor of your Adversary behind frills of complex, specialized words which he or she assumes neither you nor the jury shall fully understand. This is a ploy by the expert, as in the case of the doctor testifying immediately herein below, on behalf of the prosecutor's office, which often uses that same expert to support some premise vis-à-vis mental health, usually the capacity or fitness of a defendant to stand trial. However, as cross-examiner, you may be able to undercut the doctor's impact by having her admit the absurdity of the witness's testimony—if, in fact, it was actually the product of a hallucination. To do this, you must have the doctor admit that she never examined the patient before the 14-minute examination that she conducted specifically for this case; that her testimony is based on an assumption that the patient was recollecting something from a lucid moment; and that, if the assumption was erroneous, the patient was truly having a hallucination, and the alleged confession is meaningless. The following is an excerpt of just such Cross-examination:

Q: Have you, doctor, in your experience with chronic alcoholism, come across individuals who have hallucinations or delusions as to what has occurred in the past?

A: Yes, I have.

Q: If a person, doctor, is no longer hallucinating, no longer a chronic alcoholic, would he refer back to events when he had been hallucinating and believe them to have actually happened?

A: There are variations on that. In most instances, the individual recognizes the abnormalities of the hallucinatory or delusional experience.

Q: Doctor, this would be, am I correct, a person who has had the delirium tremens, or the DTs, and thought he saw pink elephants. When the patient recovers, he realizes that, in fact, he didn't really see pink elephants, is that correct?

A: Generally, that is correct, yes.

Q: Doctor, a person who had hallucinations as a chronic alcoholic may recall a conversation that actually took place, and he may also hallucinate a conversation that did not actually take place, isn't that correct?

A: That's correct.

Q: And when a person recognizes that what he recalls was actually a hallucination, he recognizes, in logic, that he couldn't have seen a flying building or pink elephants or anything of that sort, is that correct?

YOUR ADVERSARY: Objection.

THE COURT: Sustained.

Q: Can you always recognize, doctor, when a person describes a hallucinatory experience as opposed to an actual event?

A: Most of the time, yes, I can. Their content is usually bizarre or outlandish, making recognition not difficult.

Q: Doctor, when you speak of events that are bizarre or outlandish, are you speaking about the sort of things that people describe as pink elephants or snakes in the corner, or flying buildings, or feeling that they're flying when, of course, they're not, correct?

A: And other things.

Q: But if the hallucination is of things which are normal, such as a normal conversation with another person, then it is far more difficult to ascertain what is real, and what is not real, what was a hallucination, and what was actual, is that correct, doctor?

A: It may present a problem, but one uses other means to identify it, not only the language itself.

Q: A person being a chronic alcoholic can have a delusion or a hallucination of having a conversation, even about murder, with an individual with whom he did not have such conversation, isn't that correct, doctor?

A: That can happen.

Q: And if a person hallucinates a normal conversation, and tells you about it afterward, it is significantly more difficult to ascertain whether or not the person has told you about a hallucination, isn't it?

A: It might be more difficult.

Q: And, of course, you, not having been present at the time of the alleged conversation, would have to make a medical evaluation as to whether or not there was a hallucination or reality, correct?

A: Yes, correct.

Q: And that evaluation would be based on your past experience, not on participating in the actual event, correct?

A: Yes.

Q: And, doctor, when making your evaluation of the alleged conversation, that conversation is not something that you can weigh, measure, view under a microscope, is it?

A: No.

Q: It is a highly subjective evaluation, that is, one that comes from your own head, your evaluation, not your measuring, weighing of something solid, correct?

A: Yes, usually.

Q: Doctor, have you ever been mistaken in any diagnosis that you have made?

A: I don't think so.

Q: And, of course, doctor, you might have been wrong, and just don't know about it, correct?

A: That's a possibility.

CROSS-EXAMINER: I have no further questions.

What you have done is reduce the expert logically, by deflating the terms of her art to layman's language, reducing the witness for the jury to an ordinary witness. At the same time, you've permitted the jury to see and understand exactly what the expert is saying rather than leaving the jury sitting—usually without admitting it—in a state of confusion because of those very same confusing terms of art. Both accomplishments are essential to cross-examining expert witnesses.

To gain further insight into the Cross-examination of a witness, the following is an excerpt from a Cross-examination of Thomas A. Moore, one of New York's, and the nation's, leading medical malpractice Trial Advocates. In this example, Advocate Moore is cross-examining a doctor concerning a woman whose child was born with a defect and Mr. Moore has sued on her and the infant's behalf, inter alia (see, we use those confusing terms of art all the time ourselves) the Hospital Corporation of the City of New York.

> NOTE: *At the same time as Mr. Moore is helping to translate the esoteric language of the medical profession into layman's terms, he is also exercising very careful control of the doctor, phrasing the question with all the information he wants the doctor to consider, permitting the doctor only enough room to affirm or deny the information Mr. Moore has loaded into his question.*

Cross-Examination by Mr. Moore

Q: Do you remember being asked about the yellow meconium-stained fluid by Mr. Greenfield a little while ago?

A: Yes, sir.

Q: It has always been your opinion, doctor, in this case, with reasonable probability, that was meconium-stained fluid, from 1991 down to today, based on your expertise in the field, true?

A: Not necessarily, sir, no.

Q: You say, not necessarily, sir. Tell me, is that your opinion as you sit here right now?

A: It's consistent with meconium, and if they acted on it, I would—I would say that that was an appropriate action.

Q: Well, wait a second now, doctor. Before we talk about any action, I'm talking about yellow-stained amniotic fluid. Okay?

A: Yes, sir.

Q: Yellow-stained amniotic fluid. You've not only heard such a concept many times in your career, you have seen it, from time to time, correct?

A: I have seen yellow-stained amniotic fluid. I don't recall any information that this fluid was stained yellow. I heard that it was yellow.

Q: Doctor, did you hear the question that I asked you?

A: Yes, sir.

Q: By the way, do you, sir, as an expert in obstetrics, can you make a distinction, under oath before a court and jury, between yellow-stained fluid and yellow-colored fluid?

A: Yes, I do.

Q: Let's go back to 1991. Now, it's going to be with probability, years before this case is tried, you're expressing opinions. Not one of them is in writing, so they're all oral, right?

A: They are all oral.

Q: You want to make sure they get it right. You're the expert that they're going to, to give them opinions. You want to make sure they get it right, don't you?

A: Yes, sir.

Q: Okay. Now, sir, surely, surely, doctor, the subject of this woman's observations, recorded at the time in the chart—when I say, "recorded at the time," they're recorded in the chart about 35 minutes later, surely, those observations came up for discussion when you were giving your opinions to those that had gone to you and hired you to give them such, is that right?

A: Yes. Yes, they did.

Q: Doctor, you surely were not reticent then to give them such opinions—is that correct?—when they asked for them?

A: That's correct.

Q: Are you saying to this jury that you didn't tell them, in words or in substance, that what this woman says, yellow-colored fluid, translates to an opinion that you have that there was meconium in the fluid? Are you saying that didn't happen?

A: I'm saying that didn't happen.

Q: You had a question mark, is that correct?

A: That's correct.

Q: Tell the jury, in your opinion, one thing in the world that yellow fluid could have been as a result of, other than meconium?

A: The normal straw-colored amniotic fluid that varies from straw-colored to white to clear, since the amniotic fluid is in progress—a product of fetal urination. There's a cycle that it goes through: the baby drinks it; it goes back into the mother's circulation, comes back into the baby by the umbilical cord; the baby urinates it out; it goes back into the mother. And the color of the fluid can be crystal clear—that's not a color—it can be cloudy with skin debris in it; it can be straw-colored; it can be white; it can be colorless, and these can all be normal variations. The only person who described it as yellow was the mother. No qualified obstetrical personnel ever made a comment that this fluid was abnormal.

Q: Now, doctor, that was a long answer, but the answer to my question is: You're saying it was as a result of the urine? That's what made the amniotic fluid yellow?

A: I'm saying—

Q: Are you saying that?

A: I'm saying that the fluid is normally—varies in color depending on the situation.

Q: Doctor, you know, don't you, that in the history of obstetrics, yellow-colored amniotic fluid has never been opined to be other than as a result of meconium, in the history of obstetrics? You know that, don't you?

A: There are degrees of yellow, sir.

Q: Is that the answer to the question that I asked you?

A: You asked me about history.

Q: I said, sir, isn't it true that, in the history of obstetrics, yellow-colored amniotic fluid has never been determined to be other than as a result of meconium? And you answered to me, doctor, in response to that question: "There are degrees of yellow." That was your answer, wasn't it ?

A: That's true.

Q: Will you try to respond, doctor, to the questions that I ask you?

A: I will try, sir.

Q: By the way, do you think that a child learning colors knows that there are degrees of yellow?

A: Depends on the child and the degree of his or her education.

Q: You certainly know, doctor, that anybody sitting in this courtroom knows there are degrees of yellow, right?

A: I will not make an opinion what everybody else thinks.

Q: You knew I wasn't asking you whether there were degrees of yellow. You certainly knew I wasn't asking you that, didn't you?

A: I'm not sure I want to give you a yes-or-no answer on that. I presume it was—was that a rhetorical question?

Q: No, doctor, that was a question.

A: I presume that everybody in this courtroom knows that there are variations, but I have no medical certainty about it.

Q: Fortunately, doctor, in this day and age, as opposed to, maybe, centuries and centuries ago, obstetrics has reached the point where there's a lot of writing about it, right?

A: Yes, sir.

Q: Doctor, would you tell the court and jury one place, one article, one textbook, one source of the literature, where you have ever found, in your career, a reference to what you have said, that the urine from the baby can make the amniotic fluid yellow? Would you, doctor, cite one in the history of the annals of the literature in obstetrics, one such instance?

A: I read it on numerous occasions, but I could not give you a quote. And I've seen thousands of amniotic fluid and I've seen the variations amongst them.

Q: Doctor, I didn't ask you—your own observations, I can't—I can't be privy to, so I asked you about the literature, doctor, and you know I asked you about the literature.

A: Um-hmm.

Q: Correct?

A: Yes.

Q: Okay. Doctor, would you, since you say you have seen that many times, take the time after you leave court today and find someplace, doctor, and give it to Mr. Greenfield or someone that can bring it to this court, and find someplace in the annals of obstetrics where it's been written that the urine of the baby within the womb, within the amniotic sac, has discolored the amniotic fluid to make it yellow? Would you do that, doctor?

MR. GREENFIELD: Your Honor, I'm going to object to that direction of the witness.

MR. MOORE: It's not a direction. I'm asking, would he do it.

MR. GREENFIELD: Objection.

THE COURT: Objection is overruled.

Q: Would you do that, doctor? Take the time, please, in this important matter and find such a reference? Would you do that?

A: Yes, sir.

Q: Thank you, doctor. Sir, you know, don't you, that a baby, bathed, as I said earlier—or bathing—in discolored fluid that's as a result of meconium being passed, can be stained by it, correct?

A: Correct.

Q: You know, doctor, that this baby was determined, in the pediatric record, the nursery record, to be stained with meconium, correct?

A: Incorrect.

Q: Incorrect?

A: Incorrect.

Q: You didn't find documentation in the record that this baby was stained?

A: Absolutely not.

Q: Did you read the record?

A: I certainly did.

Q: Did you read the admission chart of the nurse?

A: I did.

Q: Did you read that it was checked that the baby was meconium-stained?

A: No.

Q: You didn't see that.

A: The baby was not meconium-stained; the amniotic fluid was meconium-stained.

Q: I see. Did you read my questioning of Dr. Clare?

A: Yes, I did.

Q: Did you see that he knew that this baby was meconium-stained?

A: He read—he read the same record as I did. He wasn't there either.

Q: Is that your response to my question?

A: Yes, sir.

Q: You saw that he knew in the questioning that the baby was meconium-stained, didn't you?

A: I can't say what I think he knew. You're asking how I say he knew? I can't tell you what I say he knew.

Q: Well, you saw his sworn testimony under oath where he agreed the baby was meconium-stained, right?

A: That was his interpretation of the record. I have mine.

Q: Doctor, you also saw that he agreed that it takes a minimum of four hours for a baby in an amniotic sac—where meconium has been passed, it takes a minimum of four hours for that baby to be stained, true?

A: Truly stained, yes.

Q: As opposed to fictitiously stained.

A: Staining implies that you can't wash it off, that it's in the skin and it remains there.

Q: Doctor, do you assume that staining is understood by people who take care of newborn babies to be staining? Do you assume that?

A: I assume it's assumed by the people who know what they are reading and writing, yes.

Q: Doctor, you saw that Dr. Clare agreed that it takes a minimum of four hours for a baby to become meconium-stained, correct?

A: Correct.

Q: You agree with him or disagree with him? Yes or no?

A: About which aspect of the question?

Q: There was only one issue in the question, doctor, that he agreed that it takes at least four hours for the baby to become meconium-stained. There's only one concept there, isn't there?

A: I'll agree to that question, yes.

Q: You not only agreed that the question was asked and answered, you agree with the testimony, true?

A: I do not agree with the testimony that the baby was meconium-stained. I agree that it takes four hours for it to happen, if it is going to happen.

Q: Doctor, I can only ask you one question at one time, right?

A: I'll accept that.

Q: Okay. I asked you if you agreed with the testimony that it takes four hours, a minimum, for a baby to become stained. Do you agree with that, doctor? Yes or no?

A: Some—someplace around that period of time, yes.

Q: Sir, if this baby was meconium-stained, and if it takes a minimum of four hours, then it follows as night to day, doctor, that at the time the bag of waters ruptured, there was meconium in the amniotic fluid, true or false?

A: True.

Q: If this woman came to the hospital and gave a history of yellow-colored amniotic fluid, that was a very important piece of history, true?

A: True.

Q: It doesn't do much good for mother and baby to chart it and then ignore it, true?

A: True.

Q: That's what was done in this case, and it was, right at the beginning, a cardinal error, true?

A: Not true.

Q: Doctor, do you think that a history of yellow-colored fluid on rupture of the bag of waters 35 minutes or so earlier, having said that it's an important issue, it should be explored?

A: Yes, sir.

Q: Correct?

A: Yes, sir.

Q: You have testified that amber or yellow fluid is a result of meconium staining, true? You have testified to that under oath, correct?

A: We now have amber or yellow? Is that the question? I mean, I want to be very clear as to what I'm answering now. We have amber or yellow? The answer is yes, amber or yellow is an indication.

Q: Doctor, amber is a shade of yellow, isn't it?

A: There are many shades of yellow. We talked about that before, sir.

Q: Have you testified, doctor, that amber fluid is meconium-stained?

A: Amber fluid? Yes, sir.

Q: And that was when you were making the distinction between amber and yellow, is it?

A: I don't think I was asked the distinction at that point, sir.

Q: If a woman arrives in a hospital with a history of a ruptured bag of waters approximately 35 minutes before, and it's the opinion, or should be the opinion, of medical personnel that that is meconium fluid, that is, by definition, a high-risk labor at that point, no ifs, ands, or buts, true?

A: True.

Q: And, doctor, to allow a first-year resident to manage such a labor would be a departure from accepted practice, true?

A: True.

23.04 Defuse the Ideas Too

In addition to defusing the language of the expert—who may not be using those terms merely to impress the jury, but rather, because they are truly the terms of that art—you must also use the same methods to defuse the thoughts and ideas of that expert. For example, an expert engineer, describing a machine which molds plastic, which machine macerated the hand of a worker (the plaintiff), indicates that the steel molding surfaces of that machine were designed to close after an infusion of hot plastic material, with 10,000 pounds of pressure per square inch. The engineer testifies that after catching his hand in the machine, the worker/plaintiff had his hand crushed. Your Adversary's theory is obvious. Since the plaintiff used that machine innumerable times, his negligence in using the machine, not misdesign of the machine, caused the injury. Your theory is that the machine was negligently maintained, and that negligence, not design, caused the injury. As the prospective cross-examiner, you have listened, as has the jury, to the expert's testimony. You have to unravel for them the points that you want them to understand. First you have to understand the points yourself. Can a steel machine be designed to close, and ram into its own parts with 10,000 pounds pressure, hundreds of times each day? Will that not cause the dies to be smashed, if not on the first blow, perhaps after the hundredth or thousandth? You rise:

Q: Mr. Engineer, you say the molding surfaces, which molded an infusion of hot plastic into dog bowls, closes with 10,000 pounds pressure per square inch each time it closes?

A: Yes.

Q: Now, this machine has a moving part and a fixed part, does it not? In other words, one part slides open, then closes onto another part which has remained stationary?

A: That's right.

Q: This part that moves and slides, it slides on some sort of track, does it not?

A: It has ball bearings in a slide housing.

Q: And this moving part has some weight to it, does it not?

A: It does.

Q: How much weight, do you know?

A: No, I was unable to take the machine apart to weigh it. I would say that the part was not too heavy.

Q: It was made of steel, was it not?

A: Yes.

Q: Weighed more than ten pounds, didn't it?

A: Yes, sure.

Q: More than a hundred too?

A: Yes, I'm sure it did.

Q: And, as it slid forward to meet its mate in molding dog bowls, did it not need some power to propel it forward?

A: Yes.

Q: And wasn't its progress forward impeded, stopped, slowed somewhat, by the friction of sliding forward?

A: Somewhat, not completely, of course.

Q: And of the 10,000 pounds of pressure that you've described for the jury, wasn't a portion of that pressure utilized in moving the part forward, and in overcoming the inertia and friction of the sliding weight?

A: Yes, I would say so.

Q: So that, by design, the machine required a substantial amount of that 10,000-pound pressure to get the two surfaces to come together?

A: Some of it, true.

Q: And, by the time the two parts close in order to mold, they do just that, they close. In other words, the machine doesn't slam or ram into itself, but closes without damaging the rest of the machine?

A: Yes, that's how it was designed.

Q: The die surfaces, the metal parts that are part of the machine to form the dog bowls, and the machine itself, are expensive pieces of equipment, are they not?

A: Yes, they are.

Q: There is a safety device built into the machine, causing it not to close if the plastic is misfed, misaligned, or anything else that might damage the die surface or the machine itself, correct?

A: True.

Q: You think that hot, melted plastic is harder or softer than a man's hand, the skin and bone of it?

A: I don't know, I never thought about it.

Q: About the same, wouldn't you say?

A: I guess.

Q: Had the safety device that is intended to cause closing parts of the machine to stop on a misfed or misaligned piece of hot plastic been working, it would also have stopped for the skin and bones of a human hand, correct?

A: It may have.

CROSS-EXAMINER: I have no further questions.

23.05 Not All the Same—But So What?

You have now the basic tools you need to Cross-examine an expert witness. There are all sorts of experts in all sorts of fields, and any attempt at cataloging them, or specifically dealing with or treating every possible expert or combination of experts, would be impossible and futile. It should suffice, however, that you know that the way to challenge the expert is to make he or she a mere mortal who is no brighter, smarter, or more logical, per se, than any other person in the courtroom. Reduce his or her language to the jury's language and reduce his or her logic the same way you reduce any other witness's logic.

23.06 Checklist for Cross-Examining the Expert

1. Do you know your subject matter?
2. Do you know the language of the particular specialty?
3. Knowing those things, reduce the testimony to layman's talk before the jury.
4. Reduce the logic of the expert's opinion the same way you reduce that of any other witness.

23.07 Sample Cross-Examinations

In the supplement section at the end of this book there are five sample extended Cross-examinations. One is a fuller examination by famous Trial Advocate Jay Goldberg of Salvatore (Sammy the Bull) Gravano, self-confessed multiple assassin; one I did myself in a homicide/multiple rape case, examining the chief DNA expert of the Federal Bureau of Investigation as to the identifying methods employed by the F.B.I. and the use of DNA to assist in that task; another is by eminent Trial Advocate James M. LaRossa; another is by the innovative Hugh Anthony Levine; and one is a fuller length Cross-examination of a doctor by the esteemed Trial Advocate Thomas A. Moore in a medical malpractice case. These are included so that you will see the blend of all the methods and tools of Cross-examination in their Cross-examinations, and also to see how the lessons put forth in the chapters of this book actually are used in real-life trials.

24.

Making the Witness Your Own

24.01 Make the Witness Your Own

As indicated in the beginning of this book, the purpose of Cross-examination is to probe, inquire, and whittle down the witnesses presented by your Adversary, to reshape their testimony into a form compatible with your own version of the issues in the case. There is often, however, another affirmative, tactical use to be made of the witnesses proffered by your Adversary; and that is to utilize the knowledge or information that the Adverse Witness possesses to partially formulate your own version of the facts, in short, to make your Adversary's witnesses your own.

24.02 What It Means

When you "make a witness your own," what is meant is that when you inquire of a witness presented by your Adversary concerning facts beyond the content of the Direct examination, it is as if you had called the witness to the stand yourself on Direct examination. In theory, you vouch for the witness as to the inquiry which goes beyond the Direct; you shall not be permitted to cross-examine the witness as to the new material; and your inquiry must be conducted without leading. In effect, for the purposes and in reference to the material on which you exceed the Direct examination, the witness becomes your own witness. Some lesser worthies than yourself become somewhat intimidated by the concept that when you make a cross-examined witness your own, you vouch for the credibility of that witness and you can't cross-examine, can't lead. So what? For the purposes that I recommend making a witness your own, that is, picking the brain of a disinterested witness, a trapped witness of whom you have substantial hold and can take advantage of with confidence, there is no need to have the protections of Cross-examination. It's not going to be a hostile, adverse encounter. Quite the contrary; the witness whose brain you choose to pick shall ordinarily be totally disinterested, but knowledgeable, a person from whom you can obtain information you couldn't get from any other of your Adversary's witnesses, and which you couldn't put into the trial yourself until much later on in your own case.

Try it; you'll like it.

24.03 Much Important Factual Information Can Be Introduced Just When You Need It

As you know, Cross-examination ordinarily is a probing of the Direct testimony. You are restricted in your probing to that information elicited on the Direct. You cannot properly cross-examine beyond that point; and certainly you can't interrupt your Adversary's case to introduce evidence you think should be before the jury at this time. If you do go beyond the scope of Direct examination and make inquiry of the witness to bring out information you think the witness knows, information you think should be before the jury, you may be advised by the court that you are proceeding beyond the Direct examination, and that you are not permitted to venture there unless you intend to make the witness your own. Often, such admonition by the judge is hurled at the cross-examiner with a tone that indicates that such a road is perilous, strewn with great pitfalls, and traveled only by the foolhardy. Such is not the case at all. It is very often quite beneficial to take an Adverse Witness, with much information about the case (usually technical, physical information), and draw from he or she—even if you do make the witness your own—information which would otherwise be difficult to obtain, which you would have to drag from a witness more sympathetic to your Adversary, or obtain from your own witness much later in the case.

For instance, you wish the jury, right at the outset of the evidentiary presentation, to understand the total physical picture of the place at which the accident happened so that they might better follow the unfolding testimony. Who will better supply that description: a disinterested policeman who responded to the scene or the alleged victim, the plaintiff? It is now, however, the plaintiff's case. Your Adversary has proffered the disinterested policeman merely to introduce the policeman's official report, which contains what your Adversary thinks is stage-setting information, in anticipation of the plaintiff taking the stand. Your Adversary's plan is to set the sympathy stage so that the jury is already primed when the plaintiff takes the stand with the fact that the plaintiff was seriously injured; that, as far as liability is concerned, the plaintiff was in the right, and the defendant in the wrong.

You are asked by your Adversary to stipulate to the introduction of the police report. Rather than routinely agreeing, inexplicably, you refuse. The judge looks askance at you as if you are an inexperienced fledgling wasting time, but you have a plan. You want to establish as part of your mosaic the entire picture of the physical scene, right at the beginning of the case. You feel that if you do not get this information in at this juncture, if you wait for the plaintiff to testify, you will become a dentist, not a lawyer; having to pull evidence out as if you were pulling teeth, fighting over every inch of ground, every street lamp, every curb marking, and every traffic signal. You feel, with some justification, that the policeman/witness proffered by your Adversary gives you a window of opportunity to set the stage, to create your own, desired atmosphere before the jury so they can best interpret the testimony about to be presented.

The police officer takes the stand and testifies that he responded to the scene, saw skid marks, and put the plaintiff in the ambulance. You cross-examine the Direct lightly; in and of itself, it is the sort of evidence to which you might as well have stipulated. However, you want to establish more at this juncture. You want to establish that the policeman did not see and does not know how the accident happened. To do this, you proceed on your own to develop information from the witness which neither the policeman nor your Adversary anticipated. (Since neither of them anticipated your tack, neither of them have prepared for such interrogation.) Thus, you catch your Adversary off guard and obtain totally spontaneous information for later use on Cross-examination of the plaintiff or other Adverse Witnesses.

For example, the police officer presented by your Adversary has testified on Direct about having been the first police officer on the scene. You rise to inquire preliminarily about the officer's arrival. Then you go off on your own quest, as follows:

Q: Officer, you've testified about the scene after you arrived there. Let me ask you this. How wide a thoroughfare is Main Street at its intersection with Maple Avenue?

A: Four lanes, two in each direction.

Q: Is there a parking lane on each side, in addition?

A: Yes.

Q: What is the surface material of the roadway?

A: Asphalt.

Q: Do you know if this asphalt was laid over cement; in other words, originally it was cement, and then later, in repaving, the asphalt was put down?

YOUR ADVERSARY: Your Honor, this is beyond the scope of the Direct examination. The officer merely testified about responding to the scene, seeing skid marks, and seeing the plaintiff leave in an ambulance.

THE COURT: That's true, Mr. Cross-examiner. These points were not covered on direct. You'll be making the witness your own if you persist.

CROSS-EXAMINER: Very well, Your Honor, I shall make the witness my own. Rather than call this witness back again at a later time, I think it would be expeditious to inquire into this area now. I certainly have no objection to having the witness considered my own.

THE COURT: Very well, if you wish. You may answer, officer.

THE WITNESS: What was the question?

Q: May the reporter read back the question, Your Honor?

THE COURT: Yes, please do. (Reporter reads the question.)

A: I think so, about five years ago.

Q: And, in places, this asphalt had torn away, was missing, causing the original cement to show through.

A: In places.

Q: And in the place where the accident happened, were there potholes present?

A: There might have been.

Q: May I have this marked for identification, Your Honor?

THE COURT: Mark it.

Q: I show you this, officer, which has been previously marked Defendant's Exhibit A, for identification, and ask you if you recognize what it depicts?

A: That's a photograph of Main Street looking east towards Maple Avenue.

Q: And does it fairly and accurately represent what the thoroughfare looked like on the day of the accident?

A: (The witness studies the photograph.) It seems to.

CROSS-EXAMINER: I offer that photograph, defendant's A for identification in evidence.

THE COURT: Show it to the other side.

YOUR ADVERSARY: I object to this photograph, Your Honor, as not being sufficiently supported by the evidence—there are conditions existing here which may not have existed at the time of the accident.

CROSS-EXAMINER: And I object, Your Honor, to counsel making a speech in front of the jury and the witness. If counsel wishes to testify, perhaps he should take the stand to be sworn. Otherwise, perhaps questions on the voir dire might be more appropriate.

THE COURT: Do you wish, Mr. Adverse Counsel, to ask the witness any question on the voir dire about that exhibit?

YOUR ADVERSARY: Yes, sir. Mr. Witness, on this photograph, defendant's Exhibit A, for identification, does everything that appears on the photograph look exactly the way it did on the day of the accident?

THE WITNESS: I can't say exactly every condition, no. I didn't check it that carefully.

YOUR ADVERSARY: That's the basis of my objection, Your Honor.

CROSS-EXAMINER: May I ask a few more questions, Your Honor?

THE COURT: Certainly.

Q: Officer, do the conditions that are depicted in this photograph, particularly the condition of the roadbed, fairly represent what existed the day of the accident? In other words, without saying that each and every pothole that appears was there on the day of the accident, was this more or less, basically and fairly, the condition that was there?

A: Yes, sir.

CROSS-EXAMINER: I again offer the photograph, Your Honor, not as an exact depiction of what was there on the day of the accident, but as a fair and accurate representation of the conditions that existed on that day.

YOUR ADVERSARY: And I again object.

THE COURT: No, it shall be received.

CROSS-EXAMINER: May I have another exhibit marked, Your Honor?

NOTE: It would be better to have premarked the exhibits to save time and make your presentation smoother and less interrupted.

THE COURT: I see you have a series of photographs there, Mr. Cross-examiner. Why not have them all marked for identification at the same time, and we'll save some time that way?

CROSS-EXAMINER: Very well, sir.

Q: Now officer, I show you this, defendant's Exhibit B for Identification, and ask you if you know what it depicts?

A: Yes, sir, that's Main Street, looking west toward Maple Avenue.

Q: And does this, officer, fairly and accurately depict the intersection, and particularly the roadbed, not exactly as it was on the day of the accident, but basically and fairly depict the physical condition of the intersection on that day?

YOUR ADVERSARY: I object, Your Honor.

THE COURT: To what? He hasn't offered the photograph in evidence. Proceed. You may answer. Please move along, Mr. Cross-examiner, this is the Direct case, and this is Mr. Adversary's witness.

CROSS-EXAMINER: I'm moving as expeditiously as I can, Your Honor. I think that the jury's having, a complete picture of the intersection will help them understand the testimony better.

THE COURT: No speeches; just proceed.

YOUR ADVERSARY: I object to the speech, Your Honor.

THE COURT: And I object to both your speeches. Proceed. Do you remember the question, officer?

A: I do. And it does.

CROSS-EXAMINER: I now offer Exhibit B in Evidence.

YOUR ADVERSARY: Now I object, Your Honor.

THE COURT: Same grounds as your objection to the other photograph?

YOUR ADVERSARY: Yes, sir.

THE COURT: Overruled, received. Let's go.

Q: Officer, I show you defendant's Exhibit C for Identification. What, if you know, does that depict?

A: Maple Avenue, looking south to Main Street.

Q: And does that fairly and accurately—not exactly—merely fairly and accurately, represent the condition of the intersection and roadway on the day of the accident?

A: Yes, sir, it does.

THE COURT: (Impatient court overrules nonobjection to save time.) Objection overruled. Received. Let's move along, Mr. Cross-examiner. I'm giving you wide latitude, but I think you could have done this on your own case.

CROSS-EXAMINER: Yes, sir.

Q: Lastly, officer, I show you defendant's Exhibit D for identification, and ask you whether you recognize what it depicts?

A: I do.

Q: And what is that?

A: Maple Avenue, looking north to Main Street.

Q: And, does this photograph fairly and accurately depict the conditions which existed on the day of the incident herein?

A: It does.

THE COURT: Received. Anything else of this witness, Mr. Cross-examiner?

CROSS-EXAMINER: No, sir.

THE COURT: Call your next witness, Mr. Adversary.

The foregoing was run at length so that you might get a better idea of the actual give and take of battle conditions. There is always something happening and always something that you must know and do to keep the trial moving and to counter your Adversary's moves. Additionally, it fairly and accurately depicts the ease with which a disinterested individual or witness will give you information, and assist you to put in evidence, as opposed to an interested witness such as the plaintiff. Had you asked the plaintiff to identify the scene depicted in the exhibits, you would have had a great deal of "I don't know," "I'm not sure," etc. As it stands now, you have all you want in evidence for the jury to better imagine the scene when the plaintiff testifies.

24.04 Don't Waste a Witness

Suppose that you had just stipulated to the officer's testimony above, or had merely watched the officer testify, had not cross-examined much—after all, he wasn't at the scene until *after* the accident happened—and then, in order to provide the jury a better understanding of the unfolding testimony of the plaintiff (the next witness), in order to introduce the photographs in order to refer to them in your Cross-examination, in order to let the jury better realize how inaccurate the plaintiff's testimony is, you try to have the photos introduced through the plaintiff himself. Imagine what the plaintiff's answers would be as to whether or not the photograph fairly and accurately represents the condition of the roadway on the day of the accident. Let's imagine what it would be like:

Q: Now Mr. Plaintiff, I show you this and ask you whether or not you know what this depicts?

A: Not really.

Q: Does it fairly and accurately represent what the condition of the roadway was on the day of the accident?

A: Not as I remember it. I don't think so.

Q: Not as to the building in the picture, but just as to the condition of the roadway surface—does it fairly and accurately depict the roadway as it was on the day of the accident?

A: Not that I can remember. There weren't all these potholes. It was a smooth asphalt surface then, as I remember it. There may have been a couple of potholes, but nothing like this. I don't know when this was taken. When was it taken?

YOUR ADVERSARY: Yes, Your Honor, may we have a representation as to when this photograph was taken, and by whom?

THE COURT: Yes, Mr. Cross-examiner, by whom and when were these photographs taken?

Now you don't think that you're getting those photographs into evidence on the plaintiff's case, do you? Certainly not. The plaintiff, playing it carefully, slowly, isn't going to give you an inch. Sure, you can later put the photographs into evidence on the defendant's case. All the points that you wanted to make with the plaintiff when you cross-examined him, using actual pictures for the jury to show how utterly inaccurate the plaintiff is, will have to be done in the abstract, with no photographs. Later on, when there's no plaintiff to twirl in circles, you'll introduce the photographs, hoping that the jury can remember all those fine points that you made. It would have been far better to use the Adversary's witnesses, use anyone's witness, and make them your own; so what? If a witness has information you want in front of the jury, make the witness your own; get it out there when you want it. Even if you make the witness your own, you'll get a lot more mileage using an independent witness to get factual material into the case than you will trying to get it out of a hostile witness or waiting until your own case.

25.

Make a Record

25.01 Make a Complete Record, No Matter What

Cross-examiners, now that you have come this long way and have read this entire book, you are almost at the end of your journey, almost at the place and time where you can put it all together. Before that and anything else that you do, you must understand that it is most important, couldn't be more important, that whatever you do, *you must make and preserve a proper and complete record.*

With all the deft twists and smooth moves of your Cross-examination, you may still suffer adverse rulings from the court. That doesn't mean you are wrong. It may mean that the judge is wrong. If judges weren't ever wrong, all those books on the shelves in the law library that contain the decisions and citations that we are so wont to quote and utilize wouldn't be there. No appeals would exist, no reversals—nothing. That isn't the way our *stare decisis* system works. Where would all the *decisis* come from if rulings and decisions of trial courts were not constantly being challenged and often reversed?

25.02 It's Not That Easy

Many of you will reply silently that, of course, you're going to make a proper record. Just as virtue really doesn't triumph until it is sorely pressed, just as being good is not much of an accomplishment until it is so easy and tempting to be bad, so too with the fact that it isn't difficult to make a record until you come across the cantankerous, obstinate, impatient, peripatetic judge. Then tell me how easy it is to make the record. It isn't the good, kind, thoughtful judge who's going to make your life difficult. It is the previously described cantankerous judge who will make adverse rulings and hammer them into you, who will also make it difficult for you to preserve a proper record. For example, you are embarking on a line of questions which you feel are essential to bringing out before the jury the unreliability of the witness, which will show his or her interest in the case and the inaccuracy of his or her testimony. The court sustains the objection of your Adversary and says the area of your Cross-examination is immaterial and irrelevant. Obviously, the court doesn't appreciate, or even comprehend, the fine point you are trying to bring out.

CROSS-EXAMINER: Your Honor, may I explain to the court the purpose of my examination in this area?

THE COURT: I understand your point, Mr. Cross-examiner. I was not appointed to this bench yesterday. Proceed.

CROSS-EXAMINER: Your Honor, I believe that I have a valid point here, and I would like to pursue it. I will give Your Honor citations. . .

THE COURT: You will give His Honor the pleasure of proceeding without a speech, if you don't mind. When I want citations, I'll ask you for a memo of law. Ask your next question.

CROSS-EXAMINER: May I approach the sidebar, Your Honor?

THE COURT: You may not. Proceed!

CROSS-EXAMINER: I'd like to make an offer of proof then, Your Honor.

THE COURT: Later. Now you'll ask your next question.

CROSS-EXAMINER: Your Honor. . .

THE COURT: If you don't ask your next question right now, I'll terminate your examination, as you have obviously completed it.

CROSS-EXAMINER: Your Honor, if I may. . .

THE COURT: Mr. Witness, thank you; you may leave the stand. Call your next witness, Mr. Adversary.

CROSS-EXAMINER: Your Honor has interfered with and curtailed my Cross-examination; you are interfering unnecessarily and improperly with the defendant's capacity to. . .

THE COURT: You are directed to sit down at counsel table and to desist from making a spectacle of yourself in the courtroom. Sit down.

CROSS-EXAMINER: I take umbrage at Your Honor's remarks in front of the jury. I am not making a spectacle of myself or of anything else. I am trying to defend my client and make what I consider appropriate objections.

THE COURT: Sit down. Sit down. Officer, put that man in his seat. Sit down and keep quiet.

CROSS-EXAMINER: There's no need for that, Your Honor. I'll sit. But I want to make the record completer clear. Your Honor is curtailing Cross-examination, improperly interfering with the trial, and precluding me from making a proper record.

THE COURT: You've brought all of this on yourself.

CROSS-EXAMINER: May I make a record, or is Your Honor directing me not to do so?

THE COURT: Call your next witness, Mr. Adversary.

CROSS-EXAMINER: I call for the declaration of a mistrial.

THE COURT: Denied. Call your next witness, Mr. Adversary.

That was neither a calm nor a pleasant scene. But if any reader thinks that such scene is far-fetched fantasy, I can point out chapter and verse where such, in essence, has occurred in more than one trial, before more than one judge. True, such a judge would not have proper judicial temperament. That doesn't mean you won't run into the same thing in your trial work. You'll know instantly that it isn't always easy to preserve the record under those conditions. It isn't pleasant or easy to stand there, in front of the jury, being berated, humiliated, beaten. It isn't easy to fly back into the hot breath of the fiery dragon. But you must.

25.03 Don't Be Contumacious

You must not be disrespectful. You must never argue with the judge's decision. The only thing you must fight for is the right and opportunity to make the record complete and record your objections. Make a proper Record. Don't argue. If the court refuses to permit you to make the proper Record, then let the Record reflect that the court refuses to let you make a proper Record. Incredibly, there is actually less time taken up if the court would permit you to make the Record, deny your application, and proceed with the trial than to create a big furor, putting your mettle to the test. Even where your Adversary or the court engages in or permits disorder and rancor, acrimony and derision, you must still make a proper record. *Nobody said it was easy.*

Summation

Here is a brief overview of the methods, procedures, and techniques which have been put forward in this book.

Cross-examination is not intended to give the trial attorney a showcase from which to dazzle the court, the jury, and his or her own client with a display of cerebral virtuosity. Nor is its purpose to improve the cross-examiner's circulation by providing an opportunity to rise, after the Direct testimony of each and every witness, to ask perfunctory, rambling questions.

The purpose of Cross-examination is to hone, to whittle down, to neutralize the testimony of the witnesses presented by your Adversary to substantiate his or her client's strengths and your client's faults. It is to subject the Direct to a baptism by fire, to melt away the fat, untruths, inconsistencies, and impurities until that testimony stands sandblast clean. Whittling down the Direct is not all the cross-examiner must try to do when he or she steps up to face the Adverse Witness. There is another affirmative and most important purpose of Cross-examination: to control and direct the Cross-examination so that the testimony of the Adverse Witnesses is diminished to fit within the cross-examiner's specific and equally planned overview of the evidence; so that, at Summation, the adverse testimony and evidence can be reconciled comfortably within the cross-examiner's theory of the case.

Evidence is the sum total of both the Direct and Cross-examination. It is not only the witness's Direct testimony, but the way that Direct testimony withstands Cross-examination which constitutes the resultant evidence the jury shall consider during deliberation. Where the Direct testimony is compatible with the cross-examiner's overview of the ultimate configuration of the issues, there is usually no purpose or necessity for Cross-examination.

The best Cross-examination is one that never takes place. Where the Direct is in no fashion harmful to, or incompatible with, the cross-examiner's position, ordinarily, Cross-examination can and should be waived.

It is also true, however, that on occasion, even though the Direct is not harmful, such as when an independent, disinterested person gives background, technical testimony, the cross-examiner may want to capitalize on the objective disinteresed knowledge of that witness to develop his or her own theory of the case, or some aspect of the case. In that instance, the cross-examiner may make that disinterested witness "his or her own" to develop additional background for cross-examining other more hostile witnesses.

When the "big-gun" witnesses presented by your Adversary score direct hits on your theory of the case, much as you might often like to run and hide, you cannot. Nor can you successfully defend your client's position by rising with contemptuous pseudo-confidence to dismiss the witness with a "No questions." When the hour is darkest for your client, when the big bombs are really falling all around you, that's the time when you must rise to begin to turn the tide by turning on the heat and sear the testimony of the Adverse Witness to melt out the fat, the exaggeration, and the untruth. That's when the cross-examiner must work to turn that evidence, if not completely around, at least into a direction which is less incompatible with the cross-examiner's position.

Remember, the "big kill' is not the cross-examiner's aim or objective. If it presents itself, by all means, embrace it. But that's easy. It is when there is no big kill that you have to, with tenacious skill and infinite patience, one question at a time, wear down and wear away—not weary—the adverse testimony by testing every nut and bolt of it. Put your Cross-examination together in a script as an orchestrated presentation, a unified whole. Then begin dismantling the Adverse Witness, first by inquiring into his or her education and any illegal or immoral background. Then test his or her capacity to see, hear, view, and observe the factual situation in the case. On occasion, in leading the Adverse Witness into a trap, you might seem to others who are not aware of your plan to be digging a hole for yourself by again guiding the witness over ground which is harmful to your client. That is only the appearance. That is only what the jury thinks and what the Adverse Witness thinks, until you pull the rug out from under him or her with inconsistencies and contradictions. Be sure you have such ammunition to use or pursue another avenue to reach your goal.

Remember the pieces of your ultimate mosaic—the evidence testimony—must be shaped and reshaped out in the open, right in front of the jurors' eyes, so that in Summation, when assembling the entire picture of your case, you have the already-shaped pieces with which to work and mount an argument. Summation is only a recapitulation, a placing of the already-formed pieces of the mosaic into the final, total picture. The pieces must already exist in final form before you rise for Summation. You cannot shape a piece of evidence at Summation. It is too late by then. You can only place the pieces that you already molded into the picture as you planned to, as you prepared to, as you had in mind when you cross-examined the various Adverse Witnesses.

Don't just hammer away at an Adverse Witness haphazardly, perhaps to actually deepen the hole into which his or her testimony has already put you. There's always something to attack, always somewhere to begin, and some item you can use to start casting doubt on the witness.

Naturally, there are those who shall counter this last statement by saying, "Well, sometimes there isn't!" And that's true. Sometimes there's a witness, say the Pope or Albert Einstein, who, when talking about his particular field of endeavor, *is* the last word, is the *nonpareil*. You may find yourself antagonizing the jury to attempt to draw such a witness into little, subtle inconsistencies which are, in the light of the particular witness, ridiculous. In that case, and that case alone, you may stand, and say confidently, as if there were obviously no harm that the witness has done to your client, "No questions."

But, how often is your Adversary going to present the Pope or a person of the preeminence of an Einstein in your case? Not often. For the most part, the witnesses are ordinary people, with ordinary intelligence, and a modicum of capacity to endure, withstand the onslaught of the bloodthirsty cross-examiner that you have become and that you are.

You need not destroy the witness, tear him or her apart limb from limb, in order to ultimately vanquish him. The word ultimately is the operative word in the last sentence. All you have to do by your Cross-examination is to sow seeds of doubt in the jurors' minds. Try to get the jurors to say to themselves, "That witness was quite sure of what happened, but he was too sure, too sneaky. There's something about him I don't trust. I'm not sure he was telling the truth. I don't know if I can rely on him." Notice that the witness does not have to be destroyed. That's not necessary. If you get a juror thinking some of these doubts, you may destroy the Adversary's case as you intended to do. That's good enough. All you must achieve is to have the jurors, or some of them, doubt something in some area of the case, and that might be sufficient for the jurors to dismiss the entire testimony of the witness.

How often in your own experience have you met people whose presentation of facts about themselves, their exploits, or something they saw or did was so pat, so smooth, and so slick that you didn't believe them? Notice that the story the person told was letter perfect and yet haven't there been such occasions when you've walked away from such a story and said to yourself,

"Baloney! I don't believe it." So too with Cross-examination. You don't have to have a witness retract or disavow his or her entire testimony to be successful. You just have to bring doubt to the mind of the jurors. This witness is too slick, too interested, and too unbelievable; their story just doesn't ring true, that's not the way people in real life see things. This guy is a smart aleck, knows too much; he's just puffing himself up to look good. Any reaction like that is a great victory, even though you may not have caused the witness to retract one word of his or her testimony. After that, the witness can insist and insist again on his or her version. The more the witness insists, the less the jury believes.

Think. Control. Cast seeds of doubt. Then you've done your job well. You never know what is going to strike a strange, doubtful note in the jurors' minds. Just work at it. Think about this: If the witness is so formidable as to sink you to the bottom of the well, then you're sunk. If you're sunk, you're sunk, and attacking, working, and hacking your way back can only help. It can't hurt. You are guaranteed to miss 100 percent of the birds you don't even aim or take a shot at. Take a shot. Get up on your feet. You know how to do it. Do it!

Cross-Examination Supplement: Real-Life Examples

The following pages contain various Cross-examinations set forth at greater length than in the body of the book. Hopefully, these examinations by various well-experienced trial Advocates give you an idea of the pace and rhythm of Cross-examination under real battle conditions.

1. Jay Goldberg: *United States v. Joseph Gambino;* United States District Court, Southern District of New York

2. John Nicholas Iannuzzi: *People v. Matais Reyes;* Supreme Court, New York County

3. James M. LaRossa: *People v. Joseph Watts;* Supreme Court, Richmond County, New York

4. Hugh Anthony Levine: *US v. E. J. Gonsalves;* U.S. District Court, Northern District of California

5. Thomas A. Moore: *Nora Martelly v. The City of New York;* Supreme Court, New York County

1. Jay Goldberg: *United States* v. *Joseph Gambino;* United States District Court, Southern District of New York

Cross-examination by Mr. Goldberg of Sammy "the Bull" Gravano.

MR. GOLDBERG

Q: Sir, you told us when you were arrested on December 11, 1990, you were charged with committing or participating in the commission of three murders, is that right?

A: Yes.

309

Q: You told us that as you understood it, if you were convicted for those three murders—for the participation in those three murders you could have spent the rest of your life in jail, is that right?

A: Yes.

Q: You were 46 then?

A: Yes.

Q: With life expectancy, you could have spent 25, 30 years in jail, is that right?

A: Yes.

Q: Okay. Now, you have not pleaded guilty, as you sit here now, to three murders, but to having participated in the killing of 19 human beings. Is that correct?

A: Yes, 19 murders.

Q: 19 people? Is that right?

A: Yes.

Q: And you actually face, as you sit here, less punishment than when you were charged with killing three people. Is that right? Is that what I understand, yes or no?

A: Yes.

Q: Am I right about that?

A: I said yes.

Q: In other words, Mr. Gravano, you face 20 years in jail—maximum 20 years in jail for taking the lives of 19 human beings and you said yes. Isn't that right?

A: Yes.

Q: But I don't recall, and perhaps I missed it. I didn't hear if Mr. Mearns had asked you whether there was a low end, a minimum period of time that the learned sentencing judge, if he saw fit, would be authorized under this plea agreement to grant you, do you remember anything like that having been put to you?

A: No.

Q: As a matter of fact, under the agreement that you worked out with the government, you replaced an exposure of three life sentences for the three murders with a possibility, if luck be with you, for 19 murders, doing no additional time? Is that so, zero on the low end, isn't that a true statement?

A: The judge isn't bound by the guidelines.

Q: Does the plea agreement not permit the judge, be he so inclined, because you haven't been sentenced yet, to impose a probationary period, a zero term of incarceration?

A: Yes.

Q: Have you not said within the last several weeks that, if luck be with you, that you could be on the street by Christmas, have you said that?

A: I don't think I said if luck be with me.

Q: Forget the luck. If fate be with you, you hope to be with us again as early as the Christmas season, have you said that?

A: I believe I wasn't asked that way, but . . .

Q: Well, I will ask you, given the festive mood of Christmas, is it your hope, as you sit here, that by Christmas you will one day free, that's your hope, isn't that so?

A: My hope is to be free one day, yes.

Q: Yes, and you have said as recently as the last two weeks, you made reference to the month of December as your hoped for goal of freedom, is that so, for these 19—

A: I think that's what a lawyer presented.

Q: And what did you say in response to what the lawyer said?

A: Yes, I hope to be out at the earliest possible date.

Q: The earliest at least after you testify, is that right?

A: I'm not to be sentenced in December, so it is actually a wrong date, but—

Q: Let me see how I understand this. When you called the government or the F.B.I. on October 24, 1990, you were sitting in a prison which Mr. Mearns refers to as the M.C.C., the Metropolitan Correctional Center, right?

A: Yes.

Q: Facing this prospect of three life sentences without parole, correct?

A: I don't believe so. I think it is just one sentence of life without parole.

Q: I mean one life without parole. Is that right, one life sentence without parole?

A: I believe that's what the sentence would have been.

Q: And you picked up the phone and you called the government. Is that right, or the F.B.I.?

A: Yes.

Q: Did you do that—and I know this may sound familiar to you—did you do this? Did you make that call because you had some conversion, some change of direction in the way in which you had lived your life? Is that why you picked up that telephone?

A: No.

Q: Okay. You picked up that phone to try to work a deal for yourself. Is that true?

A: I guess you could put it that way.

Q: Because when you went down on October 24, you met an F.B.I. agent, I think you told us several F.B.I. agents, and the United States Attorney himself, Mr. Maloney. Is that correct?

A: Yes.

Q: And you talked to them about the possibility that you wanted to come clean with your life of crime. Is that correct?

A: I believe I said something to the effect that I was turning my back on my life and I was changing direction.

Q: Let me see if I understand this. You were turning—give that to me one more time, I missed it?

A: I was turning my back on my life, my lifestyle, and I was changing my direction.

Q: Changing direction, that was October 24, 1991, is that right, and you told that to Mr. Maloney? Is that right?

A: I believe that's the date.

Q: Did you tell Mr. Maloney that, despite the statement that you made to him that you wanted to turn your back on your other life, you were going to go back to the M.C.C. and commit further extortionate credit collections, did you tell that to him?

A: No.

Q: But there is no question that after you left Mr. Maloney's office, when you told him that you wanted to turn your back on your former life, you uttered those words, intending for him to believe that you could now be trusted to turn your back on your former life, isn't that so, that is why you uttered those words to him, isn't that true?

A: No.

Q: When you said to Mr. Maloney, I am here because I want to turn my back on my former life you conveyed to him, did you not, the fact of your intention to change your way of life, isn't that a fair statement?

A: I don't know if that is what was running through my head at this particular point.

Q: As a matter of fact, despite what you said to Mr. Maloney, for the next few weeks after you went back to the M.C.C. you proceeded to arrange collections, or extortionate credit collections between October 24, 1991, and November 8, 1991, when you left the M.C.C., isn't that true?

A: No.

Q: That is not true?

A: No.

Q: Do you recall being asked this question at page 4232? This is Gravano cross in the 4,000 numbers. MR. GOLDBERG. It is a transcript, 4232. Do you recall this question having been to you—the shylocking business you were involved in continued right up until the time that you were arrested, correct?

A: Yes.

Q: In fact you even continued it there while you were in the M.C.C., did you not?

A: Yes.

Q: Are you saying here that you didn't continue engaging in shylocking right up until the day you left the M.C.C.? Are you saying that?

A: What I am saying is—

Q: Are you saying, is that yes or no?

A: What I am saying is I didn't stop it.

Q: Wait a minute.

A: It would be a complete and total tip-off to the street to stop it. It was being run while I was in prison for months, and when I cooperated I didn't go back in and tell people on the street: Stop the shylocking, I cooperated.

Q: Mr. Gravano, until I reached for a transcript, I recall the question on the floor had been, did you, sir, not after leaving Mr. Maloney's office on October 24, 1991, until November 8, 1991, when you left the prison, you left the M.C.C., did you not continue to engage in loansharking, you said no. Isn't that right?

A: I just answered you, it is, yes.

Q: The answer is now yes?

A: The answer always was yes, I didn't stop it.

Q: Well, in other words, when you went to—wherever this meeting took place—and I am not interested—on October 24, 1991, did you tell the agent not only that you were intending to turn your back on your former life, but you intended to continue to loanshark through the balance of the month of October into November, are you saying you told them that?

A: Definitely was not discussed.

Q: You didn't get permission from them to engage in any extortionate credit transactions for those remaining two weeks, did you?

A: No.

Q: As a matter of fact, even after you went to the—strike that. When you went to the meeting that we have set as October 24, 1991, you went there to convince the persons who would listen, it was your intention to convince them that you had turned your back on your former life of crime, isn't that so, yes or no?

A: No, I didn't go there with the intention to convince them.

Q: So you told them, listen, until we make this deal, until we work out an agreement I got money on the street, I got to get that, I got to get it collected even if it violates serious federal laws. You never said that to anybody, did you?

A: No.

Q: But as a matter of fact, after leaving the presence of the United States Attorney himself and F.B.I. agent, you went back to the M.C.C. and you set in motion plans to collect monies that you knew were separate violations of federal law, isn't that so, yes or no?

A: No, not true. No.

Q: All right. Then let me read this to you, sir.

MR. MEARNS: Objection, Your Honor.

THE COURT: Overruled.

Q: "Question: In fact, you even continued talking about shylocking. In fact, you even continued it thereafter while you were in the M.C.C., did you not, yes or no?"

A: "Answer: Yes."

Q: "Question: You continued to receive shylocking payments through other people?"

A: "Answer: Yes."

Q: "Question: You had people collecting money for you on these loans?"

A: "Answer: Yes."

Q: "Question: You continued to collect money right up until the time you left the M.C.C., did you not?"

A: "Answer: Yes."

Q: "Question: Right up until the November 8, right?"

A: "Answer: Yes."

Q: You made those answers, did you not, to these questions, correct?

A: Those people.

Q: Did you give these answers to the questions that I have just read?

A: Yes.

Q: The monies that you collected between the time that you first met with the United States Attorney himself, and members of the F.B.I., until the time you left the M.C.C. over this two-week period you never arranged to give that money back through any help of the government for the victims, did you, yes or no?

A: Never came to me.

Q: Never came to you?

A: It was collected by the people on the street.

Q: I see.

A: I just never stopped it.

Q: When you were arrested you had hundreds of thousands of dollars in the bank, didn't you? Didn't you have a bank account of several hundred thousands, yes or no?

A: Two hundred thousand.

Q: Two hundred thousand? None of those monies were ever used by you to make any of your victims whole? Do you know what "whole" means, to repair the damage that you had caused, am I correct?

A: Shylock customers? I don't know what you are talking about.

Q: That is one set of victims?

A: No.

Q: Is that $200,000 that you had in the bank account, that is not the whole of your wealth as of the time that you were arrested, correct?

A: No.

Q: You had additional money, right?

A: Yes.

Q: You didn't work that out, any deal or arrangement with the government to turn back as a condition of this plea of guilty any of that money to either the victims, the government of the United States, namely, the IRS or any other agency of the government, correct?

A: No.

Q: And you've said that when you went to the government on October 24, 1991, you told the United States Attorney that you wanted to turn your back on your former life, is that right?

A: I don't know if I told him that. You asked me what I did. I don't think I told the U.S. Attorney that, but that is what my motive was for, that is what I did.

Q: But your plea agreement provides that your cooperation is only for a period of two years, isn't that so?

A: I don't believe so.

Q: There is not a time limit on the time set for your cooperation provided for in the plea agreement, yes or no?

A: I believe it is not a cooperation, it is testifying. Cooperation goes on, I believe, indefinitely.

Q: Do I understand at the expiration of this two years of testifying, you feel yourself free to go back, should you be favored with a return to the street to your former life is that what you understand the two-year word means?

A: I don't believe so.

Q: But that was a term that was suggested to the government by your lawyer, isn't that right, the two-year limit on testifying, the government never said to you, you only have to testify, Sammy, for just two-year period. The government never said that to you?

A: No.

Q: That was something that you insisted upon as a condition, of facing the prospect of getting no time for the killing of 19 human beings, correct, that was your idea to put a time limit?

A: Yes.

Q: And let me ask you something. Did the government ever say to you, listen, Salvatore Gravano, you can keep all the ill-gotten gains that you have made from loan-sharking, gambling, labor racketeering, murder, or was it your lawyer who argued in your presence with the government that there should be, no restitution required for you, whose idea was it that you can keep the money?

A: It was never discussed.

Q: Never discussed. They never said to you, Mr. Gravano. You are a person who I think went to the eighth grade?

A: Approximately.

Q: Correct. You were trained as a ladies hairdresser, is that right?

A: No, I was never a hairdresser.

Q: Wasn't that your training?

A: No.

Q: Did you ever go to hairdressing school?

A: Yes.

Q: Was it ladies hairdressers?

A: It was hair cutting.

Q: Hair cutting, okay. And the government never said to you, listen from your humble beginnings, and there was a period of time, was

Q: there not, when you reported, you and your wife in the year 1982 a mere $24,000 and change in taxable income, right?

A: I believe so. That is what the numbers are.

Q: So now—here you are in December of 1992 a millionaire, correct?

A: (No response.)

Q: And you described yourself as a millionaire, have you not, at the time of your arrest?

A: Yes.

Q: Did the government ever say to you: Listen, Gravano, it is clear to us that this fortune which you have amassed has not been through hard legitimate work, but has been through evil doings, and you should provide a fund for the victims who remain on the earth, as well as other people who have suffered financial loss. Did the government ever say that to you?

MR. MEARNS: Objection to the phrasing of the question.

THE COURT: Overruled.

Q: Did they say that to you, sir?

A: No.

Q: You certainly never offered it, right, as part of cleansing your soul, you never said to the government, listen I want to make my peace?

A: I didn't cleanse myself. I never said I cleansed my soul. The answer to that is, no, as well.

Q: You are here, sir, because you will do what it takes, you will spare no words or statement if you feel that it can increase your chances to return to the streets, isn't that a fair statement?

A: No.

Q: Are you here because you feel conscience stricken over your participation in the murder or demise of 19 human beings, you are not here for that reason, are you?

A: I am here because I was debriefed about what I know in this case, and I said exactly what I know. I am compelled to be here.

Q: Are you not, sir, as you sit here, in any way restrained or upset by any feeling of conscience about the loss of life, for example, for Joe Colucci who you say you killed, is that right?

A: Sure.

Q: You are. As a matter of fact, Joe Colucci had been your friend, is that right?

A: Yes.

Q: You are here having taken an oath, hoping—this is what I am asking you—hoping that this jury will trust your word, isn't that a fair statement?

A: I am here to say the facts of what I know.

Q: And you want the jury to trust, isn't that a fair statement, of what you say, isn't that correct?

A: That is not my job. I am here to tell the truth of what I know.

Q: You told other people who you knew in the course of your life things, for example, you had conversations with Louie Milito shortly before his death, to the effect, that he could trust you, that there would be no harm coming to him from you. Didn't you say that in words or substance to Louie Milito?

A: Sure.

Q: You gave him your word?

A: Sure.

Q: You knew Louie Milito all your life?

A: If he would have acted a certain way.

Q: You knew Louie Milito and Louie Milito knew you longer than these ladies and gentlemen?

A: He was a friend of mine and he was a man.

Q: Let me finish my question.

THE COURT: Excuse me. Listen to the question, and, please permit the witness—the witness will let you finish your question—and you will let the witness finish his answer because if both of you speak the same time this reporter will have some difficulty.

MR. GOLDBERG: Fine. We're sorry. My apologies.

THE COURT: Thank you.

Q: Louie Milito knew you longer than this jury knows you, isn't that so?

A: Of course, I said.

Q: Louie Milito knew you for 15 or more years, isn't that so?

A: At least 20.

Q: Twenty years. And you were a friend of Milito, isn't that so?

A: Yes.

Q: Were you a friend of his family?

A: Yes.

Q: You were a friend of his wife and his daughter, isn't that so?

A: Yes.

Q: You told on a given day Louie Milito to meet you at a particular location, is that correct?

A: Yes.

Q: You planned to murder him or have him murdered, isn't that a fair statement?

A: There came a point.

Q: Well, when you called him, did you call him on the phone?

A: No.

Q: Did you have someone call him?

A: Someone else called him.

Q: The mission was to cause him no alarm in asking him to come to that place, isn't that right, wherever it was?

A: That is true.

Q: But the man without question did. Before this man departed his home in Staten Island and journeyed for the last time in his life to a given location, the plan was set in motion to murder him, isn't that right?

A: Yes.

Q: As you sit here do you have any feeling of conscience with respect to his murder?

A: Yes, absolutely.

Q: And once you murdered him, or participated in his murder, did you go to his wife and daughter and tell them that you would help find the person who had murdered Louie Milito, did you do that, yes or no?

A: They came to me. I did tell them that, yes.

Q: They believed in you; is that right?

A: They believed I would help them.

Q: They trusted your word, is that right? Right? Is that a fair statement as far as you could glean?

A: Yes.

Q: They felt, as far as you could glean from the way they looked up at you after you said that you would help them, that they had faith in you, is that right?

A: Yes.

Q: All the while, sir, unbeknownst to them, you had killed the husband of Mrs. Milito and the father, obviously, of Ms. Milito, correct?

A: Yes.

Q: You had been in a business venture with Louie Milito before he met his demise, isn't that so?

A: Yes.

Q: You have said, have you not, on one or more occasions that you never killed in a fit of rage, did you ever say that to anyone?

A: Yes.

Q: In other words, your murders were done not out of anger, but they are planned in terms of what it could mean for you in terms of your pocketbook; isn't that so?

A: No.

* * * * * * * * * * * * * * * * * * * *

Q: Do I understand, sir, that at the tail end of your examination, you told this jury that you had pleaded guilty to two instances where you actually obstructed justice by intruding into the jury box to fix the outcome of case, is that what you pleaded guilty to?

A: Yes.

Q: One of those cases involved Eddie Lino?

A: Yes.

Q: Is that a drug case?

A: Yes.

Q: Was it a federal case?

A: Yes.

Q: Was it in this very building?

A: I would imagine so.

Q: You intruded in effect into the jury box by bribery and corruption of a person who had sworn as a juror to render justice, is that right, you did that?

A: I was a go-between for the captain in our Family and the people in the jury, yes.

Q: You pleaded guilty to doing that, isn't that so?

A: I participated, yes.

Q: You did that on one or more occasions, correct, yes or no?

A: Yes.

Q: But you say to this jury that they can trust your word, that you are telling the truth, is that what you are saying?

A: I said that I am here according to my deal telling the truth from what I know.

Q: And do I take it, withdrawn. Did it ever figure into your consideration to say to the Government you have charged me with crimes. I will tell all that I know and throw myself on the mercy of the Court. I don't need a plea agreement. Did you ever say that to the government?

A: No, I don't believe so.

Q: In other words, you have been involved in business deals in the course of your life, have you not?

A: Yes.

Q: At times you have been represented by lawyers in business deals, is that right?

A: Yes.

Q: Here you had a lawyer, is that right?

A: Yes.

Q: You didn't go in and say to the government listen, I have killed 19 human beings. I have done labor racketeering, extortion, armed robberies, gone on stickups, or did stickups, armed robberies. I want to turn my back on my former life. I will tell you all that I know. And I have full confidence in the judicial system that I will get what is coming to me. Did you ever say that to the government?

A: Not in those words, but that is what I did.

Q: That is what you did. But you told us that on December 11, 1990, a judge, a magistrate or a judge of the District Court had decided that you were such a threat to the community that you weren't even granted bail following your arrest on December 11, 1990, isn't that so?

A: Yes.

Q: You were such a threat to the community that you hoped to rejoin by Christmas that you were put in prison without any chance of bail following December 11, 1990, is that right?

A: Yes.

Q: And you are telling the ladies and gentlemen of this jury that you harbored one single scintilla of thought of going in, and telling these people, Mr. Dowling and Mr. Gabriel and members of the prosecution team, all the terrible things that you had done in your life, trusting without any restraints being put upon the judge to deal with you as his learned wisdom dictated, you never did that, did you?

A: That is what I did, I came in—

Q: I am sorry. I am sorry. I interrupted. Go ahead. Sir, this—whoever the judge is, no longer is authorized under the law to give you a life sentence, isn't that so?

A: I believe so.

Q: In other words, by agreement between you and your lawyer and the government, the learned judge is no longer to sentence you to life, two life sentences for taking the lives of 19 people, correct?

A: I believe it is a cap of 20.

Q: Cap of 20, which means if things really go bad for you, the judge in a maximum can sentence you to 20 years, correct?

A: I believe that is the high top level.

Q: But if things, as I said earlier, go good for you, the holiday season will be very good for you, hopefully, is that right?

A: I have no idea.

Q: Now, sir, was there ever a time when you tried to convey to anyone that the result of your upbringing was such that it led you into a life of crime, did you ever say anything of that kind to anyone that you were such a product?

A: I said I grew up in the tough neighborhood.

Q: Did you say it was a tough neighborhood, or did you tell a jury of human beings that you were a product of a ghetto life, did you say that to a jury, yes or no?

A: Yes.

Q: And you knew that when you said that you were a product of a ghetto life, you were trying to get sympathy when you uttered those words in front of a jury, isn't that so?

A: No. Absolutely not.

Q: But you were not the product of a ghetto upbringing were you, yes or no?

A: What I did was correct my answer there, and I said that it was not exactly a ghetto, but it was a tough neighborhood.

Q: Did you not say, did you not use the word, before I look at the book, that you were a product of a ghetto upbringing, did you use those words, yes or no?

A: I believe I went on to say that the ghetto might be a stretch of the word, but I came from a tough neighborhood.

Q: Your parents are hard-working honest people, who worked 15 hours a day in a dress factory. They bought a $6,000 bungalow in the country, okay?

A: What I said is I grew up in a tough neighborhood with rough guys. We stole, we robbed, we quit school. That is what I said. It had no reflection on my mother and father or their business or how they worked. I never said I came from a broken home or bad home, I never did.

Q: Are there other siblings in that family aside from yourself?

A: Yes, I have two sisters.

Q: There are others in the family aside from you, is that right, two sisters you said?

A: Two sisters.

Q: And did anyone within your family structure, to your recollection, engage in the kind of conduct that you have outlined for this jury?

A: No.

Q: Let me ask you, if you will, to recall a man by the name of Frank Fialla, does that name strike a bell with you?

A: Yes.

Q: Is he one of the people who met his demise on June 27, 1982, through your actions?

A: Yes.

Q: When Mr. Fialla died he was involved in some potential business transaction with you, is that right?

A: Yes.

Q: In other words, there you were the seller and he was the purchaser of some disco, is that what was planned, is that right?

A: A building and disco.

Q: A building, a disco. There was some $650,000 involved, is that right?

A: Yes.

Q: You arranged for him to be murdered, is that right?

A: Yes.

Q: Then there came a point in time when you are left with monies because of his death that had to be reported on a tax return, is that a fair statement?

A: Yes.

Q: I am going to show you a document previously furnished by me to the government, and ask that it be marked defendant's Exhibit D for identification. Am I correct that Fialla died, was murdered, after he had given you $650,000, is that correct?

A: The money was in escrow.

Q: I see. And then there came a point where you met with your tax preparer and had to prepare a tax return to explain that $650,000, correct?

A: Yes.

Q: I am going to show you, and I take it, your wife's name is Deborah?

A: Yes.

Q: I am going to show you a document which has been furnished to me by the government pursuant to law, and ask you is this your tax return for the year 1983?

A: Yes, I believe so.

MR. GOLDBERG: I am going to offer it in evidence.

MR. MEARNS: No objection.

THE COURT: It will be received.

Q: Now, sir, let us take a look at how the $650,000 is explained. This is, now I am going to read it, with Your Honor's permission. And in your tax return that you signed, this is how you explained how you kept the $650,000, this is what you say: "Deal did not go through until January '83. Deal was aborted by purchaser." I am reading from the document. What you are saying there, is that you kept the $650,000 because the deal was aborted by Mr. Fialla to purchase it, do you understand that?

A: That is not so.

Q: That is in the document. As matter of fact, the deal didn't go through because you aborted Mr. Fialla, isn't that a better statement?

A: No.

Q: Well, the deal didn't go through as you tell the Internal Revenue Service, deal did not go through because the deal was aborted by the purchaser. The purchaser was Mr. Fialla, is that right?

A: It did not go through in 1982 or '83.

Q: This is your tax return, can you read it to the jury with His Honor's permission, it says within the parenthesis?

A: I rather you read it.

Q: You rather I read it, okay. Deal did not go through until January 1987. Deal aborted by the purchaser. You were telling the Internal

Revenue Service that the reason the deal didn't go through, is that Mr. Fialla had aborted the deal, had pulled out of the deal, you understand that by the use of that language? It is an accounting term. When in fact, as I said earlier you are the person who arranged the abortion of the purchaser, isn't that a better statement?

A: The abortion?

Q: The end, the demise of Mr. Fialla, the purchaser, isn't that what happened in this case?

A: Yes. And then the deal did not go through.

Q: Because it would be very difficult to have him show up at a closing because of all the dirt on him, isn't that a fair statement?

A: So then the money went back to the family and the estate. It is because you make—

Q: Isn't that right, Mr. Gravano? The deal was "aborted" by the purchaser, as you wrote on your tax return, because you arranged for him to be aborted, to be murdered?

A: Yeah, all right.

2. John Nicholas Iannuzzi: *People* v. *Matais Reyes; Supreme Court, New York County*

Cross-examination by Mr. Iannuzzi

Q: Dr. Deadman, please, first of all, if you would be kind enough and by the way, if any question that I ask you has a tendency to confuse you, would you advise me of that? Because probably I'd be more confused in asking it than you are by the question. But in the event that I don't have it properly, would you let me know that?

A: Yes.

Q: In connection with the reports that were done by the F.B.I. laboratory, does the F.B.I. laboratory that generated these reports have an independent function other than the F.B.I. itself?

A: The laboratory is a division within the F.B.I.

Q: And is it a commercial venture to the extent that it does reports and analysis for other law enforcement agencies for a fee?

A: No. We're funded by Congress to provide this service to law enforcement agencies.

Q: So, basically, it isn't an independent company such as Lifecodes or Cellmark or something to that effect?

A: That's correct.

Q: And in connection with the DNA analysis, I believe you indicated DNA analysis is basically hinged on two aspects of genetics, is that not correct, one being molecular and one being population genetics?

A: Well, both of these fields obviously are part of the procedure that we utilize in a case like this.

Q: And molecular biology basically has to do with the determination of fluids, bodily fluids, and their relationship to each other, wouldn't that be correct, not necessarily for identification, but in reference to medical science? *A molecular biologist does research into the correspondence between molecules, parts of the blood and so forth, is that not correct?*

A: Well, I would say molecular biology is a science that looks at living things, living organisms, from a molecular approach. And by a molecular approach I mean you're concerned with the chemical reactions that take place, the chemical substances that are involved in life. Molecular biology is an extremely broad field that looks at many different aspects of the chemistry of life.

Q: All right, and they, when I say they I mean molecular biologists, make these comparisons and perhaps draw scientific theorems or theories in connection with the relationship of the molecules to each other and to the other bodily fluids, would that be correct?

A: Molecular biologists generally are not interested in comparing things. They're interested in identifying defective genes or in identifying certain malfunctions in a person's biological processes. But the one thing that is somewhat unique about forensic DNA analysis is the interest in comparing samples to try to determine if there is consistency in two different samples.

Q: So would it be fair to say that the molecular biologist isn't interested in comparisons but rather in identifying certain genes?

A: That's true. They generally are not interested in doing what we're doing in the crime laboratory.

Q: And in the crime laboratory, when you are comparing genes, you're basically comparing genes that may have been identified by, or have in fact previously been identified, by molecular biologists?

A: Yes. All of the probes that we're using have been identified by researchers outside of the F.B.I., and I would assume most of those would be under the term molecular biologist.

Q: And you yourself are not a molecular biologist?

A: I have background in organic chemistry and biochemistry, which is a major part of molecular biology.

Q: Is the answer no, you are not a molecular biologist?

A: I have experience in aspects of molecular biology.

Q: Are you a person who has a degree, a Ph.D., in molecular biology?

A: No.

Q: Have you published any papers in connection with molecular biology?

A: I have not.

Q: And have you of your own knowledge, not what you've used from other people's research, identified independently genes as a molecular biologist?

A: That's never been any part of what I've been involved in, the identification of genes.

Q: So that the genes that you compare have been, in fact, identified by others and that you have in some fashion familiarized yourself or been familiarized with them for the purposes of criminal identification?

A: Well, we have certainly worked with many of these genes and the probes used to detect these genes and have studied them extensively to see if, in fact, they are suitable for our analysis.

Q: And, you've testified to the effect that what ultimately, you cannot—let me just see if I can phrase this correctly—when you make your analysis, you can not basically get to an ultimate conclusion that certain bands or loci are exactly consistent with others, is that correct?

A: Yes.

Q: In other words, you can't measure with total precision that yes, indeed, this is exactly the same as another band, correct?

A: That's correct.

Q: So that when you take a sample and you go through your six-step procedure, and you ultimately end up with an autorad, and you make a visual comparison, that visual comparison can get to the point where you or someone in the lab could say this *could* be included or could be an inclusion, and that this *could* be an exclusion, or it's inconclusive, correct? Are those the three possible results?

A: Well, I would not use the word—I would say this is an inclusion, this is an exclusion, or this is inconclusive.

Q: But those are the three possible results?

A: If you obtain sufficient DNA to work with. In some cases you do not obtain enough to work with.

Q: And, of course, the conclusions have to do—this visual conclusion, that is to say, this is includable as a possible match, correct?

A: Again, it's not an exact match. I'm not sure if possible is the correct adjective. A match is a match.

Q: So basically when—and if perhaps I don't use exactly the proper terminology, forgive me—you can indicate by the visual examination that is an exclusion, that is to say for sure this is not a match, correct?

A: Yes.

Q: Or you can't tell if this is a match, so it's inconclusive, correct, for whatever reason?

A: Inconclusive, yes, is something that comes about for various reasons.

Q: So the results could be that the sample could be inconsistent or that it's not a match, or that this is consistent with a match?

A: That's correct.

Q: And that's about as close as you can get in the science of DNA analysis without statistical interpolation?

A: Yes. Well, I can interpret a match situation without a statistical analysis because—based on my experience, both my own experience and my experience of the forensic DNA analysis community.

Q: However, you cannot indicate to this court or to any other court or anybody that any sample is an exact match of any other sample, right?

A: That's correct.

Q: And that goes with all of the power of science that you have at your command in the F.B.I. lab, and all of the other DNA people who work on this cannot say when they see two bands, that these are exact matches. You can't do that, can you?

A: That's correct. Nobody can do that.

Q: They can't be measured by machines or by eyes or by anything, right?

A: That's correct.

Q: And within the framework of making determinations, when you're attempting to make an identification, and you come down to the match, you say this match is consistent with the subject, as opposed to this *is,* for sure, the subject. The best you can say is this is inconsistent with the subject's blood type.

A: Yes. The results in a case are consistent with the DNA coming from this person.

Q: Not that this is absolutely positively this person, correct?

A: That's correct.

Q: And basically that's because at the level that we're at now, this is what would be called the limitation of technology, right?

A: Yes, the technology is limited to the other—we're limited by the technology to the extent that we cannot measure these bands exactly.

Q: And as a matter of fact, have you not testified on other occasions that when you do the comparison, that you never get exactly the same correspondence for the location of the loci, when you do the DNA analysis a second time?

A: It would be very rare to measure two bands exactly the same twice, whether with two different samples or even the same samples. It would be very rare to determine that those two bands have exactly the same size because of measurement imprecision.

Q: So that if you had known blood from a known person, because of measurement imprecision, it would be very rare to get the same result two times in a row, right?

A: The same exact size two times in a row, yes.

Q: If you would take your own blood and know that it was yours, you still wouldn't be able to, because of measurement imprecision, come up with the same results on your own blood, right?

A: Yes. We have looked at that many times.

Q: And so in comparing the blood of unknown individuals or a known individual with a possible sample, to say with precision that known person and the unknown sample are exactly the same is absolutely impossible, right?

A: That's right. You can't say that.

Q: And so, the ultimate bottom line of DNA comparison, after all the charts and all of the everything that we've been through today, is that taking the gels and X-rays and the radiation and everything else, the bottom line is, on looking at an autorad, there is not a human being alive who can say this blood exactly and precisely matches that blood.

A: That's correct.

Q: And so, the only way that the F.B.I. lab—and by the way, molecular biologists, scientists who have dedicated their lives to determining the composition of blood in order to perhaps locate the defective genes or genes that affect life, are not in any fashion involved in identification of DNA or DNA for the purposes of identification, isn't that right?

A: Well, we have certainly worked with many molecular biologists.

Q: I understand that, but may I just ask you this: Are molecular biologists who are involved in scientific research involved in DNA identification?

A: Most of them have very little experience in DNA identification and really don't know what's involved.

Q: And as a matter of fact, they've been involved in molecular biology or—I'm sorry, molecular genetics far longer than the 18 months or 24 months that the F.B.I. lab in Washington has been set up using it for identification purposes, isn't that right?

A: That's true, but they have not been involved in forensic DNA analysis.

MR. IANNUZZI: If Your Honor please, could you, so that perhaps we can move along, ask the witness to answer questions, and if there's something else, I'm sure Mr. Prosecutor could bring it out on redirect.

THE COURT: Ask your next question.

Q: The only way the F.B.I. lab and people who are involved with the use of DNA for identification have to make comparisons of what you have already testified cannot by any means be a precise measurement is to make extrapolation by statistical multiplication, correct?

A: We can assess the significance of our match result in a particular case by conducting a statistical analysis. That's one of the ways of doing it.

Q: When you say you have a matching result, the fact of the matter is that there isn't a precise match, correct?

A: I never defined match result as meaning that the bands are exactly the same size, if that is what you mean.

Q: I am asking you if there is ever a precise match?

A: I cannot say the two bands are exactly the same size if that is what you mean by precise match.

Q: That's what I mean. So what you do is evaluate the assessment of the nonprecise match by multiplication? Is that right?

A: I can assess the frequency of matching bands in a particular case.

Q: But if you take—and perhaps it is because I am not any kind of a geneticist, I don't even ascribe to having any experience as you do, but if you multiply an imprecise match as many times as you wish, it doesn't make it at the end result more precise than it was before you multiplied it, does it?

A: You're talking about—matching of bands is one operation; statistical analysis of those matching bands is a second operation.

Q: Does the multiplication of the imprecise base pairs we're talking about, imprecise matches we're talking about, when you multiply it, does that eliminate the imprecision?

A: Again, they don't have anything to do with each other. The matching process is one operation—the statistical analysis of bands that are matching is a second operation.

Q: What I am asking you is this. And I'll try to phrase it in a way that it makes sense to you as a scientific expert—the imprecise match, no matter how many times you multiply it, it doesn't become more precise? There's no way of making that more precise, just statistically more probable. Is that correct?

MR. GIRGENTI: Your Honor, this question had been asked and answered.

THE COURT: Three times. He may not have answered to your satisfaction. He answered the way he believes he can answer that question.

Q: Is the multiplication involved in the statistical approach necessary to address the limitation of technology that exists today?

A: No, the statistical approach is an attempt to assign some significance to matching DNA profiles.

Q: Sir, are you familiar with the treatise, "The Fixed Bin Analysis for Statistical Evaluation of Continuous Distribution of Alielic Data from VNTRA Loci for use in Forensic Comparison?"

A: I am.

Q: As a matter of fact, you participated in putting the document together?

A: I did, yes.

Q: And I ask you to look at page 13 and ask you if I am reading it correctly when it says, "a statistical approach is needed which will address the limitations of technology, the genetics of VNTR'S, and the available data bases." Does that paper that you helped put together say that?

A: Yes it does.

Q: And in analyzing alleles, isn't the analysis that you do in the F.B.I. lab to—and that which you did here, based on a statistical approach, a comparison of theoretical numbers?

A: Yes, statistical analysis is part of the examination procedure used in the F.B.I.

Q: And after you get the autorad and you get to the point where you make the match which you have already acknowledged at that point you've done all the analysis that is going to be done from the point of view of the physical specimen and the blood itself, and the radiation, and the X-ray, that's all been done to the point that you're looking at an autorad, you reach a point when there is no more scientific analysis of the blood that is going to be done at this point, correct?

A: Well, then measurements are made of the autorads after they're developed, on the computer.

Q: And, even with the computer, sir, and with everything else you have available to you to measure the physical blood, you're still at the same point, that is to say, there is no way to measure precisely, by use of a computer, human, android, any other thing, right?

A: You keep using the word precise. There's a precise way of measuring. There's no way of measuring the bands exactly. They can't be measured precisely. They cannot be measured exactly.

Q: They can be measured precisely and that precise measurement can not show that they're exact right?

A: Correct. We cannot measure them exactly. We can measure them with good precision.

Q: You can precisely tell they're not exact, right? Not even a computer can do that?

A: We can precisely measure them.

Q: And you can precisely measure the fact—and you know with all your knowledge of DNA, that they cannot be measured exactly? Right?

A: That's correct.

Q: At the F.B.I. lab you use a window of tolerance, an acceptable shift of 2.5 percent up or 2.5 percent down, in measuring or assessing whether the blood or semen sample of a known compares to an unknown sample? You allow a measurement window of 5 percent from top to bottom, right?

A: Well in our laboratory, we know that measurement imprecision can vary as much as 2.5 percent in either direction.

Q: And as matter of fact, by the way, when Mr. Prosecutor asked you a question, he asked you whether or not the system that you use is accepted by the other labs across the country. Those other labs don't use as wide a window as the F.B.I., correct?

A: I would say most laboratories would use the exact same window we use.

Q: Is it your testimony that Cellmark uses a 2.5 window, just as you do?

A: Well, I am talking about the private laboratories, the crime laboratories, that will be using our procedures . . .

Q: Let me do it this way. I am not asking whether other labs that have been taught and use the F.B.I. system use your window. I am asking whether the people independent of the F.B.I. such as Cellmark use the same window of tolerance. If they give themselves as big a break as the F.B.I. does?

A: Cellmark uses plus or minus 1 millimeter as their window of tolerance. In other words, they use 2 millimeters tolerance when they compare samples generated from different gels.

Q: Is that more or less than the F.B.I.?

A: It probably is less than the F.B.I. I am not sure of what that 2 millimeter measurement could be in terms of percentages.

Q: And how about Life Codes? They don't use a 2.5 window in any direction either, do they?

A: Their two bands have to be 1.8 percent apart.

Q: So that, basically, the two entities that have been cited in the documents that you helped put together, "Fixed Bin Analysis," both use lesser windows of tolerance than the F.B.I., correct?

A: As a part of their procedure, their windows are smaller. We believe them to be incorrect.

Q: Regardless of whether you agree or disagree, they, in fact use smaller tolerances than the F.B.I.? Correct?

A: They have a smaller quantitative match criterion than we do.

Q: Let me ask you a question, doctor, do you know the words yes and no?

MR. PROSECUTOR: Objection.

THE COURT: Sustained.

Q: Now, all of these variables of which we have spoken here several times already, when you get the final result, all these variables then have to be put through a mathematical computation or statistical analysis to give probability of whether the life fluid that you're measuring belongs to an individual or doesn't, right?

A: One interprets—one develops experience with these variables that we have talked about in working with the system. The variables again have nothing to do with the statistics.

Q: Basically, there are the variables and then there's the statistical analysis of the material that has all of these variables going for or going against it, correct?

A: But the variables in the system have to do with the matching and the variables in the systems have to be understood by the people using that system.

Q: However, with these variables, you get to a point where, you can not say from looking at any one of these charts that the blood that I have on the autorad *absolutely, positively belongs to this defendant, right?*

A: That's correct.

Q: And that's after all the analysis, all the variables that you did, you cannot, as you sit there right now, testify that this blood that you analyzed, absolutely, positively belongs to this defendant?

A: That's correct.

Q: So, in order to make a determination beyond that, to make your DNA more probable, you do a statistical analysis, correct?

A: We do a statistical analysis to assess the significance of a DNA match.

Q: And the statistical analysis that you then do has to do with the data base and sampling of blood from other people in the population, correct?

A: Yes.

Q: And you have to compare the blood of the subject to how many times in our city, how many times in the world this combination of things occurs? Right?

A: We determine or we estimate that by using individuals in a sample of the population. Using such a sampling, we can generate the DNA frequency that allows us to estimate the frequency of bands in a population.

Q: And even when you finish with all of these probes, with all the computers, and all of the machines that the government of the United States has at its command, you cannot as you sit here right now, say even after your statistical analysis that this blood absolutely, positively belongs to the defendant?

MR. PROSECUTOR: Your Honor, I object. This is by my count at least—

THE COURT: (to Dr. Blank) You can't say it, just one person in the world that has that? Is that right?

THE WITNESS: That's correct, you cannot make positive matches.

Q: So that basically what you're doing with the statistical analysis is gauging probabilities? And trying to do them with a spread as wide as possible so as to see that if one in 49 million or the one in 200 million is about as close as you can get to precision or exactitude—let me withdraw the word precision or exactitude—is that right?

A: Again, we can conduct the statistical analysis to assess the meaning of a DNA match. We attempt to do it in a way we believe to be an appropriate way of dealing with population samples and dealing with the technology that we have available to us.

Q: By the way, to a great extent, your analysis has to do with the population base that you're using, correct?

A: The numbers that we develop as a result of a statistical analysis certainly depend on the population samples you're dealing with.

Q: And you have indicated that the F.B.I. has determined a Hispanic population base?

A: Yes.

Q: Now, what people have you included in the Hispanic population base?

A: Our Hispanic population data base deals with individuals from two geographic regions. From Florida and from Texas.

Q: You are, of course, familiar, I know, with Dr. Lewontin from Harvard University, are you not?

A: I have read some of his writings, yes.

Q: Dr. Lewontin is a well-known population geneticist in the field?

A: Yes.

Q: Is he well-respected?

A: He is by some people. He's not by other people.

Q: Would you accept Dr. Lewontin as a knowledgeable individual in the area of population genetics?

A: Yes.

Q: And when Dr. Lewontin indicates that to assign the designation Hispanic to a data base is a biological nightmare, would you disagree with that?

A: Well, I am not sure exactly what he means by that.

Q: Dr. Lewontin has said that the Hispanic data base includes people of Mexican, Puerto Rican, Guatemalan, Cuban, Spanish ancestry, would you disagree with that?

A: That's probably true, yes.

Q: In your F.B.I. data base, have you sampled Mexican, Puerto Rican, Guatemalan, Cuban, Spanish ancestry, people?

A: We have sampled people that live in Texas that are Hispanic and people that live in Florida that are Hispanic.

Q: The answer is, if I am not being unfair, that the F.B.I. has not made a determination, within its list of "Hispanic data base" of people who are specifically, say, Guatemalan, Cuban, Spanish, or Puerto Rican?

A: Again, we're working with people from two different areas in the United States, and one can talk about individuals and what their ethnic background would more likely be living in those two areas.

Q: In Texas, and in Florida, when you did your data base, did you make any determination as to whether or not the people that you took samples of were Guatemalan, Puerto Rican, Spanish, Cuban backgrounds?

A: No. Background information of that type is not taken.

Q: And, of course, when Dr. Lewontin suggests to you that Mexicans have large and variable Indian ancestry, would you disagree with him?

A: No, I would agree with that.

Q: When Dr. Lewontin suggests that Guatemalans are almost pure Indian, would you disagree with that?

A: Yes, basically.

Q: When Dr. Lewontin says that Puerto Ricans have little or no Indian ancestry, but considerable African ancestry, would you agree or disagree with that?

A: I would agree with the first part. I am not sure about the second part.

Q: When Dr. Lewontin indicates that Spaniards and Argentinians have no Indian or black African ancestry, would you agree or disagree with that?

A: Well, I could assume that would be true for individuals from Spain. I am not really sure about Argentina. I would assume that they would have quite a mixture in Argentina.

Q: American Indians have gene frequencies that depart from other world populations in an extreme way, correct?

A: In some unconventional genetic markings, I believe they do, yes.

Q: Indians are extreme in blood group O, many populations being almost pure O, correct?

A: Indians are a different racial group than Caucasians and blacks and they have different gene frequencies for those types of markers.

Q: In your sampling, when you took the samples in Texas and in Florida, did you make provisions to determine whether you were accessing people of Spanish with no black or Indian ancestry?

A: No, we assumed that the Texas population would have a large percentage of Indian blood in them.

Q: That was an assumption, not even scientifically measured in any way, that was used to set this F.B.I. standard, correct?

A: I think most people, including Dr. Lewontin, would make that assumption.

Q: You're assuming what somebody else would assume, but do you know, of your own knowledge, or scientific research, whether or not there was a specific determination within the F.B.I. "Hispanic data base" for Spanish people with no Indian or black background?

A: I would assume you'd have to go to Spain to get individuals that would fall into that category.

Q: Is it your testimony that in Texas and in Florida there are no people who are descendants of Spanish people from Spain? Is that what your testimony is?

A: Probably very few.

Q: Do you, as a matter of fact, have knowledge to that effect?

A: No. That would be just my guess as to that.

Q: By the way, what does Hispanic mean to you? Does that mean people who are generally Spanish from around the world?

A: It means to me ethnic groups that are from Mexico, from the southwestern part of the United States, from Cuba, Puerto Rico, those individuals would be considered part of the Hispanic group.

Q: So that Spanish people are not included in the Hispanic data base, Spanish people from Spain or descendants, they are not in your data base, is that correct?

A: Certainly Mexico, Puerto Rico, Cuba would contain considerable Spanish blood since they were colonized by the Spanish several hundred years ago.

Q: So, therefore, it would seem—although you don't know for sure—that there are few Spanish people from Spain, and descendants of Spanish people from Spain, without Indian or without black blood, in your "Hispanic" data base?

A: I would just say since Spanish were here many hundreds of years ago, there are probably very few individuals with pure Spanish blood without admixtures of black, American Indian, in them.

Q: By the way, doctor, what is the makeup of the blood of individuals from Puerto Rico? So far as white, black, and Indian is concerned and please refer to your notes and the specific statistics that you use in the F.B.I. laboratory.

A: Well, I would just say that there is, in fact, probably, an admixture of Caucasian, black, and Indian blood in Hispanics from Puerto Rico. Primarily, probably black and Caucasian.

Q: What I am asking is, do you have in the makeup of the F.B.I. Hispanic data base that is used to make DNA interpretations of Hispanic people in the United States, a breakdown of the individuals who have been used in the sample for the purposes of determining their background?

A: No. We know only that there are individuals that are Hispanic from two geographic regions in the United States.

Q: And would you say that the presence of Indians' blood and the amount of it, which you are only assuming, would it cause gene frequencies quite separate and apart from the gene frequencies of other people?

A: Admixtures are going to cause some differences in gene frequency, with the particular markers we're dealing with, since they're present in all individuals, with not large differences in the racial groups. I would think that some Indian blood here or there would not have a major effect.

Q: Aren't Indians, or Indian blood, doesn't it have an extreme for M? Do you understand M?

A: That's another genetic marker.

Q: And aren't there extremes in connection with M, ranging from 75 to 90 percent?

A: I am really not sure of that particular marker.

Q: And are they not extremely aberrant in their RH type, with high frequency of small k, capital DE?

A: I am not familiar with the genetic markers per se in the American Indian population.

Q: In making your Hispanic analysis, you're making a statistical analysis based upon a data base the composition of which, in all charity, you haven't the foggiest idea of what's in it, except that they came from Texas and Florida, right?

A: And those individuals who identified themselves as Hispanic, and we approach the Hispanic population in a way designed to compensate for the unknowns in those two collections of individuals.

Q: The people filled out or responded to the fact that they were Hispanic, correct?

A: That's one of the ways of putting them in the category of Hispanic.

Q: Did they have to fill out some kind of a document to show their background, where their folks came from, where their grandfolks came from, so that you would be able to feed that into the computer in Washington and come up with a specific breakdown of the data base called Hispanic?

A: We do not have that specific information.

Q: So that there's no information whatever as to the makeup of the Spanish people in the Hispanic data base, except that they said they were Hispanic, right?

A: And the knowledge about the individuals that lived in those two particular geographic regions.

Q: The general demographic that in Texas there are probably a lot of Mexicans, and in Florida there are a lot of Cubans, right?

A: That's part of it.

Q: What is the other part of it?

A: There may be Puerto Ricans in Florida.

Q: May be? The words are *may be.* You don't know because you don't have the information, correct?

A: That is a guess on my part.

Q: There was no effort made by the F.B.I. to make a closer analysis of the folks that were put in the Hispanic data base except for the general demographic: there are a lot of Cubans in Florida, there are a lot of Mexicans in Texas, right?

A: Again, we designed our approach to assessing allele frequencies or determining the appropriate allele or band frequency to use because we know there are different racial groups in Hispanic populations. We designed our approach differently.

Q: Did you in any fashion do a determination of individual groups, let's say, let's do Puerto Ricans and just do them separately so we have some data information as to how Puerto Ricans differ from Cubans? Do you have that in Washington?

A: We have not done that, yet.

Q: Have you anything that tells you how Cubans differ from Guatemalans?

A: No, we do not.

Q: Do you consider Argentinians and Brazilians Hispanic, or would it depend on whether they identify themselves as Spanish?

A: It would probably depend on what they identify as; if they're from Germany, they wouldn't be Hispanic. If they were from other European—

Q: Doesn't it actually boil down to how the question was asked of them. Are you Spanish? They would probably say yes?

A: They would say they're Hispanic, yes.

Q: And do you have any determination as to how Puerto Ricans differ from South Americans who speak Spanish?

A: We never compared the two. Again, we did not think there would be anything to suggest significant differences between the two.

Q: Whether you think it would or wouldn't, you have no empirical knowledge or statistical knowledge or computerized knowledge in connection with yes, there is a difference or no, there isn't. Just a guess right now, isn't it?

A: We know we have four population data bases. We know how blacks and whites differ, we know how blacks and Hispanics differ. We know how whites and Hispanics differ. There's essentially very little difference in these different population data bases. These markers are present in all populations. There are frequency differences, but they are not large differences.

Q: And, basically, the reason you're saying that is because you haven't done any analysis whatever in reference to the Spanish people and how they differ amongst themselves? It is entirely an assumption on your part, isn't it?

A: We know how the Spanish people differ within the two groups. We look at Texas and Miami, we know how they differ, how whites compare to blacks. There are not large differences.

Q: As a matter of fact, the differences between white and black data bases is sometimes less extreme than, say, between people from Eastern Europe and Italy, isn't that correct?

A: That's possible, but I do not think it likely for these particular markers.

Q: Maybe not for these particular markers, but haven't you seen—and if you'd like to, I'll show you the statistics, that Poles differ more from Italians than they do from other races; that there are fewer differences between white and black than there are between Poles and Welshmen?

A: Well, if you're referring to Dr. Lewontin's data, some say that what he wrote was subject to question, and—

Q: Would you suggest also that there is some question in connection with Mourant? Are you familiar with his work?

A: I have read references to the book that was written by him. Or her. I'm not sure if it's a he or a she.

Q: And would you say that Mourant and the various studies that were done by Mourant are incorrect?

A: Some of them are probably correct. Some of them are probably incorrect. All that is a compilation of data from many, many investigators.

Q: And all your Spanish Hispanic data base is compilation of data from many investigators, isn't that right?

A: It's a compilation of data from two locations, one in Texas, one in Florida.

Q: And have you made a determination, sir—not you personally—but has there been a determination made within the Spanish data base that you use as to the makeup of Puerto Rican blood, specifically, an individualized—

A: No, we have not set up or have not developed a "Puerto Rican" data base.

Q: So that in connection with someone who might be, or have background from Puerto Rico, in making a determination as to the frequency of this blood, you don't know if he is one in 49 million or one out of every 3 people who live in his neighborhood in Puerto Rico, do you?

A: I guess I don't know for sure, but I can certainly give my opinion as to which would be more likely.

Q: Would your opinion be based on blood sampling from Puerto Rico as opposed to your assumption?

A: It would be based on my knowledge of the tremendous variability of these genetic markers we've been discussing in this particular case in all populations.

Q: Will it be based on scientific information as opposed to your guesstimate, sir?

A: I would say my experience in this particular field of science.

Q: Eighteen or 24 months of it, right? And in this 18 or 24 months you, sir, can make a determination off the top of your head as to the blood frequencies of all 4 or 5 billion people in the world, right?

A: I've been involved in this for four years, and I'm—

Q: I'm sorry, four years as opposed to 2 years—

A: I'm extremely well-read in terms of what other people are doing besides the F.B.I. laboratory. These markers are tremendously variable *in* all populations, including Hispanics, including all racial groups.

Q: Let me ask you this, sir. Could you make a distinction with medical or scientific certitude that the blood of Carlos Defendant is distinct, and I'm talking about of your own personal research knowledge, is distinct from the people of the southern half of Puerto

Rico? Can you say that it is that distinct without having ever taken a sample of it?

A: I'm not sure what you're asking me. Are you saying do I believe his blood—

Q: No, no, not what you believe. I ask you, sir, because you are a scientist, and that's why you were presented here, as an expert, can you say with scientific exactitude that the blood of Carlos Defendant is indeed quite different than the blood of the people in the southern half of Puerto Rico—forget the northern half—without having taken a sample of it.

A: Well, I've never compared it to a population sample from Puerto Rico. But the same multitude of types that exist in all populations are going to be present on the island of Puerto Rico.

Q: When you say that, sir, it's not based on any study that you've done or anybody else has done, as far as you know, it is based purely on your guesstimate, right?

A: I would say it's based on my knowledge of the distribution of these markers in all populations.

Q: So is the answer that your answer is not based on an actual study that you know of?

A: That's correct. I have not looked at a population sample from Puerto Rico.

Q: And you will acknowledge that within certain groups, for example, with the Indian group, there is great variability within certain groups, right?

A: Not necessarily for these markers.

Q: For pure, pure Indian blood, the people who have pure Indian blood, are quite distinct from nonpure Indian blooded people, isn't that right?

A: With respect to some markers, they are. Quite distinct.

Q: And can you say with scientific exactitude, sir, that the same does not exist in Puerto Rico?

A: Again, I don't think I could testify exactly to anything, but I certainly can give you my opinion based on my own information, the

F.B.I.'s information, plus the companies that have Hispanic data bases consisting of Puerto Ricans, that there is tremendous variability in these markers. Because the F.B.I. does not have a Puerto Rican data base, that does not mean that Lifecodes, Cellmark, or other companies do not have Puerto Rican data bases. They use the same probes we use. They see the same tremendous variability we see in our populations.

Q: Have you used Cellmark data base to make this determination in this case?

A: No, I have not.

Q: Okay. Have you used Lifecodes to make the determination in this case?

A: No, I have not.

Q: And when, sir, you say that Mr. Carlos Defendant is one out of 49 million or one out of 25 million Hispanics, I want you to answer this question, if you will. Which 25 million Hispanics?

A: I would say that would be an estimate that would apply to the United States, Hispanic individuals in the United States. That would be our best estimate as to the frequency of the defendant's DNA profiles in the Hispanic population of the United States.

Q: And by the way, I'm sure that you are aware of the fact that Mr. Carlos Defendant doesn't come from either Texas or Florida, but from New York. Now, that's not a question, but let me base a question on it. Have you done a study of the blood types and frequencies of the Puerto Rican and Spanish population of the city of New York?

A: The F.B.I. has not. Lifecodes, I think, has a population data base of the New York Hispanic population.

Q: And, of course, we've already established that you didn't use Lifecodes statistics, you only used the F.B.I.'s. So, the answer is that you have not had access to a blood sampling of the Puerto Ricans living in the greater New York area, right?

A: That's true, but I can use Lifecodes data because we do use common probes which recognize the same DNA.

Q: Did you in this case?

A: I have not used the Lifecodes data base, no.

Q: So that when you made the estimate, you made the estimate of a Puerto Rican living in New York without in any fashion checking with any statistical analysis of the blood types of the Puerto Ricans who live in New York, right?

A: That's correct.

Q: And is it your—other than your guess, or your assumption or your probability based on your experience, was there an actual study done to determine if the people who reside in the geographic area of New York and who intermarry with each other or with different groups, if they have similar or different blood frequencies than Carlos Defendant?

A: Well, you're comparing an individual to a population. I don't think you can do that.

The Cross-examination continues, but I think you have a good sampling of exact scientific testimony.

3. James M. LaRossa: *People* v. *Joseph Watts;* Supreme Court, Richmond County, New York

Cross-examination by Mr. LaRossa

Q: Do you remember, sir, testifying that you were involved with others in a conspiracy to murder a man by the name of Fred Weiss?

A: Yes, I do.

Q: No question about that, is there?

A: No question.

Q: You don't recall when this was?

A: What year?

Q: Well, let's start with year.

A: 90, 91, 92 before I went to jail.

Q: 90, 91, or 92?

A: 92 or 93 before I went to jail.

Q: Did you tell us, sir, that you went to a house on Staten Island which was under construction with others?

A: Yes.

Q: And did you tell us that a man by the name of Annunziata was going to meet Weiss and bring him to the construction site?

A: Yes, I did.

Q: And that when Annunziata brought Mr. Weiss into that house the plan was to assassinate him, is that right?

A: Correct.

Q: That didn't trouble you, did it. Sir?

A: Did it trouble me?

Q: Yes.

A: It was part of my life.

Q: The answer is no it didn't trouble you?

A: It was part of my life.

Q: So is the answer no it didn't trouble you?

A: The answer is it was part of my life.

THE COURT: Can you answer that yes or no. If you can't, say you can't.

A: I can't.

Q: You can't. Was there anything morally stopping you from participating in this?

A: No.

Q: Now you know, sir, that you could have gotten up to twenty-five years for this conspiracy, don't you?

A: Yes.

Q: And you knew, sir, when you started to cooperate with the federal government that you were going to get a whitewash on that, isn't that right? You know what I mean by a whitewash, don't you?

A: Yeah, I believe so.

Q: And you did get a whitewash on it, didn't you?

A: Yes, I did.

Q: And, sir, you have no compunction being one of the people participating to kill Frederick Weiss, isn't that right?

A: It was part of the life.

Q: You're never going to be prosecuted for that crime, are you?

MR. DRURY: Objection asked and answered.

THE COURT: Sustained.

Q: Louie Milito, remember that gentleman?

A: Yes.

Q: Did you, sir, help others in burying Louie Milito's body?

A: Yes.

Q: He was dead at the time, wasn't he?

A: Yes.

Q: Did you know, sir, what the penalty for being an accessory after the fact of murder is, do you have any idea what it was?

A: No.

Q: Did you know, sir, in the federal system you could have been charged with a crime punishable up to fifteen years?

A: Yes.

Q: Were you charged with that crime?

A: No, I wasn't.

Q: Will you ever be charged with that crime?

A: I don't believe so.

Q: You'll never do a day for it, right?

MR. DRURY: Objection.

THE COURT: Sustained. Asked and answered.

Q: Did you have any hesitation about burying this man?

A: It was part of the life.

Q: Any moral dilemma? Were you unhappy about it?

A: Was I happy about it, I don't know what you mean.

Q: Was it morally troubling you?

A: It was part of the life. I did whatever it was.

MR. LAROSSA: Could I see the tax returns? None of them are in evidence.

THE COURT: D.B. 73.

Q: Let me show you what's been marked D.B. 71, sir, 1990 that's your tax return for the year 1990, right?

A: Yes.

Q: And sir, it was signed and filed, was it not?

A: You say I signed it.

Q: Sir, that's a copy of it, you signed the tax return?

A: Did you say I signed it?

Q: Didn't you sign your tax return?

A: That's what I'm looking for, I'm asking you what page.

Q: This is not a signed copy, sir?

A: Oh, this is not a signed copy.

Q: If you look at the second page?

A: If you say this is my tax return I believe you.

Q: Sir, when you signed that tax return in 1991?

A: This isn't signed.

THE COURT: Well, that's a copy, if you find the original you signed the original I assume.

THE WITNESS: Yes, Your Honor but I don't remember signing it.

Q: Turn to the second page will you, sir?

A: Yes, sir.

Q: Go down to the bottom of the second page you see a man's name on it all the way down at the bottom?

A: Yes, on the left side.

Q: Who is it?

A: I can't read it.

Q: You can't read that. Who prepared your tax returns in 1990?

A: I don't know.

Q: You don't know?

A: No.

Q: Sir, are you questioning the fact that you signed a return and filed it?

A: I'm not denying the fact that I signed it, I just said this wasn't signed, I'm not denying it.

Q: It's not signed, sir?

A: Okay I'm not denying I signed the original.

Q: When you signed it, it was false, wasn't it?

A: What's in here is false?

Q: You know what's there.

A: What's not there.

Q: What's there is a small portion of what you earned?

A: What I signed here is for real, it's what's not in there.

THE COURT: It's not a statement of your full income.

THE WITNESS: Right that's what I'm trying to say, I'm not arguing with him, Your Honor, he's very, you know.

Q: Mr. Borghese.

A: Yes.

Q: You signed that was a false return?

A: I agree.

Q: You knew it was false?

A: What's in here is the truth.

Q: It is? That's all the money you made that year?

A: It's what's not in here. What's in here is the truth and I signed it, yes.

Q: Mr. Borghese, you know, do you not, that when you didn't put all the money that you stole from people in that return for the year 1990 you didn't put it in, that violates the law?

MR. DRURY: Objection as to the term stole.

THE COURT: Overruled.

Q: Isn't that right?

A: Yes.

Q: When you did it you knew you were violating the law?

A: Yes.

Q: You knew you were committing a felony?

A: Yes.

Q: And you're never going to be charged for that felony, are you?

A: I don't believe so.

Q: You say you don't believe so, you mean you won't right?

A: I don't believe so.

MR. DRURY: Objection.

THE COURT: All he can say is what he believes, he can't say it for a fact.

Q: When you signed that agreement, they agreed not to bring any more charges against you, isn't that right?

A: I don't believe so.

Q: You don't believe so. What do you think that agreement gave you?

A: That I'm going to have to see somebody about taxes.

Q: Paying your taxes, paying your taxes not doing five years for false tax returns, you see that as a distinction, sir. You understand if you violate the tax law you're charged with a crime, you can go to jail, don't you?

A: Yes, I do.

Q: You can go to jail for five years, isn't that right?

A: Yes.

MR. DRURY: Objection asked and answered.

THE COURT: He's trying to get to the next point the objection overruled.

Q: Now, sir, that can't happen for your violation of the 1990 tax return, isn't that right?

A: I don't believe so.

Q: You don't believe that it can happen?

A: Right.

Q: Let me show you what's been marked D.B. 75 which is a tax return for the year 1992; D.B. 77 which is a tax return for the year 1993, and D.B. 79 which is a tax return for the year 1994. You have those returns, sir?

A: Yes, I do.

Q: They're copies of the returns that you filed for those respective years, isn't that right?

A: I guess so.

Q: And when you signed and filed those returns, you knew they were false, isn't that right?

A: Yes.

Q: And you knew that when you signed and filed those returns you were violating the federal tax law, isn't that right?

A: Yes.

Q: And you knew, sir, that you could be charged criminally for filing false tax returns, isn't that right?

A: Yes.

Q: And when you signed those, you knew that you perjured yourself by signing a false tax return, isn't that right?

A: Yes.

Q: And you know, sir, that you cannot be charged for those crimes under your agreement with the United States Government, isn't that right?

A: I believe so.

Q: Did you file a tax return in 1995?

A: Excuse me?

Q: Sir? Did you hear the question?

A: No, I didn't.

Q: Did you file a tax return for the year 1995?

A: No.

Q: Did you file a tax return for the year 1996?

A: No.

Q: Now, sir, this agreement that you entered into with both the district attorney and the government, the United States Government that you would not be prosecuted for crimes other than those that you pled to, had a provision in it about forfeiture of assets, didn't it?

MR. DRURY: Objection, judge. The document speaks for itself.

THE COURT: Yes, but he can ask the witness about it. Go ahead.

Q: Sir.

A: Repeat the question.

Q: You knew, sir, that this agreement that you entered into with the government and the district attorney's office had a provision in it regarding forfeiture of assets?

A: I didn't know.

Q: You didn't know that?

A: No.

Q: I want you to take what's been marked D.B. 1 and go to page six, sir. By the way, this is the agreement you signed, isn't it?

A: I'll take your word for it.

Q: Well, you don't have to take my word for it. Go to the last page?

A: Yes, it is.

Q: You signed it?

A: Yes, I did.

Q: Now, page six, you see page six?

A: Yes.

Q: You see paragraph number eight?

A: Yes.

Q: The second sentence of that paragraph talks about civil adminis-trative proceedings, does it not?

A: You're asking me?

Q: I'm asking you to read it, sir.

A: I'm reading it. I don't understand what it says.

Q: You don't understand it?

A: (Witness shakes head negatively.) No.

Q: Do you understand this sentence: It is further understood that this agreement does not prohibit the United States, any agency thereof, or any third party, from initiating or prosecuting any civil or administrative proceedings, directly or indirectly involving the defendant, including, but not limited to, proceedings by the Internal Revenue Service relating to potential civil tax liability or forfeiture of assets. You understand what that means, don't you?

A: Would I be looking at you like this, if I understand?

THE COURT: The answer is no?

THE WITNESS: What does that mean? They can get me?

THE COURT: At least your money.

Q: Did you ask your lawyer what this meant?
A: No.

Q: Sir, don't you know that the government could seize your assets, out of your tax proceedings, if they chose to. Don't you know that?
A: No, I didn't.

Q: You didn't understand that by reading that paragraph?
A: The lawyer read it. I just went by what he did.

Q: Well, did you ask him about it?
A: Nah.

Q: Didn't ask her, didn't ask him?
A: I believed whatever he said was good, was good. I signed it. That was it.

Q: Well, the bottom line is, it doesn't make any difference what you understood their agreement to be, because you hid all your money, didn't you?
A: I hid it?

Q: Yes.
A: Not too good. You found it the other day.

Q: Well, maybe I'm a little better than the federal government, sir. But has anybody else tried to find it, Mr. Borghese?

THE COURT: Sustained. He doesn't know that.

Q: Do you know whether anybody's tried to find it?

MR. DRURY: Objection.

THE COURT: Overruled. Do you know if anybody's gone after your money, as far as you know, that was forfeited?

THE WITNESS: To take it?

THE COURT: Yes, to take it.

A: No.

Q: Anybody from the United States Government come and ask you about the money?

A: No.

Q: After Mr. Drury found out and talked to you about it last week, did anybody from the state come and ask you about the money?

A: To take it?

Q: Yes.

A: No.

Q: Nobody's going to take it from you, right?

MR. DRURY: Objection.

THE COURT: You can ask him what he believes.

Q: You believe nobody's ever going to come and take that from you, right?

A: I hope not.

Q: Because you're on the team, right?

MR. DRURY: Objection as to "on the team."

THE COURT: Rephrase it, please.

Q: Sir, you believe, do you not, that as long as you continue to cooperate with them, satisfy them, do what they want, they're not going to come and take your money, isn't that right?

A: Say that again.

MR. LAROSSA: With the court's permission.

THE COURT: All right. Please read the question back.

Q: Sir?

A: Yes.

Q: And, sir, you told the United States Government, and the district attorney of Staten Island, that you had a phoney job for a number of years, didn't you?

A: Yes, I did.

Q: And, sir, they never bothered to try and take that annuity check away from you, which you had never earned, right?

A: Did they try to take it?

Q: Yes, did they?

A: No.

Q: They just let you take it, deposit it, and cash it?

A: They let me take it to pay lawyers.

Q: And, sir, you told them, did you not, that 94 Hancock Street was being used for crimes, didn't you?

A: Who, state or the F.B.I.?

Q: Both of them.

A: It was used for gambling, yes.

Q: And you told them that, didn't you?

A: Yes, I did.

Q: And, sir, they knew that that property was sold, right?

A: Yes.

Q: And nobody tried to seize—

A: I don't—excuse me, I don't know if they knew it was sold, but I told them I was selling it.

Q: And nobody stopped you from selling it, right?

A: No.

Q: Nobody seized the asset because it was being used for an illegal activity, did they?

A: No.

Q: And nobody sought to grab 59 Walker Street, did it—did they?

A: What were they going to do with that—with that, excuse me.

Q: What were they going to do with that? Was that used for gambling?

A: At Walker Street?

Q: Yes.

A: Yeah. I forgot. It was.

Q: Anybody seize it?

A: No.

Q: Anybody stop you from selling it?

A: No.

Q: Now, sir, someday in the near future, when you're released from jail, the United States Government is going to work it out so that you get a new name, right?

A: Yes.

Q: And you're going to get a new Social Security number, aren't you?

A: Yes.

Q: And you're going to get a new background in terms of education, isn't that right?

THE COURT: A new background.

MR. LAROSSA: Sir.

THE COURT: Clarify the prior question. "You're going to get a new background in terms of education," that might be confusing.

Q: They're going to give you a different high school that you went to, instead of the one you normally did, right?

A: Yeah, I guess so.

Q: And if people try and checkup on you financially, they're going to find that yours clean as clean can be, isn't that right, under the new name?

A: Is—

MR. DRURY: Objection as to "clean as clean can be," judge.

MR. LAROSSA: I think everybody—

THE COURT: Rephrase the question, please.

Q: Well, sir, after this trial and the few days you've been here, anybody in the audience and anybody who reads the papers, or sees anything, knows what you've been up to all your life, right?

MR. DRURY: Objection.

THE COURT: All right. Rephrase the question.

Q: Sir, your life, as it stands right now, has not had one concrete job since you were 20 years old, right?

MR. DRURY: Objection as to concrete.

THE COURT: All right. Mr. LaRossa, just ask the question.

Q: How about a real job, is that better?

THE WITNESS: I'm confused. Does he want the answer yet?

THE COURT: No, Mr. Drury's objecting, and I'm sustaining the objection. That means you don't have to answer the question. The last question was: Have you had a real job since you were 20 years old? Can you answer that question?

A: Job that's on the books. No. I answered that.

Q: No, a real job. A job where people go to work and get paid?

A: No. I answered that yesterday, no.

Q: Have you had a bank—you, have you had a bank account in the last 30 years?

A: I don't think so.

Q: Have you had a stock account?

A: No.

Q: Now, this new person that's going to be you, whatever name you put to it, is going to be given a background with jobs, right?

A: Is it?

Q: Yes.

A: I don't know that.

Q: You don't know that. They didn't tell you that in the witness protection program?

A: I didn't talk to them.

Q: You never talked to anybody in the witness protection program?

A: About when I get out?

Q: No, are you in the witness protection program right now?

A: Yes, I am.

Q: And they didn't tell you what the terms and conditions are?

A: No, they don't tell you nothing until you're ready to get out.

Q: They tell you that they were going to give you money when you get out?

A: No.

Q: Help you get—set up in a new home?

A: Yes.

Q: In a new location?

A: Not a new home.

Q: Help you get a job?

A: Yes.

Q: They tell you that?

A: Yes.

Q: Give you money to get on your feet?

A: Yes.

Q: And your background under that new name will have no scars on your background, isn't that right?

A: I don't know what you mean—

MR. DRURY: Objection.

THE COURT: Overruled.

Q: You know what I mean, don't you?

A: I don't know what you mean. You mean credit?

Q: I mean, you're going to be like a newborn baby with a new name, right?

MR. DRURY: Objection.

THE COURT: All right. Sustained.

Q: Are you under the belief that when you get out, and you're in the witness protection program, your new background won't show all the prior crimes and other bad things that you've done, and if anybody tried to check it, they wouldn't find out, right?

A: Oh, you should have said that. Crimes. Sure. It would be different. I didn't understand.

THE COURT: The answer is yes. Please move on.

MR. LAROSSA: I'm waiting for him to stop making a speech.

THE COURT: All right. Please.

Q: You lived a life of crime, did you not?

A: Yes, sir.

Q: Gambling?

A: Yes, sir.

Q: Loansharking?

A: Yes, sir.

Q: A life of deceit, is that right?

A: Yes, sir.

Q: Abuse of the people?

A: No.

Q: No. Each time you smacked somebody, did you think that was being abusive to people?

A: Well, three times in 30 years isn't a bad record; or three times in 40 years isn't a bad record.

Q: Okay. Buried bodies without any remorse?

A: Yes.

Q: No compunctions about conspiring to kill people?

A: It was the life.

Q: What?

A: It was the life.

Q: No hesitation to lie to people if it was in your self-interest?

A: It was the life.

Q: No hesitation to commit perjury when it was in your self-interest; for example, your tax returns?

A: No.

Q: Your unemployment insurance?

A: No.

Q: Your probation report?

A: No.

Q: And now, sir, after you've inked and signed the cooperation agreement, do you believe you're a different person?

MR. DRURY: Objection.

THE COURT: Sustained.

Q: Do you believe you're now a law-abiding citizen?

A: Well, I don't think I'll be committing any more crimes.

Q: Do you believe you're law-abiding now?

THE COURT: All right. This is argumentative.

MR. LAROSSA: It's not, sir. It's what his—it's what he believes his future is.

THE COURT: It's—then it's a—Rephrase the question.

Q: Let me ask you a question, sir. Would you commit perjury now?

A: No.

Q: Would you commit perjury under any circumstance?

A: No.

Q: Would you commit perjury if you could wipe that $100,000 fine out?

A: No.

Q: Would you commit perjury if you could walk out of the courtroom right now?

A: No.

Q: So you're a different person now than you were before you signed that agreement, right?

A: I'm the same person, with a different outlook.

MR. LAROSSA: I've had enough.

4. Hugh Anthony Levine: *United States* v. *E. J. Gonsalves,* U.S. District Court, Northern District of California

Cross-examination by Mr. Levine

> *NOTE: Mr. Levine is using an image projection device, putting the prior statements on a screen for both the judge and the witness to view simultaneously.*

Q: Let's put it this way: insofar as his declaration says what it says, then, you didn't talk to him again until April 1st, you don't contradict that, do you, as you sit here?

A: No.

Q: All right. Now, then between March 25 of 1993, and April 1 of 1993, you operated in connection with this investigation without consultation with Mr. Lyons, correct?

A: Yes.

Q: And you did so without consultation with anyone else in the United States Attorney's office, correct?

A: Yes.

Q: Now, on March 26 of 1993, in your discussions with Tom Hershey, you told him that you had a search warrant for Newt and for Roper and for a couple of pickup trucks, too, right?

A: Correct.

Q: And you told him that you knew what he had been doing regarding uninspected meat and Newt, as your declaration states on page two, right?

A: Yes.

Q: And did you give him evidence to convince him of that, say some things to him to convince him of that?

A: No. I think I just made those statements.

Q: Did you make statements to him to the effect that you could prove that he was guilty of federal offenses?

A: I don't recall making those statements.

Q: Let's put it this way, agent: you didn't paint a rosy picture for Tom Hershey; you painted a picture that you believed that he had been involved in violations of federal law, that you could prove it. Right?

A: Right.

Q: And that you were there with a search warrant to search about it, right?

A: Right.

Q: And that you basically had him dead to rights? That is what you led him to believe?

A: We had a pretty good case against him, yes.

Q: You also told him that you knew that Louise Hershey and John Hershey were criminally involved with him. Isn't that so?

A: We knew they were involved.

Q: You told him that you knew they were involved?

A: Um-hum.

Q: Is that a yes?

A: Yes.

Q: And you gave him indications to convince him of that also, didn't you?

A: No.

Q: You attempted to convince him at the very least that you could also prove their guilt of federal criminal charges, right?

A: No. We knew they were involved. The scenario was that we knew they were involved, but we didn't think the extent was anything great at that time.

Q: So you then went on to tell him that you wanted his cooperation regarding the Newt Frankfurter, Inc. investigation, correct?

A: Correct.

Q: And that you wanted to perhaps work a deal for his cooperation, correct?

A: Correct.

Q: And then he was told by those state agents that the state marijuana charges could possibly be dropped against him, correct?

A: Correct.

Q: And did the subject of testimony or possible testimony come up in your conversation with Tom Hershey on that day?

A: Yes.

Q: You don't remember this whole discussion verbatim, do you?

A: No.

Q: And you didn't make any notes, right, you, yourself?

A: No.

Q: Would you agree with me, again, that there is no mention in agent Quinn's notes of testimony, possible testimony by Tom Hershey? Would you agree with me on that, or should we put them up again?

A: No. That's fine. I agree.

Q: You agree with me, don't you?

A: Yes.

Q: And yet, you know that his declaration filed in this court in connection with this motion refers to a discussion of testimony, don't you?

A: Yes.

Q: And so you know about paragraph 6 of agent Quinn's declaration where he swears, "I recall that Tom Hershey was reluctant to testify, and that he was afraid. He probably said he did not want to testify. Tom Hershey was told that, if not necessary, he would not be called to testify. However, no one promised Hershey that he would not have to testify." You're aware of that being in agent Quinn's declaration, correct?

A: Yes.

Q: And then you agreed that there's no mention of testimony in his notes at all?

A: I agree.

Q: And there's no mention of testimony in his memorandum of inter-view at all, right?

A: Yes, that's true.

Q: And in that, respect, his notes are not complete, are they?

A: In that respect, no.

Q: Your recollection is not complete, either, is it?

A: Probably not.

Q: Now, for example, in your phone conversation with Mr. Lyons on March 25 of 1993, there was no mention of keeping Tom Hershey's cooperation secret, or trying to, was there?

A: No.

Q: There's nothing in the rough notes about that, is there?

A: No.

Q: There's nothing in the revised notes about it either, is there?

A: No.

Q: And yet, there were discussions with the Hersheys on that subject, right?

A: Yes.

Q: And Tom told you, as you testified—page 14—that he did not want to testify?

A: That's correct.

Q: And he was adamant about it, wasn't he?

A: Yes.

Q: And, agent Hasheider, is it your testimony that you just ignored what he said about that?

A: Well, he said he didn't want to testify, but that still didn't say that he wouldn't testify.

Q: Well, sir, let me just read what you said on Direct examination about this "ignore" stuff:

"**Question:** page 15, Mr. Lyons on line 3—"and when he made that statement, this is a statement that he didn't want to testify, how did you respond to him?

"**Answer:** Well, I don't know if I had any response at all. Witnesses do this all the time to me. That's atypical. Nobody wants to testify.

"**Question:** Right. Did you reassure him in any way, or did you just ignore the statement?

"**Answer:** I ignored it."

You recall so testifying, right?

A: Yes.

Q: Now, regarding "ignored it," what do you mean, you just didn't respond?

A: No. When I said, "ignored it," what I meant is just what I stated previously, in that we got witnesses all the time that are reluctant to testify and don't want to testify, but that isn't saying that they won't testify. So from the standpoint of saying, there is a difference in my mind about between not wanting to testify, and saying they don't want to, and saying, "No, I won't."

Q: That's not the question, agent. This is the question: when you ignored it, as you've testified on direct that you did, does that mean that you were silent about it, you made no statement or utterance?

A: No, that isn't what that means.

Q: All right. What I am asking—did you make any response to it?

A: Well, I said there is a possibility he may not have to testify as usual with cases. Very few of these cases go to trial, as you pointed out earlier.

Q: Now, are you changing your testimony on Direct examination that you ignored it?

A: No.

Q: Do you want to help us out here on how you could ignore on the one hand and make a statement to him that it's not a definite, but he might have to testify on the other hand? Can you reconcile that here for us?

A: No, I can't.

Q: The truth is that you did not ignore it by making no response, isn't that so?

A: (No response.)

Q: You didn't make no response to him saying, "I don't want to testify," did you?

A: No.

Q: You just didn't hear that and then stare blankly at his face and say nothing, did you?

A: No.

Q: And, sir, if you did not ignore what he said to you, are you positive about what your response to him was?

A: Yes, I am.

Q: You agree with me that the notes and the reports are silent on this issue as we have established a few minutes ago?

A: Yes.

Q: You never wrote anything on this subject about testimony until your declaration over two years later, isn't that true?

A: That's correct.

Q: Did any agent in your presence do anything other than ignore what Tom said about not wanting to testify?

A: Did any agent—repeat the question.

Q: Do anything besides ignore him?

A: I don't know.

Q: Well, let's go back to agent Quinn's declaration, page two, paragraph 6. This is what we read a little while ago. He wrote, he swore, "I recall that Tom Hershey was reluctant to testify and he was afraid. He probably said he did not want to testify. Tom Hershey was told that, if not necessary, he would not be called to testify. However, no one promised him that he would not have to testify." Now, did that happen? What he is swearing here in his declaration, did that happen?

A: I believe so.

Q: Well, can you tell us how, if you ignored Tom, how he was told that?

A: No, I can't.

Q: Your testimony here that you ignored Tom was wrong, wasn't it?

A: Yes, it was probably incorrect.

Q: Okay. Now, again in your Direct examination, page ten, line 18, Mr. Lyons asked you:

"**Question:** Did you discuss whether or not he would testify on any point in the investigation?

"**Answer:** No." Do you recall so testifying on direct?

A: Yes.

Q: And, again, how can you explain agent Quinn's declaration that I just read if you gave a truthful answer on direct testimony here?

A: I probably was wrong in my recollection, sir.

Q: So at the very least, you would agree with me that some of your direct testimony in this case is mistaken?

A: That part is, yes.

Q: And then the other part about ignoring him you've already told us was mistaken, too?

A: That's one and the same, is it not?

Q: No. This is page 10, and that's another page, and I don't want to quibble with you about that. Let's put up these notes of agent Quinn. Can you read those, agent Hasheider?

A: Yes.

Q: You'll see. I hope—no, you won't see because it is on the wrong page. You'll see 4:40 P.M., N.H. reassured the H's and John, right?

A: Yes, I see it.

Q: And I'm reading it right, aren't I?

A: Yes, I guess. That's what it says, "N.H. reassured the H's and John."

Q: The "it's" are the Hersheys and John?

A: Yes.

Q: And that's at 4:40 P.M., right?

A: Okay.

Q: What they needed reassurance about was their fear of being revealed as cooperating, isn't that so?

A: I don't recall what that's in reference to.

Q: Well, forgetting that for a moment, isn't it true that they needed reassurances about their fear of being revealed as cooperating with your investigation?

A: They were definitely concerned about that, yes.

Q: It was more than concerned, wasn't it, isn't that a bit mild to describe it? Didn't they communicate to you a clear fear of physical retribution to them and their loved ones if they cooperated with your investigation?

A: I believe so, yes.

Q: And didn't they actually give you some examples of things that had occurred in the past to support that fear?

A: Allegedly, yes.

Q: Now, the most obvious of which, were it to be revealed that they were cooperating, was if Tom Hershey testified, isn't that so?

A: True, correct.

Q: And, sir, the truth is that the reassurance that you gave the Hersheys and John at 4:40 was that Tom would not have to testify, isn't that so?

A: No.

Q: Well, if you had ignored him about his expressed fear about not wanting to testify, do you agree that he might need some reassurance on that subject?

A: Yes, he may.

Q: All right. Now, in the presence of Tom Hershey, Louise Hershey, and John Hershey, you called off your planned execution of the federal search warrants at Newt and Roper, correct?

A: Correct.

Q: And Tom expressed to you actual fear of reprisals from the Ringo brothers against him and his family if it was disclosed that he cooperated with the investigation, correct? He flat-out told you that, didn't he?

A: Yes.

Q: It was a recurrent theme with him, wasn't it?

A: Yes.

Q: And it was the main consideration or problem that the Hersheys had about cooperating, wasn't it?

A: Yes.

Q: In other words, Tom Hershey wasn't negotiating with you about what he would plead to, or how much time he would do, or things of that sort? What he was mainly concerned with was physical reprisals from the Ringos, right?

A: I guess so.

Q: Well, you know so, don't you?

A: Well, it was a concern of his, but—

Q: It's the way he came across to you, wasn't it?

A: That he was fearful of the Ringos; he said it numerous times.

Q: And so did Louise Hershey, isn't that so?

A: She may have said it, but I remember hearing it from Tom.

Q: John Hershey when he arrived said the same thing, didn't he?

A: Yes, he did.

Q: All right. Now, speaking of the arrival of John Hershey, he arrived at 4:20 P.M., is that right?

A: Is this according to Mr. Quinn?

Q: Well, that's what I am asking, but I should give you the benefit of the right note. And, so, we have a note: "4:20 P.M., son John arrived in blue chevy truck," correct?

A: That's what it says, yes.

Q: And it is 4:20 because it's 4:16 and 4:21, right? (Referring to time references before and after the specific item.)

A: Correct.

Q: Now, you testified on Direct examination at page 17, Mr. Lyons asked you,

"**Question:** Okay. At some point in time did John Hershey arrive at the premises?

"**Answer:** Yes.

"**Question:** Was this before or after Tom made the call?

"**Answer:** After.

Q: Do you recall that?

A: Yes, I do.

Q: And the call that you are referring to is the call that was tape-recorded by Tom to George Ringo, correct?

A: Correct.

Q: And isn't it true that actually before that call was made, "son, John, dialed the operator on the phone in order to get the time stated on the tape preparatory to the call?"

A: Yes, that's what it says.

Q: 4:51 P.M. John dialed operator for Tom to check recorder. And then, 4:54. Redialed time after equipment check. 4:55. Redialed time and, then Neal dialed the 5:10 call and Tom asked for George, and, 4:57. The call was over. Right?

A: Right.

Q: So it is clear at least from agent Quinn's notes that the call to Newt did not occur before John Hershey arrived, as you testified on direct, but after, isn't that so?

A: That's correct.

Q: And when you so testified on direct, you were mistaken?

A: When I testified on direct, I'm assuming that was my discussion with John. So the time is—you're correct.

Q: Won't you agree with me that on direct in this respect you gave mistaken testimony?

A: Yes.

Q: Now, one moment, please. (Pause to put the witness's declaration on the projector.) Your declaration states that, "I told him, Tom, that we knew that John Hershey and Louise Hershey were involved." Isn't that right?

A: That's correct.

Q: And you remember that without me needing to put it in front of you?

A: Yes.

Q: Okay. Let's just compare that to what you testified here in your Direct examination, page 9. Mr. Lyons asked you, "In your investigation what information did you have about John Hershey or Louise Hershey?"

"**Answer**: We had some sketchy information that they were involved but not to any great extent." Now, you didn't say to Tom Hershey that you had some sketchy information they were involved but not to any great extent. You flat-out said that you knew that John and Louise were criminally involved with him. Is that so?

A: We knew they were involved, yes.

Q: You told him that you knew they were involved?

A: That's correct.

Q: You didn't say in terms of a sketchy information, you flat-out told them that you knew they were criminally involved, right?

A: Yes.

Q: And when John got there, he was told the same thing, wasn't he?

A: Yes.

Q: And, now, John Hershey had no exposure in the state drug case, as far as you knew, isn't that so?

A: That's my knowledge, yes.

Q: He wasn't charged with it, right?

A: No.

Q: He didn't even live with his parents at the place where the marijuana growth had been found, right?

A: Right.

Q: And the state agents didn't offer John Hershey any incentives about that, that they might drop any state drug charges against him because there wasn't any, right?

A: Right.

Q: And the same was true with respect to Louise Hershey, right?

A: Correct.

Q: Now, according to your memorandum of interview of John Hershey, dated March 26, 1993, John—just read this very last line. This is your memory of the interview of John Hershey, dated March 26, 1993?

A: Yes, it is.

Q: And it is about your interview of him at his parents' residence in Oakdale on that same date?

A: Yes.

Q: And the last line, quote, "he initially advised his father not to co-operate but changed his mind after talking over the proposed cooperation agreement." Close quote.

A: Right.

Q: And this is your own memo, right?

A: Right.

Q: Now, he, obviously—he did this advising his father not to cooper-ate after Mr. George Ringo had left that phone message for Tom to call him, right?

A: Right.

Q: And, now, John Hershey's advice to his father made in your pres-ence presented an obstacle to you in your effort to secure Tom's cooperating, didn't it? I mean, here was his son telling him, "Don't do it, Dad," right?

A: I don't understand what you mean here.

Q: Well, when he advised his father not to cooperate, that was con-trary to what you wanted, right?

A: Exactly.

Q: And it was an obstacle to you that the son would be telling his fa-ther not to do what you wanted the father to do, right?

A: Right.

Q: And—

A: But by that time, Tom had already agreed to cooperate.

Q: Well, let me ask you this, sir: the arrival—let's go back to the other sheet. We got the arrival at 4:20 of John, correct?

A: Yes.

Q: And let's just shift over to page 3—I don't have the right page. And then 31 minutes later, at 4:51 P.M., 31 minutes after his arrival at 4:20 we have John dialing the operator to get the time onto the tape for that phone call that he was going to make, right?

A: Right.

Q: So we have this 31-minute time frame in which John arrives and he is advising his father not to cooperate, and by the end of that time frame, he's actually helping you set up the monitored phone call, correct?

A: Correct.

Q: Now, basically in those 31 minutes, agent Hasheider, John Hershey went a 180-degrees from advising his father not to cooperate to co-operating, himself, right?

A: No. That interview that you have there was conducted on the porch at 5:10. That memorandum of interview is generated from my discussion with him at 5:10. I did not interview John until later.

Q: Putting aside when you interviewed him, what your memorandum says is not what he said to you. It's what he said to his father. He initially advised his father not to cooperate, right?

A: Correct.

Q: Okay. Now, that happened—that didn't happen at 5:10 P.M.? That happened not long after 4:20 P.M., right?

A: Yes, probably.

Q: Right. And what I am saying is 31 minutes later he's had a change of mind about that because he's now assisting you and his father in cooperating, right?

A: Right.

Q: Okay. Now, he made self-incriminating statements, John Hershey, about his involvement, did he not?

A: Yes.

Q: And he made statements incriminating his father in the meat operation, did he not?

A: Yes, he did.

Q: And he said that he, too, had helped butcher meat and delivered it to Newt, did he not, he, meaning, John Hershey?

A: Yes.

Q: And he even talked about his own abuse of marijuana, didn't he?

A: Yes.

Q: And also Louise Hershey made incriminating statements about her involvement, is that right?

A: Yes.

Q: Along the same lines?

A: Um-hum, yes.

Q: And back on March 25th, the day before, in your conversation on the phone with Mr. Lyons, you never discussed the issue of cooperation by Louise Hershey or John Hershey, did you?

A: No.

Q: And there is nothing about it in the rough notes, is there?

A: No.

Q: Nothing about it in the revised notes, right?

A: No.

Q: And in your declaration, your declaration in support of this motion, page 3, paragraph 9, regarding March 26th, you state, quote, "I have no recollection of any discussion of a deal for John or Louise Hershey." Period. Close quote, correct?

A: Correct.

Q: Now, sir, that's not an accurate statement, is it?

A: Yes, it is.

Q: You did discuss cooperating with John Hershey on March 26, didn't you?

A: No, I did not. John Hershey told me that he was feeling remorse for his parents, and then he heard the offer that we were giving Tom, he's the one who went and talked to his father about it because he was feeling remorse, because he claimed that those marijuana plants in the basement were his, and his father was taking a rap for it.

Q: All right. Now, agent Hasheider, there came a time when the United States Department of Agriculture made a substantial purchase of meat in order to have a controlled delivery to Newt Frankfurter, Inc., correct?

A: That's correct.

Q: And that purchase was made basically because Tom Hershey wasn't getting any cattle from Eddie Roper to use to make the controlled delivery, correct?

A: Yes.

Q: So you had to fall back to a plan b, which was to just go buy some meat, right?

A: Yes.

Q: The meat was bought early on in April 2, right?

A: No. It was bought before then. We took delivery of it on the morning of April 2nd.

Q: Okay. Fine. And you had to get the money together through your channels on August—I mean on April 1st, right?

A: I didn't handle it. I don't know how the financing was done.

Q: You just don't open some drawer and pull out the money and go to the meat store, right?

A: Correct. Correct.

Q: There has to be a requisition for it, doesn't there?

A: I believe so.

Q: In writing, right?

A: Yeah.

Q: Submitted to a superior, right?

A: Correct.

Q: Got to be passed upon by the superior as to whether they are going to authorize the disbursement of government funds, right?

A: I assume that's the way the process went.

Q: How much money are we talking about here, anyway?

A: $1,400, maybe.

Q: So not an insignificant amount of money, right?

A: No.

Q: So, all of that, really, the approval to buy the meat and the paper-work regarding the funds, that really all occurred on March 30, didn't it?

A: I don't know because my agency didn't handle it.

Q: Well, it occurred before—let's just set the time line here. What date was the controlled delivery actually made?

A: April 3rd.

Q: And that's a Saturday, right?

A: Correct.

Q: It had been planned to make it *on* the Friday, April 2nd?

A: Right.

Q: But it couldn't be made ready on time for Tom to get it there on Friday, April 2nd?

A: Yes.

Q: And the delivery of the meat, you took delivery on the morning of April 2nd, hoping you could make the controlled delivery later that day, right?

A: Correct.

Q: You had to pay for the meat before you took the delivery and that occurred on April 1st, right?

A: I believe so. I don't know.

Q: You just said before that you paid for the meat before you took de-livery of it, right?

A: I don't know that, sir, because my agency didn't handle the pur-chase of the meat. I was only assuming what happened.

Q: As the case agent, don't you know in fact, from whatever source, that the plan, the plan was to buy the meat because you couldn't get it from Roper, actually was approved on March 30th?

A: Yes, that's fair. Yes.

Q: And, well, there's probably some records around that confirmed that, aren't there?

A: No.

Q: So you had the plan to make the controlled delivery of store-bought meat, and you had the meat before there was ever any written agreement between Mr. Lyons, or the U.S. Attorney's office, and Tom Hershey, through his attorney, correct? Isn't that so?

A: I guess so.

Q: You had the meat; you paid out 1,400 bucks for it; you had the whole plan for it back on March 30th, which was before there ever was any agreement, or any writing, memorializing the agreement between the United States attorney's office and Tom Hershey?

A: Right.

Q: Okay. And as a matter of fact, the reason that there ever came to be such a writing was because it was initiated by Tom Hershey, not by you, isn't that so?

A: What writing?

Q: The letter that eventually went from Mr. Lyons to Mr. Spiering, on April 2nd, came about because Tom wouldn't go any further in his cooperation without something in writing, isn't that so?

A: No.

Q: Well, he certainly was agreeing to make the controlled delivery to the point that you bought the meat before there was any writing memorializing an agreement, isn't that true?

A: Right.

Q: And the notes you had of your phone conversation with Mr. Lyons don't refer to a writing, having an agreement in writing, do they?

A: Which phone conversation are you talking about?

Q: I'm talking about the March 25, 1993 one, where you made the notes?

A: Correct.

Q: Nothing in there about having an agreement in writing?

A: No.

Q: All right. And there's nothing in the revised notes, either, about having an agreement in writing, correct?

A: Correct.

Q: Now, what was the volume of this meat, by the way, weight, roughly?

A: Approximately 1,347 pounds, or something like that.

Q: You didn't go out and commit the United States government to an expenditure of some $1,400 to take possession of 13 hundred and some pounds of meat without an agreement that Tom would deliver it, did you?

A: No.

Q: And on whose authority, by the way, was this purchase of meat made?

A: Whose authority?

Q: Yes.

A: Somebody within the food safety inspection service.

Q: Someone higher than you?

A: Yes.

Q: It was a rush situation, wasn't it, getting this meat and making this controlled delivery?

A: The time of it was of essence, yes.

Q: And, actually, that had been told to Tom Hershey on March 26, that there was a narrow window of time here that you're dealing with. Isn't that so?

A: That's correct.

Q: That's in the notes of Mr. Lyons, isn't it?

A: Uh-hum.

Q: Meaning, yes?

A: Yes.

Q: And, of course, not only did you not buy all that meat and all that money without an agreement with Tom Hershey, but you had to go and arrange all of the personnel, that would be involved to go into Newt after the controlled delivery was made, right?

A: Correct.

Q: And do you recall now when it was made, approximately how many agents were involved in that entire operation?

A: Not without looking at the plan, no.

Q: It was a lot, wasn't it?

A: Yeah.

Q: And a lot of cars involved, too, right?

A: Yes.

Q: And all of this orchestration surrounding this controlled delivery, this didn't occur without an agreement with Tom Hershey, did it?

A: No.

Q: Now, when was that agreement formed?

A: He agreed to cooperate the day we did the warrant at his place. He verbally agreed on it.

Q: Was it his act of agreeing to cooperate that formed the cooperation agreement?

A: Hmm, no, because we knew that, as per Mr. Lyons' instructions, he had to have an attorney and a formal agreement had to be formalized between the attorneys.

Q: But to just back up and not—pardon my metaphor—beat a dead horse, before that ever occurred you went ahead and made the plan and got the requisition for the money and bought the meat and took delivery of this meat, right, before there was any agreement formalized between Mr. Lyons and the attorney for Tom. Isn't that what happened?

A: That's correct, then, I guess, according to the time frame.

Q: Right. So, without the involvement of Mr. Lyons and any written agreement between Mr. Lyons and some attorney for Tom, you did that phone call, that controlled phone call, to George Ringo on March 26th, right?

A: Correct.

Q: And you did that debriefing of Tom and Louise Hershey at Knights Ferry Park on March 30th?

A: Correct.

Q: In which they just told you everything?

A: Correct.

Q: And you set up that controlled delivery of that meat which you hoped would occur on April 2nd, right?

A: Right.

Q: And all that was done without any agreement in writing, right?

A: I guess so. Correct.

Q: Isn't it true, sir, that you just planned to keep on going with a controlled delivery plan that was in place without any agreement in writing?

A: No.

Q: —until Tom insisted on it? Isn't that the way it came about?

A: No.

Q: Well, did you stop at some point and say, okay, now I got this plan to do this controlled delivery and I got 1,457 bucks that we paid to a meat place, and I'm now sitting on 1300 and some pounds of meat. I guess it's time to get an agreement in writing. Is that the way it happened?

A: Not at all.

Q: Isn't it true that it was you who called up Mr. Lyons and told him, "It looks like we have an agreement?"

A: Yes.

Q: And when you told him, "It looks like we have an agreement," there was no writing memorializing that agreement, right?

A: No.

Q: And there was no phone discussion between Mr. Lyons and Mr. Spiering, yet, right?

A: Correct.

Q: And, yet, you're telling Mr. Lyons, "It looks like we have an agreement," right?

A: Correct.

Q: And you will agree with me, won't you, agent Hasheider, that it was Tom Hershey who insisted on speaking with Mr. Spiering before he would go any further with the cooperation, before he would make that controlled delivery?

A: No.

Q: Agent Hasheider, did the subject of Tom Hershey testifying or not testifying ever come up between you and Tom Hershey after March 26 of 1993, until June 22nd of 1993, when you testified that you phoned him from Mr. Lyons' office?

A: I don't recall.

Q: So you have no recollection of that subject ever coming up in that roughly 3-month period of time, right?

A: The only time I can recall is that he said something that he didn't want to testify was at the—may have been at the park.

Q: Knights Ferry Park, on March 30th?

A: Yes.

Q: So let's say that did happen, and then your recollection did not come up from, say, March 30, 1993, until June 22nd of 1993, when you phoned him from Mr. Lyons's office?

A: I don't recall it coming up again, no.

Q: By the way, that call from Mr. Lyons' office to Tom Hershey on June 22nd of '93, did you record that—was it recorded, I'll say?

A: The call?

Q: Yes, the phone call?

A: To—excuse me.

Q: Mr. Hershey. You testified on Direct examination back in October that one day you were in John Lyons's office, and it was discussed that Tom is going to have to go into the grand jury, and you placed a call to Tom Hershey from Mr. Lyons's office. Do you remember that?

A: No.

Q: Do you remember that?

A: A call from Mr. Lyon's office?

Q: *Yes?*

A: No, there wasn't.

Q: Was there any call from Mr. Lyons' office to Tom Hershey recorded, to your knowledge?

A: I don't recall making—I don't recall making a telephone call from Mr. Lyons' office.

Q: All right. I just need a moment to flip through some pages, Your Honor. (Pause) What I am talking about this is on pages 44, 45— and Mr. Lyons asked you, "Now, did there come a point in time in which you had a telephone conversation with Tom Hershey about the fact that he was going to be subpoenaed to testify before the grand jury?"

"**Answer:** Yes.

"**Question:** And when did you have that conversation with him?"

"**Answer:** On the 22nd of June."

All right. It was your office. That may have been confused you. You made this call from your office? What I am asking you, again, that phone call wasn't recorded?

A: No.

Q: Did you make any notes of it, of that conversation?

A: No, I don't believe so.

Q: Was there any other agent present who made any notes of it?

A: No.

Q: Did you have a subpoena then for Tom Hershey?

A: I don't believe so, because we were still under the assumption that Mr. Hershey was going to cooperate.

Q: And you would never need one, is that what you mean?

A: Exactly.

Q: All right. Okay. Now, you did eventually feel compelled to serve Mr. Hershey with a subpoena for the grand jury and that occurred on March—on June 24 of 1993, correct?

A: Right.

Q: —the day before his scheduled appearance, right?

A: Correct.

Q: And you testified about riding in with Mr. Hershey to go to the federal building for that purpose, right?

A: On the 25th, yes.

Q: And the two of you talked about mostly car racing, is that correct?

A: Correct.

Q: Is it your testimony that Mr. Hershey, from the time of that phone conversation from your office on June 22nd to him, until the time that he was in Mr. Lyons' office and said he wasn't going to testify, never expressed any concern about testifying? Is that your testimony?

A: No. He probably said that he didn't want to testify. It's hard for me to distinguish. He said that numerous times, but he never said he wouldn't testify.

Q: Well, in that period—I mean, by that point of time, June 24, 1993, Newt had burned in an alleged arson fire, right?

A: Right.

Q: And Louise Hershey—you had information—had relocated to Mexico, is that right?

A: What?

Q: You had information that Louise Hershey out of fear of reprisal from the Ringos had moved or gone to Mexico, didn't you?

A: No.

Q: Let me ask you this: when you told Tom Hershey that he was going to have to testify in a grand jury and you said you then went on to talk about car racing, did he ever ask you who would be present when he testified?

A: I explained to him the grand jury process; that he would be in front of 23 people, yes.

Q: Did he ask if Newt, or its lawyers, or people would get a transcript of what he testified to?

A: I don't recall.

Q: Did he ask you if the grand jury proceeding would be opened to the public?

A: I informed him that it's a secret, closed proceeding when I described it as being with 23 people.

Q: Did he ask you to postpone it?

A: No.

Q: Did he ask you if Louise Hershey could come in with him?

A: No.

Q: Did he ask you if she could be there, be present with him?

A: No.

Q: Did you ever suggest to him that he might be taken into custody if he didn't show up to testify?

A: No.

Q: Are you telling us, agent Hasheider, that after all of the fears that Tom Hershey expressed about reprisals, and fear of testifying and fear of being exposed, if he cooperated, that this no longer, when it came time to go over to the U.S. attorney's office, this no longer presented any problem for him?

A: I don't know what he was thinking but, apparently, not.

Q: In other words, it's your testimony that he did nothing or said nothing to communicate to you in anyway that this issue any longer presented a problem?

A: No.

Q: Can you—did he tell you what caused him not to show up for that meeting at Spangler's restaurant that he didn't show for?

A: My recollection is that he said that he had transportation problems, that his car had been repossessed, or something of that nature, and wasn't able to get there.

Q: Did you believe that?

A: Yeah.

Q: You were upset about that, weren't you?

A: Well, yes.

Q: And you communicated that upset to him, didn't you?

A: I'm sure I did.

Q: Did Tom Hershey ever tell you why he refused to testify in the grand jury?

A: My recollection is the same thing that he has been saying for sometime, in that he was fearful of the Ringos.

Q: Did you ever hear Mr. Lyons ask him that question in the office that day, when he refused, why he's refusing to testify?

A: I don't recall him asking that no.

Q: Is it your testimony, sir, that when that occurred, you were caught by surprise?

A: That—

Q: You were caught by surprise?

A: What?

Q: That he wouldn't testify?

A: Yes.

Q: That's your testimony?

A: Yes.

MR. LEVINE: Your Honor, I don't have any further questions. Thank you very much.

5. Thomas A. Moore: *Nora Martelly v. The City of New York;* Supreme Court, New York County

Cross-examination by Mr. Moore

Q: Dr. De Brovner, you found several departures from accepted practice in the care of this mother and baby, didn't you?

A: No.

Q: You reviewed this case in 1991?

A: Yes, I did.

Q: You had some opinions in 1991?

A: Yes, I did.

Q: You communicated those opinions in 1991?

A: Yes, I did.

Q: By the way, you knew that this case was far from trial in 1991, didn't you?

A: Yes, I think that was reasonable.

Q: Doctor, when a case is far from trial, as opposed to when it's close to trial and on the court trial calendar, in reviewing it, you know that it may be years before you testify, if you're going to testify in the case, correct?

A: Correct.

Q: Under those circumstances, doctor, doesn't it help to memorialize your opinions in writing, so that years later you have them to refresh your recollection about what you found in your analysis at the time?

A: It might be helpful, it might not be. If I have communicated to the attorney very close to the time that I reviewed the case, the attorney had taken whatever notes are appropriate and was able to share those notes back to me when and if the case got to trial.

Q: Did I ask you anything other than it might help you to memorialize your opinions at the time, if you knew and expected it might be years before you'd ever have to express those opinions in a court of law?

A: I said, it might be helpful, it might not.

Q: Doctor, in this case, I assume, as in any other case I've cross-examined you in, even though forming opinions years before your testimony, you do not have one word in writing, right?

A: It was not requested and there is no word in writing, that is correct.

Q: You know, of course, that if you did have anything in writing, at the time you testify, myself or anybody cross-examining you would be entitled to see them and question you about your opinions that were in writing. You know that, don't you?

A: Yes, I do, sir.

Q: By the way, sir, you gave opinions with what's called "a reasonable degree of medical probability," or "a reasonable degree of medical certainty"; correct?

A: Yes, sir.

Q: And you understand that that's the level to which opinions must rise to be considered in a court of law in this state, correct?

A: Correct, sir.

Q: How long did you say you've been doing this? Fifteen years, I believe you said, is that correct?

A: That's what I said, sir.

Q: All right. Now, sir, back in 1991, since you didn't put anything in writing, I assume you had oral contacts with a lawyer or lawyers for the Health and Hospitals Corporation concerning your opinions, is that correct?

A: That's correct, sir.

Q: And, doctor, you've read, by the way, not only Depositions in this case, but, I assume, prior to coming here today, some testimony that has been taken down and typed up, that has been heard before this court and jury. You've been furnished with such, correct?

A: That's correct, sir.

Q: Doctor, smoking, smoking is a red herring that will only lead triers of the fact down a wrong road in this case, would you agree?

A: I'm not sure I understand the import of your question, sir.

Q: Let me ask you this: Back in 1991, it was never your opinion, with a reasonable degree of medical probability, that any cigarettes this woman may have smoked in early pregnancy, before it was confirmed that she was pregnant, in any way adversely affected this baby. That was never your opinion, with a reasonable degree of medical probability, correct?

A: Correct.

Q: By the way, did anybody on the behalf of the Health and Hospitals Corporation ask you your opinion on that issue?

A: They may have, and I would have said that it had no effect.

Q: And, doctor, it was never your opinion in 1991 or 1992 or 1993, 1994, 1995, 1996, or as you sit here today, it was never your opinion that any failure to follow nutritional advice by this woman in any way adversely affected her baby? That was never your opinion, true?

A: True.

Q: And you'd tell them that, too, if they asked, wouldn't you?

A: Yes.

Q: Who was directly supervising Dr. Agustin in the care of mother and baby in this case, doctor?

A: According to Dr. Clare there were senior resident, chief resident and perhaps an attending involved in the care.

Q: Is that your answer?

A: Yes, sir.

Q: Doctor, you understand supervision, correct?

A: Depends on its context, sir.

Q: Do you know the meaning of the word supervision, doctor?

A: I am sure there are many definitions, sir.

Q: Did you say there were various definitions of supervision?

A: Yes.

Q: Doctor, is supervision a common English word?

A: Yes, sir.

Q: Is it a concept known to medicine, doctor?

A: It's used in medicine and nonmedicine context.

Q: And in the same way, doctor, with the same meaning, correct?

A: I guess it's used in different ways in different context.

Q: Doctor, are there degrees of supervision?

A: Yes, sir.

Q: Would you say that an attending physician on call in the hospital, but somewhere other than observing this mother and baby, would be directly supervising a resident who is caring for the mother and baby, would you say that, doctor?

A: I don't have enough information to answer that.

Q: Would you say, doctor, that a chief resident not observing and analyzing this mother and baby, but someplace else with some other patient or whatever, would be directly supervising one who is, would you say that, doctor?

A: If that was the fact, I would agree with that, yes.

Q: You would say that a chief resident not involved in the care of a mother and baby but doing something else would qualify as directly supervising one who is, is that your testimony to this jury and his honor?

A: No, I think you asked me in the negative and I said that if the chief resident was not involved in observing or obtaining adequate information about this patient from the resident he would not be adequately supervising this patient. I agreed with you, but I didn't know there was—that the facts were in evidence.

Q: Doctor, you also, therefore, agree that the same would be true concerning the attending?

A: You didn't—

Q: If I asked you if the attending was on call in the hospital, as it's been testified to but was not observing and familiar with this mother and baby and analyzing by being present, that physician could not be directly supervising one who was, true?

A: Are we going to adopt this as the question and not the previous one? I will be happy to answer this one for you.

Q: Would you please answer the question, doctor?

A: The answer to this question is that is correct.

Q: And if there was, doctor, a third-year resident, a senior resident as you obstetricians call them, who was not observing and analyzing this mother and baby's condition, that physician could not be directly supervising one who was, correct?

A: I think I need some information as to observing and analyzing.

Q: They were the words I used relative to the attending and the chief resident. I mean somebody there directly supervising. If he's not there he can't be directly supervising, true?

A: I am not quite clear what "there" is, sir.

Q: I am talking about by the patient's side.

A: By the patient's side? I am not sure it's absolutely necessary that they be at the patient's side to have adequate information to adequately supervise.

Q: Doctor, direct supervision you agreed has to be furnished by a licensed physician to a nonlicensed physician, that was the starting point in this area, true?

A: True.

Q: Direct, doctor, has a definite meaning in English, doesn't it?

A: Direct as refers to the physician not as reference to the patient.

Q: Are you assuming in this case that there was a licensed physician directly supervising Dr. Agustin in his management of this labor?

A: I have no information to the negative.

Q: You already answered that if there was not that would be a departure from accepted practice, true?

A: True.

Q: By the way, when did you find out for the first time that Dr. Agustin was not licensed to practice medicine in the State of New York in 1984?

A: About a quarter of twelve today.

Q: No one on behalf of the Health and Hospitals Corporation ever volunteered that to you, correct?

A: Correct.

Q: You said you were at least intellectually curious to know whether Dr. Clare was right that Dr. Agustin was a second-year resident or I was right in my declaration that he was a first-year resident. Remember saying that?

A: Yes, sir.

Q: Are you different than anybody else, doctor, that when you don't know, you inquire?

A: Depending on the nature of the situation. Sometimes I do and sometimes I don't. Depends whether it's appropriate.

Q: Let me ask you this, doctor, did you try to allay that intellectual curiosity by asking someone on behalf of the Health and Hospitals Corporation, Mr. Greenfield or another from the time you first found out of this dispute up to now, did you try and find out what the answer was; was Dr. Agustin a first-year resident or second-year resident?

A: If I felt it was pertinent to my opinion I would have inquired. If I didn't think it was pertinent to the opinion I was asked to give I would not have inquired.

Q: We still don't know whether you inquired or not, doctor. Please answer the question I asked you. Did you or didn't you?

A: I don't think I did.

Q: You don't think you did?

A: I know I did not.

Q: Let me, doctor, ask you, I am sure you'll agree with the following proposition, that if good practice dictates in the care of a patient that the physician who is involved be directly supervised by someone else, the identity of that direct supervisor should be somewhere reflected in that chart; you think that's good practice?

A: No, sir.

Q: That's not good practice?

A: That's the Department of Obstetrics and Gynecology at Metropolitan Hospital to determine, not for this chart to reflect.

Q: Are you saying that appropriate documentation wouldn't dictate that if somebody has to, in practicing medicine, be directly supervised by someone that the identity of the direct supervisor shouldn't be documented?

A: May not have to be documented on this chart. Certainly ought to be documented in departmental procedure.

Q: Who was directly supervising Dr. Agustin on this fateful day, do you know?

A: Do I know the specific name, no, I don't.

Q: I say who?

A: Specific person. I don't know the name of that specific person.

Q: Did you ever make any effort to find out from 1991 down to today?

A: I was enlightened by Dr. Clare's testimony and I am also aware of the policy of city hospitals and how they function.

Q: Doctor, can you please answer my questions?

A: I will do my best, sir.

Q: Have you made one effort to find out who was directly supervising Dr. Agustin in the care of this mother and baby in labor?

A: The specific person, no.

Q: Weren't you asked, doctor, to give opinions about the standard of care in this case?

A: I was.

Q: And you just said that if this gentleman, Dr. Agustin was not under direct supervision that would be a departure in accepted practice?

A: Yes, sir.

Q: When this woman comes in with a history of yellow-colored amniotic fluid, doctor, the concept of her amniotic fluid should be uppermost in the mind of those caring for her, true or false?

A: True.

Q: Did you see, doctor, that there's not one word about her amniotic fluid in the examination that was performed upon her when she arrived in the hospital?

A: Yes, sir.

Q: Doctor, there are two possibilities in that record, aren't there, either there was fluid leaking or there was no fluid leaking, true?

A: True.

Q: Either one would have to be documented, true or false?

A: The fact that there was—

Q: Doctor, did you hear my question?

A: I need clarification.

Q: You need clarification. Either one. I asked you, there's only two possibilities, doctor, either the fluid was leaking or it was not correct?

A: Correct.

Q: Either finding, doctor, either finding. You know what either finding is referring to the two, either and two, they go together, right? Doctor, it's your answers. You know, what I am talking about, don't you?

A: Would you please repeat the question?

Q: Doctor, in being concerned uppermost about the fluid, the possibilities are that there was some leaking or there was none?

A: Correct.

Q: Correct?

A: Correct.

Q: Since it's uppermost in the minds of those caring, either one of those observations, either leaking fluid or no leaking fluid should have been documented, yes or no?

A: Conclusion that she had ruptured—

Q: Did you hear my question, doctor, was clearly a yes or no and you answer it yes or no?

A: Yes.

Q: Would you please, for this court and jury, answer it yes or no?

A: Yes, it was documented.

Q: It was documented?

A: Yes, sir.

Q: Did you see me ask in essence the same question of Dr. Clare?

A: It was documented, sir.

Q: Did you hear my—

A: I don't remember you asking him or not asking him. I don't remember how he replied.

Q: Doctor, you know it's not documented, don't you?

A: The record says spontaneous ruptured membranes. That implies that it was ruptured and that there was fluid. Fluid continues.

Q: Did you read Dr. Weinbaum's testimony?

A: I sure did.

Q: This gentleman with his subboards in high-risk or maternal fetal medicine?

A: Yes.

Q: You say it was documented in the record when this woman was examined upon arrival as to whether there was leaking fluid or no leaking fluid, is that your testimony?

A: By the—

Q: It is your testimony, right?

A: Yes, it is.

Q: Yes. Show us, doctor, where that is documented in the record? Take your time.

A: By the conclusion that the patient—that the doctors agreed that the patient had ruptured membranes. When a patient comes in it's up to the doctors to document the fact that she indeed has ruptured membranes. The fact they concluded she had ruptured membranes indicates to me that they were satisfied that she did.

Q: We are still waiting, doctor, to see whether it's documented that the fluid was leaking or not leaking at that time?

A: They could not document that the patient had ruptured membranes without the fluid leaking otherwise there's no way they could tell.

Q: That's how you tell. Doctor, if that fluid was not leaking it could be a sign of another consequential observation in this case, true?

A: No.

Q: By the way, doctor what is gushing fluid in a woman at term other than ruptured membranes, tell the jury?

A: Assuming it's not urine there is no other.

Q: You think, doctor, that a woman would know the difference between a gush of urine and her bag of waters rupturing? You think she knew the difference between those two?

A: Yes, I do.

Q: A hundred percent of the time, right, doctor?

A: I would assume so.

Q: Therefore, doctor, the history of gushing fluid tells the physician a hundred percent of the time that the bag of waters has ruptured, true?

A: Gushing is a word that I would say would indicate that by her I heard that I would think there could not be anything else. Fluid does not always gush.

Q: But, doctor, if the would-be mother has experienced something that even she tells, the patient, her bag of waters ruptured or broke as it in quotes, sea of water, water broke, yellow in color, that's the bag of waters rupturing, true?

A: I would say that's the assumption, yes.

Q: Now, doctor, if there was a gush and no fluid leaking at the time of admission to the hospital, you read Dr. Weinbaum's testimony concerning that eventually, didn't you?

A: I read his testimony, yes, sir.

Q: And he said, doctor, that would be or could be indication of Oligo-hydtamnios or insufficient fluid, true?

A: I read his testimony and that's what he did say.

Q: Now, doctor, if there was Oligohydtamnios there might well be initial gush when the woman arrived in the hospital, no leaking, correct?

A: In this particular case this patient had sonography admit amniotic fluid so we know there was no Oligohydtamnios in this particular case.

Q: When was the last sonogram?

A: Within a couple of weeks of the time.

Q: You know in a couple of weeks there can be significant depletion in the amniotic fluid, you know, don't you?

A: Depends how significant is significant. It can decrease.

Q: Your answer is it depends how significant is significant?

A: Right.

Q: Is that your answer?

A: Right. There's no way this patient—

Q: Doctor, I will ask you the next questions.

A: Thank you.

Q: You want to give answers like that I will ask the next question?

A: Thank you, sir.

Q: You are welcome. Did you, sir, still say that it wasn't important for them to document in this chart whether or not there was leaking fluid or not leaking fluid when this patient arrived in the hospital?

A: It is important for them to ascertain whether or not there was leaking fluid, yes.

Q: Doctor, you know what the word document means correct?

A: Correct.

Q: Is it important, yes or no, to document that fact, either leaking or not leaking, yes or no? Tell the jury and his honor.

A: If it goes to that conclusion it's important to document it. They concluded that it did and that's all they had to do.

MR. MOORE: Your Honor, with all due respect, judge, could the witness with all due respect when a question can be clearly answered unequivocally I ask would the witness please be directed to do it, judge?

THE COURT: Doctor, the rules of evidence in New York require on Cross-examination if the question can be answered with a yes or no answer you have to answer it that way. If you can't answer it with a yes or no answer you indicate you can't answer it with a yes or no answer.

THE WITNESS: Thank you, Your Honor.

THE COURT: Those are the rules.

Q: And, doctor, obstetrics is a specialty, even though many times the obstetrician is not really needed, correct?

A: Correct.

Q: Babies have been born in the fields for centuries, correct, doctor?

A: Correct.

Q: Babies are born on subways; they're born in taxicabs; they're born many, many places other than hospitals, correct?

A: Correct.

Q: But the reason for obstetrics, doctor, becomes painfully obvious when babies do get into trouble, correct?

A: Correct.

Q: And obstetrics can save them, correct, doctor?

A: Sometimes.

Q: Under the circumstances of this case, doctor, if there was proper monitoring and it was found that this baby was getting into distress, then action had to be taken at that point, correct?

A: Correct.

Q: And under those circumstances, doctor, this baby could have been saved, true?

A: I would hope so, but I couldn't say so.

Q: Doctor, you would hope so, in accord with the probabilities that when intervention by experts is made, the reason for intervention works, in likelihoods and in probabilities, correct, doctor?

A: I can't—can't agree with that, sir, no. It doesn't always happen that way.

Q: Doctor, haven't you just said the antithesis of what I asked you? Didn't I ask you about likelihoods and probabilities and didn't you say, you can't always say that? In other words, if there's intervention in a hundred percent of the cases, there may still be damage. That's what you're saying, correct?

A: That's correct.

Q: But I'm not asking you that, doctor. I'm asking you, isn't the reason for intervention to avoid damage?

A: Yes.

Q: And therefore, hopefully, doctor, more likely than not, it does.

A: Each case is different.

Q: Of course.

A: That's all I'm saying. Can't say that in this case it would have made any difference or not. I just can't say that.

Q: You can't have any likelihoods of probabilities?

A: In this particular case, I can't say that.

Q: I see. Doctor, let me ask you this: Did they give you Wendy's—the Plaintiff's next child's—birth record to review?

A: Yes, sir, I know.

Q: The plaintiff's next child was born at St. Luke's Hospital, correct?

A: No, sir.

Q: They didn't give you that?

A: No.

MR. MOORE: May we have this document marked for identification, Your Honor (indicating)?

THE COURT: Yes, mark it for identification.

(Plaintiff's Exhibit 10 marked for identification.)

COURT OFFICER: Show it to the witness?

MR. MOORE: Thank you. (Said exhibit handed to Mr. Moore.) May I just be given a moment, Your Honor? (Pause.) Doctor, you see, in that case, with Nora Martelly's third child, who was in court here today and who is a normal child in every way, that in that case, on the monitor, they picked up that there was a lack of variability after meconium was passed, and they did a cesarean section for fetal distress and they delivered a baby who is now healthy in every way? You see that, don't you?

A: May I read?

Q: You just take your time—Doctor, can you answer the question?

A: You're paraphrasing. Would you like me to read—

Q: Did you think, doctor, that I was quoting, word for word, from the record?

A: I do not think that your paraphrasing expresses what the record says, sir.

Q: Doctor, you take all the time in the world to look through that record.

A: Yes.

Q: Isn't it true, doctor, that they diagnosed fetal distress based on the passage of meconium and poor variability of the fetal heart on the monitor, and they did an emergency cesarean section? Doctor, don't hesitate to take as much time as you want to answer the question as I frame it. It's my question, doctor, would you please answer it? Take your time.

A: The record indicates, meconium—judge, the record is not as it is being purported to be. I cannot answer it yes or no, sir.

THE COURT: Well, that's your answer.

Q: By the way, doctor, I just held up one page to you.

A: I'm looking at the same page.

Q: There are many other things, right?

A: That's—that's right, sir.

Q: Okay. Doctor, did they find a reduced variability on the fetal monitor?

A: Yes, they did.

Q: Was there the passage of meconium, doctor?

A: Yes.

Q: Did they get the consent from the patient to do cesarean section?

A: Yes.

Q: And did they go ahead and do it?

A: Yes, sir.

Q: And do they say, in another part of the record, that there was fetal distress, doctor?

A: If it says it in another part of the record, I'm not sure; I haven't looked at it. This is the page you showed me (indicating), where they also talk about giving Pitocin augmentation to the patient with meconium, and that is not necessarily what this court [sic] testified to earlier was a standard of care. So I'm not quite sure that I agree that this is what it says.

Q: Doctor, we're not talking about standard of care now. We're talking about intervening when needed and saving a baby. Remember those questions, doctor?

A: It's my understanding that this was to be used as—showing what standard of care was, sir.

Q: That's exactly what it can't be used for, doctor, because it's five years later. We can't use 1989 standards for 1984. You know, doctor, that's why we have to go back for textbooks at the time, when we question witnesses about standard of care. Doctor, I offered that based on my questioning of you about intervening when there's problems, but if you do it timely you save babies. Remember your problem with that, doctor, that it doesn't happen a hundred percent of the time? Then I asked you, isn't it more likely than not? You can't even agree with that. And then I asked you about this woman's other baby.

MR. GREENFIELD: Your Honor, I'm going to object. Is Mr. Moore going to be testifying or is he going to be asking questions?

MR. MOORE: Judge, that's a question summarizing the basis for why I asked the witness. He's under the assumption that I offered this record as an issue on standard of care.

A: This particular case, those things were present, intervention oc-curred and this baby is apparently alive and well. That is this par-ticular case and there's no quarrel with that.

Q: Doctor, variability is such an important issue on reading a monitor, correct?

A: Very important.

Q: And, doctor, variability, however, is something that is better inter-preted the more expert the observer, correct?

A: If it's subtle, yes.

Q: And, doctor, subtle loss of variability on an external monitor may turn out to be very severe loss of variability on an internal monitor, correct?

A: Possibly.

Q: In this case, the mother only had an external monitor at most, in the labor room, correct?

A: Yes.

Q: When this woman was in the labor room and when they say she was attached to the monitor, they did not attach an internal moni-tor, true?

A: True.

Q: By the way, doctor, it sounds almost like a throwaway at this point, but isn't it a fact that a high-risk pregnancy, where the bag of waters has ruptured and where the cervix is three centimeters dilated, should be the subject of internal monitoring? Wasn't that the standard in 1984?

A: If the station of the head permits it and the external tracing is not giving an adequate readout, then an internal monitor can be more variable—more accurate.

Q: Doctor, the fact is, isn't it, that since the internal monitor is much more accurate, particularly when it comes to variability, that in 1984, if they had ruptured membranes, the cervix sufficiently dilated and a presenting head, in this case at minus two, they should have attached an internal electrode? True or false?

A: Internal electrode would have been preferable.

Q: And that wasn't done in this case, correct?

A: Correct.

Q: By the way, doctor, on the issue of internal electrode and a standard practice in terms of a high-risk pregnancy in 1984, do you find Edward Hon, H-o-n, his article, even though in a neonatology book, "Neonatology, Pathophysiology and Management of the Newborn," the chapter "Management of Labor and Delivery," by Edward Hahn, would you say that's a generally authoritative work, doctor, you reserving the right to disagree with any particular portion?

A: I'm quite familiar with Dr. Hon's work, but I'm not at all familiar with that article, so I could not say, sir.

Q: Doctor, I'm not asking you whether you're familiar with the article. The fact is that Dr. Hon, Edward Hon, at that time at the University of California, subsequently at Yale, was the American pioneer in continuous electrical fetal monitoring, true?

A: He was among several, yes.

Q: And you, doctor, would not agree that his article, "Management of Labor and Delivery," would be a generally authoritative work, you reserving the right to disagree with any particular portion?

A: I cannot say that everything that a given individual wrote is authoritative, especially without knowing what it was.

Q: Doctor, you know that the standard of "generally authoritative" is not that everything the person wrote is gospel or absolute, it's just that he is an authority, correct?

A: He is a well-thought-of obstetrician. I cannot say that there are not people who disagree with him on almost every point.

Q: That's not the issue.

A: Sure, it is. Sure, it is.

Q: When he talks, people listen, to use a phrase, true?

A: That's not my definition of "authoritative."

Q: I'm not asking you for your definition—When he talks, people listen.

A: Absolutely right, true.

Q: Because he knows they consider that he knows what he's talking about. That's why they listen, right?

A: There are many reasons why people listen to important people.

Q: In the early 1980s, there was probably no more recognized figure in the field of electrical fetal monitoring than Edward Hon, true?

A: He was an important figure. There were quite a few others that were doing similar work.

Q: Can you answer the question as I posed it?

A: You said nobody more important. The answers, I couldn't say that.

Q: Doctor—

A: If you read back the question, I'd be happy to answer it.

Q: Doctor, the question was, there was probably no more important figure in the field of electrical fetal monitoring in the early 1980s than Edward Hon, isn't that true?

A: Probably no more important. I wouldn't be able to, say that.

Q: Tell the jury one person that you know that was more recognized as an authority in that field than Edward Hon.

A: Barry Shiffrin (phonetic), in Los Angeles.

Q: Do you recognize Dr. Shiffrin as an authority?

A: I'm not recognizing him as an authority, also. You asked me, who was probably more important. That's a totally different question.

Q: So there's nobody in the United States of America, in the 1980s, that spoke with, quote-unquote, authority in the field of electrical fetal monitoring? Is that your testimony to this jury?

A: The testimony is that—

Q: Is that your testimony, doctor?

A: You'll have to ask the question in a different way. I cannot answer it the way you asked it.

Q: Sir, for many, many years now, you have refused, in a court of law, to recognize any of the standard texts as generally authoritative, you reserving the right to disagree with any particular portion, correct?

A: Correct.

Q: And, doctor, you know, don't you, that in 1983, on my questioning, your answer was different, and you've changed since to this with respect to the use of texts in cross-examining you, true?

MR. GREENFIELD: Objection, Your Honor.

MR. MOORE: I'll back that up.

THE COURT: Overruled.

Q: You know that, is that right?

A: I have no idea.

Q: Well, doctor, by the way 1983, is it fourteen years ago that you were in your infancy, so to speak, as an expert coming to court because you said earlier you have been doing it about fifteen years, right, doctor?

A: That's about right, sir.

Q: I would like to quote, doctor, from sworn testimony by you September 20, 1983, Carlton Reade, individually and as Administrator of the Estate of Marie Reade versus Edgar O'Casio. You were asked these questions, doctor, by me, page 68 (reading):

"Question: By the way, doctor, you find authoritative, don't you, *Williams On Obstetrics,* it's a well-recognized text in the field, isn't that correct?

"Answer: It's a well-recognized text. I cannot say I find every sentence in the book authoritative.

"Question: Well, that's not the question. The question, is it generally authoritative, doctor, and you reserve the right to disagree with any particular portion, right, sir?

"Answer: Yes."

Q: I am sure you don't remember that testimony, doctor, but I pose the questions almost exactly the same today haven't I? I asked you if these books, Danforth, Williams, the chapter by Edward Hahn, were generally authoritative, you reserving the right to disagree with any particular portion, and you have said every time today no, correct?

A: That's correct.

MR. MOORE: I have no further questions of you.

Index